THE CULTURAL LIFE
OF IMAGES

Theoretical archaeology group (TAG)

THE CULTURAL LIFE OF IMAGES

Visual Representation in Archaeology

Edited by
Brian Leigh Molyneaux

London and New York

First published 1997
by Routledge
11 New Fetter Lane, London EC4P 4EE

Simultaneously published in the USA and Canada
by Routledge
29 West 35th Street, New York, NY 10001

© 1997 Selection and editorial matter,
Brian Leigh Molyneaux
© Iindividual chapters the contributors

Typeset in Bembo by Florencetype Ltd, Stoodleigh, Devon

Printed and bound in Great Britain by
Biddles Ltd, Guildford and King's Lynn

British Library Cataloguing in Publication Data
A catalogue record for this book is available from the British Library

Library of Congress Cataloguing in Publication Data
The cultural life of images: visual representation in archaeology /
edited by Brian Leigh Molyneaux.
p.   cm.
"Theoretical Archaeology Group."
Includes bibliographical references and index.
1. Imaging systems in archaeology.   I. Molyneaux, Brian.
II. Theoretical Archaeology Group (England)
CC79. I44C85   1997
930–dc20

ISBN 0–415–10675–3

CONTENTS

ILLUSTRATIONS

FIGURES

TABLE

CONTRIBUTORS

Richard Bradley, Department of Archaeology, University of Reading, Whiteknights, PO Box 218, Reading RG6 2AA, UK.

Timothy Champion, Department of Archaeology, University of Southampton, Highfield, Southampton, SO17 1BJ, UK.

Alan Costall, Department of Psychology, University of Portsmouth, King Henry Building, King Henry Street, Portsmouth PO1 2DY.

Richard A. Fox Jr., Department of Anthropology, University of South Dakota, Vermillion, South Dakota, 57069, USA.

Clive Gamble, Department of Archaeology, University of Southampton, Highfield, Southampton, SO17 1BJ, UK.

Simon James, Education Service, The British Museum, Great Russell Street, London WC1B 3DG, UK.

Brian Leigh Molyneaux, Department of Anthropology, University of South Dakota, Vermillion, South Dakota, 57069, USA.

Stephanie Moser, Department of Archaeology, University of Southampton, Highfield, Southampton, SO17 1BJ, UK.

Lynette Russell, 10 Fanny Street, Moonee Ponds, Victoria 3039, Australia.

Michael Shanks, Department of Archaeology, St David's University College, Lampeter, Dyfed, Wales, SA48 7ED, UK.

Brian A. Sparkes, Department of Archaeology, University of Southampton, Highfield, Southampton, SO17 1BJ, UK.

Wiktor Stoczkowski, UPR no 315 CNRS, 27 rue Damesme, 75013 Paris, France.

Carolyn Trant, 17 St Anne's Crescent, Lewes, East Sussex BN7 1SB, UK.

GENERAL EDITOR'S PREFACE

Why does the world need archaeological theory? The purpose of the Theoretical Archaeology Group series is to answer the question by showing that archaeology contributes little to our understanding if it does not explore the theories that give meaning to the past. The last decade has seen some major developments in world archaeology and the One World Archaeology series provides a thematic showcase for the current scale of enquiry and variety of archaeological interests. The development of a theoretical archaeology series complements these thematic concerns and, by focusing attention on theory in all its many guises, points the way to future long term developments in the subject.

In 1992 the annual Theoretical Archaeology Group (TAG) conference was held in Southampton. Europe was our theoretical theme at this the EuroTAG conference from which the first volumes in this series originated. We stressed two elements in the structure of the three-day conference. In the first place 1992 had for long been heralded as the time when the single market would come into existence combined with moves towards greater European unity. While these orderly developments could be planned for and sessions organized around the role of archaeology and the past in the construction of European identity, no-one could have predicted the horror of what would occur in former Yugoslavia. Throughout 1992 and beyond, the ideologies of integration and fragmentation, federalism and nationalism vied with each other to use the resources of the past in vastly different ways.

The second element recognized that 1992 was a notable anniversary for theoretical archaeology. Thirty years before, Lewis Binford had published his first seminal paper, 'Archaeology as Anthropology' in *American Antiquity*. This short paper was a theoretical beacon in an otherwise heavily factual archaeological world. From such beginnings came the influential processual movement which, in its early years, was referred to as the New Archaeology. Thirty years has clearly knocked the shine off such bright new futures. In the meantime archaeological theory had healthily fragmented while expanding into many areas of investigation, previously regarded as off-limits to archaeologists and their mute data. Processualism had been countered by post-processualism to either the enrichment or irritation of by now partisan theoretical practitioners. Euro TAG marked the anniversary with a debate involving the views of Lewis Binford, Chris Tilley, John Barrett and Colin Renfrew, supplemented by opinions from the floor. Their brief was to outline the theoretical challenges now set before the subject. The audience heard various programmes of where we might go as well as fears about an uncertain theoretical future. Both optimism and pessimism for another thirty years of theoretical excitement were to be found in almost equal measure. However, the clear impression, exemplified by the number of people (almost 800) who attended TAG was that the strength of any future theoretical archaeology now lies in its diversity.

How different in numbers attending and diversity of viewpoints from the early days of TAG, an organization whose aims have always been simple: to raise the profile of discussion about the theories of the past. The need for such a group was recognized at the first open meeting held in Sheffield in 1979 where the programme notes declared that 'British archaeologists have never possessed a forum for the discussion of theoretical issues. Conferences which address wider themes come and go but all too frequently the discussion of ideas is blanketed by the presentation of fact'. TAG set out to correct this balance and achieved it through an accent on discussion, a willingness to hear new ideas, often from people just beginning their theoretical careers.

EuroTAG presented some of the influences which must now contribute to the growth of theory in archaeology as the discipline assumes a central position in the dialogues of the humanities. As expected there was strong participation from European colleagues in sessions which focused on Iberia and Scandinavia as well as discussions of the regional traditions of theoretical and archaeological research in the continent, an archaeological perspective on theory in world archaeology, the identity of Europe, and multicultural societies in European prehistory. Set beside these were sessions devoted to human ancestry, food, architecture and structured deposition. Two archaeological periods expressed their new-found theoretical feet. Historical archaeology argued for an escape from its subordination to history while classical archaeology embraced theory and applied it to its rich data. Finally, the current issues of value and management in archaeology were subjected to a critical examination from a theoretical perspective.

The visual language of archaeology has often been ignored. This volume explores a multiplicity of viewpoints and a variety of visual media that taken together point to a rich seam of future archaeological research. Images have always been used to present the past. What we now appreciate is that they were also instrumental in inventing archaeology as an academic discipline. Moreover, the inertia of the image channelled the direction and scope of subsequent archaeological inquiry. The structure of theoretical archaeology today owes more than it cares to acknowledge to the images and representations which break up the blocks of text devoted to the subject. Consequently, one aspect of our current theoretical agenda must be to examine the ancestry of the images we use in order to assess their powers of theoretical persuasion. The challenge, taken up by many of the papers in this volume, is also to provide the context for that analysis.

Clive Gamble
April 1996

ACKNOWLEDGEMENTS

The EuroTAG organizing committee consisted of Clive Gamble, Sara Champion, Simon Keay and Tim Champion. They were helped by many staff and students from the Department of Archaeology at the University of Southampton and particularly by Cressida Fforde and Olivia Forge who did the lion's share of the organization in the final days. Thanks are also due to Peter Philips who videotaped the debate and to Mike Corbishley, Peter Stone and Eric Maddern who organized videos and storytelling while the art of Carolyn Trant and Sylvia Hays provided the art exhibition. Financial support was received from the Prehistoric Society, the TAG travel fund, Oxbow books, Routledge and the University of Southampton.

INTRODUCTION

The cultural life of images

BRIAN LEIGH MOLYNEAUX

Images made in the past and images made to represent the past are equally difficult to analyse. They capture the ideas and imaginings of artists in the visual energies of form, line and colour, but their messages are largely hidden. For prehistoric art, the chief villain is time. For archaeological representations of the past, the issues are no less complex. It is common to use pictures in academic research as props for ideas expressed in other forms. Images may be created with an eye to aesthetic quality, but they tend to be 'representations' of ideas, or 'illustrations' of objects or 'reconstructions' of events. They are rarely considered as objects that also communicate directly to viewers, as objects of analysis in their own right. What such pictures actually convey to readers or audiences, the nature of their silent messages, is rarely discussed. The main goal of this book, in chapters about art and perception (Costall), art and illustration (Bradley, James, Trant), photography (Shanks), ancient art (Molyneaux, Sparkes), and recent historic and modern representations of the past (Champion, Fox, Moser and Gamble, Russell, Stoczkowski), is to reveal the cultural life of images, exposing their power and influence as direct statements about social ideas and relations, visual messages that may be as strong and distinctive as those conveyed in texts.

PICTURES AND WORDS

Many scholars think it is impossible (following Wittgenstein) for images to exist outside language. Artworks often mean little without the caption and the art history, the critic and the museum guide, to tell the viewer what to appreciate and how. The viewing seats in an art museum challenge the visitor to sit and contemplate, but they are often empty. Understanding a picture requires the education and direction of attention to its meaningful aspects.

At the same time, written language seems empty without imagery. In the early days of print, manuscripts and books had wonderful animated or vegetative letters and colophons, and maps were crowded with pictures – all still imbued with the magic and mythology of the antiquarian view of the past. In the early days of modern science, Galileo incorporated the first telescopic images of Saturn in his text as a sentence element, the same size, scale and status as the surrounding words (Galileo Galilei 1613, p. 25, noted and illustrated in Tufte 1990:120–21). Even now, scientific words display their ancient descriptive past (as clavicle, the common scientific name for the collar-bone, derives from the Latin for key because of its resemblance to the curve of a medieval vault key or its hinges; see Fleck 1979:133–5). Knowledge itself is a landscape in the English language, consisting of 'fields' which we 'explore' in our 'search' for understanding (Salmond 1982).

The bond between art and language and the seen world seems right and unavoidable (see Mitchell 1994), but from an analytical view, this sensible integration is a problem. The use of naturalistic imagery implies a direct relationship between the representation and the world, transparent and without interpretive obstacles. The ideas represented claim truth to nature. This is why spectators and readers are comfortable with images of natural things: in art because such depictions do not seem to require much textual intervention (a tree is a tree, rather than a bourgeois or New Age mystification of nature); and in texts because word pictures demand less privileged knowledge, less of the jargon that sets academics apart from the general public (something tree-shaped, rather than arboriform). Indeed, a picture of a human may be recognized outside the relativistic domain of language, whether one speaks !Kung or Hindi or English; human actions and familiar objects may be detected without a guidebook.

The idea that representations of natural things convey information as simply and directly and truthfully as nature itself is very seductive. It is not surprising that naturalism (here defined as close adherence to nature or reality – as nature is believed to be) is an important tool of propagandists, whether in politics, religion, or advertising, as it lends credence to their claims (see, among others, Hobsbawm and Ranger 1983, Adams 1994, Champion 1996, Fox 1996, Molyneaux 1996, Russell 1996, Sparkes 1996).

It is also not surprising that science withdraws from this lively but highly metaphorical world for objectivity's sake. Normal science drops the familiar and imagined – archetypal and allegorical humans, superhumans, monsters, animal, and plant species – for the unimagined, paring text down to its unlively essentials, choosing the dead and forgotten (Latin), rather than the living, to describe life.

Yet modern science cannot proceed without imagery. Visualization is essential in theoretical work, providing a material environment (in the form of models, diagrams, and other images) within which intuition can operate and, more subtly, allowing the connection of ideas with natural processes. A loss of visualization caused a period of 'spiritual and human confusion' in physics during the development of quantum theory between 1913 and 1927 (Wolfgang Pauli, quoted in Miller 1978). It was taken for granted in Classical physics that physical processes would provide continuity with what we observe, but when Heisenberg developed quantum mechanics, represented solely as formal mathematics, links to the natural world, and therefore visualization, were lost; the unsettling dislocation persisted until Nils Bohr created a new visual aesthetic of wave/particle duality that rejoined physical theory with our experience of the world (Miller 1978).

The pictures used in scientific description are apparantly neutral illustrations and photographs. Illustration and photography are only ostensibly neutral, however (see Bradley 1996, James 1996, Shanks 1996). In their appearance of being exactly what they represent, claiming truth to nature and so to science, they persuade the viewer with a naturalism no less saturated with meaning than other forms of art. Of course, scientific results are not socially constructed to the extent that scientists work with their hands to discover, invent and replicate natural processes (*contra* some constructivists and cultural relativists, as discussed in Gross and Levitt 1994). This active engagement with material things brings them in touch with the material world. But they get no closer than the Yanomamo shaman, preparing and applying natural stimulants and medicines. Each scientific or nonscientific representation of knowledge – recognized as artistic or not – is shaped in specific circumstances of production within a specific time, space and sociocultural milieu.

Ludwik Fleck compares early and contemporary anatomical descriptions and drawings in his 1935 work 'Entstehung und Entwicklung einer wissenschaftlichen Tatsache: Einführung in die Lehre vom Denkstil und Denkkollektiv' (Fleck 1979) to illustrate the existence of different 'thought styles' in scientific observation. Using drawings of the human skeleton, he shows that the seemingly objective illustrations of his time are no less ideographic than those of earlier times (see also Rudwick's (1976) 'visual language' concept in geology). The significance of such an approach to representations is not simply that it underlines scientific relativism and exposes the changing visual styles of science. It also shows how the images helped to reinforce and promulgate attitudes in the scientific community (Fleck's work anticipated and influenced Kuhn's (1962) conceptualization of the scientific paradigm (Kuhn 1979)).

This visual impact may be described as a metaphorical reinforcement. Representations enlarge and strengthen existing messages appearing in other forms (see Champion 1996, Fox 1996, Molyneaux 1996, Sparkes 1996). This is explicit in image/text combinations, as various as Egyptian dynastic art, the image-poems of George Herbert (1593–1633), William

Blake's illuminated books, postmodern art and all illustrations. It is implicit in arts and crafts, as non-verbal carriers of social information (see, for example, Wobst's (1977) analysis of headwear and Wiessner's (1984) analysis of San beadwork).

Images are especially effective in the reinforcement of power and ideology. During the fifteenth century, Dutch paintings of events from the Bible often included images of wealthy patrons and donors. These actual people were included as minor actors in the imaginary scenes, most often kneeling in prayer. Vinograd (1991:180–81) explains that this gave such paintings the status of eyewitness accounts, thereby reinforcing the truth of the religious events, but there is more to this striking juxta-position. In the circumstances depicted, power and privilege stand side-by-side with religion. Only the fact that the artist averted the eyes of the donors from Mary and Jesus or other sacred figures prevented an official, and outrageous, apotheosizing of the powerful – at least for those contemporary spectators educated in the iconography of the time. By this subtle detail, the artists ensured that the donors looked beyond scenes they could not actually have witnessed. But the conceit was probably lost on the masses who viewed such paintings in the churches. Their reaction may have been what was intended by such displays: that the wealthy were closer to God (for contrasting discussions of the directness and veracity of Dutch art, see Alpers (1983) and Adams (1994) with reference to the seventeenth century).

The sheer visibility of pictures as material forms gives strength to whatever messages they convey (cf. McLuhan's (1964) notions of 'hot' and 'cool' media, in which terms, pictures are usually 'hot' (dense with information) as compared with the equally perceivable spaces around them). This perceptual reinforcement describes the alteration of some aspect of the perceived environment in order to increase the probability that it will be attended to by a diversity of perceivers. The manipula-tion of information to direct attention may be intentional: one may have to shout to be heard. A critical point here is that such reinforcement may also vary with shifts in the informational environment itself – one may have to shout above the noise to be heard. This 'straining for effect' often attends the declining of a style or fashion in cultural things (see Kroeber 1944, Kubler 1962). This suggests that content analysis (for example, Berelson 1952) has a potentially significant role to play in the study of pictures, in the study of variation in the 'shape of meaning' as it is affected by variation in ideological reinforcement (see Molyneaux 1991, 1996).

Perceptual reinforcement is a crucial attribute, as it suggests not only that images have existence outside the language of texts but also that images, and image-making, cannot be entirely circumscribed by cultural, social or perceptual relativism. Trobriand Islanders, for example, carve the prows of their Kula trading canoes with elaborate designs that are dazzling to the eye – an effect they hope will soften up their trading partners (Gell 1992). Although Gell (1992:46) argues relativistically that the dazzle is only relevant because it is seen as a sign of magic emanating from the board, the sign of magic is also inseparable from the physical sensation (see Morphy 1992 for an Australian example). As the perceptual psychologist Gibson (1966:26) reminds us, 'No symbol exists except as it is realized in sound, projected light, mechanical contact, or the like. All knowledge rests on sensitivity'. The use of intense visual stimuli in a similar way helps generate the power of persuasion that is used so effectively today in advertising and entertainment, as the beautifying of non-essential commodities lures the consumer (Haug 1986).

If another model is needed to illustrate this notion of material and social integration, it is perhaps Mead's (1972) concept of organism–environment interaction. As Lewis (1981:132) sums it up, 'objective reality cannot be defined as wholly external to the organism (materialism) or wholly internal (subjective idealism), but rather it is the production of organism–environment interaction'.

It is therefore appropriate to examine both social and material attributes of pictures, a task engaging the efforts of materialists and idealists alike (see Costall 1996 for a discussion of competing perceptual theories).

THE SITUATION OF PRODUCTION

In order to examine the effects of metaphorical and perceptual reinforcement, the essence of the power of images, it is necessary to study them within the context of their production. The simple, compelling reason for this is that the artist, no matter how invisible in scientific and other academic contexts, works within a situation mediated by social and material forces – hence, Fleck's 'thought styles' (and see, for example, Rudwick 1985, 1992).

Unfortunately, within Western tradition, the suppression of individuality in the scientific method causes science to be generally uninterested in artists and the artistic process. Without such information, representations can only convey generalities. In archaeology, they may be treated as lifeless objects, sorted into stylistic categories and used to chart cultural differences and changes. In anthropology, the circumstances of their creation may be less significant than their function, as they are interpreted as part of some social process, such as religion or the display of social identity.

These aspects of study are all necessary, but there is so much more that may potentially be discovered in a representation about the contemporary society behind it. Elkins (1996:201) has recently claimed that: 'Our smallest units tend to be images in their own right (depicted figures,

portraits, objects, symbols) and when it comes to individual marks . . .
we generally prefer theorizing about their nature to studying them'.
In a 'close reading', beneath the generalizing of form, style and subject,
each artwork is unique and may contain information specific to its
time and place of production. The generation of distinctiveness, even
where neutrality, continuity and commonality are what is desired,
happens because artists (and those who guide them) respond both
consciously and unconsciously to the information around them. The
artist is not a social automaton who simply reproduces a picture already
in the mind, but the first spectator, working with hand and eye within
the environment of information that represents a picture (cf. Wollheim
1991:101–2).

Artists and spectators all join a discourse that is already in progress,
and we may learn more about the social forces that generate pictures
within this discourse from formal variation in individual pictures, as
elements of information are manipulated as part of perceptual and
metaphorical reinforcement (see Molyneaux 1996).

THE INERTIA OF PICTURES

The reinforcement of ideas in some images is very powerful. Historical
or religious tableaux depicting great people, times and events provide a
very intense, dense, and engaging shorthand for entire eras and highly
complex situations. Each image captures literally or figuratively a moment
frozen in time, but it may eventually stand for an eternity. Picture a
scene intended to represent Upper Palaeolithic times (for example, in
Moser and Gamble 1996 and Stoczkowski 1996); the image may stand
for more than fifteen thousand generations of human life! This is an odd
concept, the compression of time and space into a single image. It is an
archaeological conceit no less fantastical than that of a religious person
who maintains that the ancestors are still with us. Yet we are bound to
picture, knowing that while each image may be marked by a caption,
protected within a text within a book, it will still have a life of its own.

The problem is that picturing overcomes time, and scholarship, by
capturing the imagined essence of an event in an easily remembered,
replicated and transported form. If it is a human event, it is even more
resistant to change. As Kubler observes, we tend to discard tools and
technology we no longer need, but we retain art, as 'symbols which are
still valid in human experience, unlike the superannuated discards of
medieval labor' (Kubler 1962:80). Pictures and other visual representations therefore have a tremendous inertia, or staying power, that may
persist long after the ideas behind the images have gone out of fashion.

Such persistence, and often, anachronism, may be seen in art
throughout history, in Egyptian tomb paintings of kings (Molyneaux
1996), Greek images of themselves and other peoples (Sparkes 1996),

statues and images in France of ancient Gaulish warriors (Champion 1996), imaginative reconstructions of 'Custer's Last Stand' (Fox 1996), depictions of Palaeolithic people and life (Moser and Gamble 1996 and Stoczkowski 1996), and images of Australian Aborigines (Russell 1996).

Rock art research (not covered in this book) provides a good illustration of the problems of reinforcement and inertia in representations. Prehistoric rock art is simple, direct, and most often lacking an archaeological context – a signal that, like abstraction, its cypher-like images demand interpretation. There are indeed a vast number of interpreters (the author included: for example, Molyneaux 1983, 1995). To make rock art even more potent, it is solidly situated, bound to the earth – proof of its primitiveness and fundamentality and therefore open to additional musings on its place in the landscape. How easy it is for rock art professionals, enthusiasts, and native people interested in its original meanings and functions to deride the notion of art for art's sake. There are probably few rock art images that are not held sacred by someone today. Still, for all the discourse, we will never be certain whether we are closer to understanding its origins. This is surely an obvious point to anyone except those who make a spiritual interpretation. Many researchers accept this by concentrating on the preservation, protection or promotion of the art, or studying modern interpretations as they change with the shifting political and social agendas of our time. Through all this, the images sit passively, reflecting colour and form to anyone who sees them. The curiosity about origins and so, interpretations, goes on, and will go on, as long as the rock art remains in sight.

SEEING AND READING

Like the rocks that bind images to the earth, or the walls that frame works of art, books capture illustrations and hold them as things that can be known. The confidence with which we read is extended to our tacit acceptance of the picture surrounded by words. This is, however, only the conceit of the insider. To an outsider, the pictures may simply stand against rows of strange characters or stripes on a sheet of paper. In such an alien environment, shorn of its received and confident wisdom, the text becomes an object as the picture is assumed to be, something that the graphic designer may appreciate, to whom text may be simply a matter of lines and always in competition for space with pictures.

There is a need to see pictures in this alien, natural light, if only to sense their silent power. It is true that all art is seen through the filter of expectations, and all research is conducted under the metaphorical weight of tradition, but it is also true that 'reading texts . . . is no substitute for experiencing the works of art they purport to illuminate' (Goldstein 1988:195). It is dreadfully ironic, but not at all shameful, that in the end, such experience usually ends up producing more words about pictures, as it does here.

By confronting the seen and represented world, the writers of this book have done what pictures and other images silently demand: to be attended to directly, treated as worlds in themselves, seen as positive forces leading opinions, rather than following words.

REFERENCES

Adams, A.J. 1994. 'Competing communities in the "Great Bog of Europe". Identity and seventeenth-century Dutch landscape painting.' In W.J.T. Mitchell (ed.), *Landscape and Power*. pp. 35–76. Chicago and London: University of Chicago Press.

Alpers, S. 1983. *The Art of Describing. Dutch Art in the Seventeenth Century*. Chicago: University of Chicago Press.

Berelson, B. 1952. *Content Analysis in Communications Research*. New York: Free Press.

Bradley, L. 1996. (this volume).

Champion, T. 1996. (this volume).

Costall, A. 1996. (this volume).

Elkins, J. 1996. 'On the impossibility of close reading. The case of Alexander Marshack.' *Current Anthropology* 37:185–201.

Fleck, L. 1979 [1935]. *Genesis and Development of a Scientific Fact*. Translated by F. Bradley and T.J. Trenn. T.J. Trenn and R.K. Merton (eds). Chicago and London: University of Chicago Press.

Fox, R.A. Jr. 1996. (this volume).

Gell, A. 1992. 'The technology of enchantment and the enchantment of technology.' In J. Coote and A. Shelton (eds), *Anthropology, Art and Aesthetics*, pp. 40–63. Oxford: Oxford University Press.

Gibson, J.J. 1966. *The Senses Considered as Perceptual Systems*. Boston, MA: Houghton Mifflin.

Goldstein, C. 1988. *Visual Fact over Verbal Fiction. A Study of the Carracci and the Criticism, Theory, and Practice of Art in Renaissance and Baroque Italy*. Cambridge: Cambridge University Press.

Gross, P.R. and Levitt, N. 1994. *Higher Superstition. The Academic Left and Its Quarrels with Science*. Baltimore and London: Johns Hopkins University Press.

Haug, W.F. 1986. *Commodity Aesthetics, Ideology and Culture*. New York: International General.

Hobsbawm, E. and Ranger, T. (eds) 1983. *The Invention of Tradition*. Cambridge: Cambridge University Press.

James, S. 1996. (this volume).

Kroeber, A.L. 1944. *Configurations of Culture Growth*. Berkeley and Los Angeles: University of California Press.

Kubler, G. 1962. *The Shape of Time. Remarks on the History of Things*. New Haven and London: Yale University Press.

Kuhn, T. 1962. *The Structure of Scientific Revolutions*. Chicago: University of Chicago Press.

Kuhn, T. 1979. 'Foreword.' In Fleck, L., *Genesis and Development of a Scientific Fact*. T.J. Trenn and R.K. Merton (eds). Chicago and London: University of Chicago Press.

Lewis, D.G. 1981. 'Mead's contact theory of reality: the manipulatory phase of the act in the constitution of mundane, scientific, aesthetic, and evaluative objects.' *Symbolic Interaction* 4:129–42.

Mead, G.H. 1972. *The Philosophy of the Act*. Chicago: University of Chicago Press.

McLuhan, M. 1964. *Understanding Media. The Extensions of Man*. New York: McGraw-Hill.

Miller, A.I. 1978. 'Visualization lost and regained: the genesis of the quantum theory in the period 1913–27.' In J. Wechsler (ed.), *On Aesthetics in Science*, pp. 73–102. Cambridge, MA and London: MIT Press.

Mitchell, W.J.T. 1994. *Picture Theory*. Chicago and London: University of Chicago Press.

Molyneaux, B.L. 1983. *The Study of Prehistoric Sacred Places: Evidence from Lower Manitou Narrows*. Archaeology Paper No. 2. Toronto: Royal Ontario Museum.

Molyneaux, B.L. 1991. 'Perception and Situation in the Analysis of Representations.' Unpublished PhD thesis, Department of Archaeology, University of Southampton, England.

Molyneaux, B.L. 1995. 'Representation and valuation in Micmac prehistory. The petroglyphs of Bedford, Nova Scotia.' In Teski, M. and J. Climo (eds), *The Labyrinth of Memory*, pp. 159–71. Westport, CT: Greenwood Press.

Molyneaux, B.L. 1996. (this volume).

Morphy, H. 1992. 'From dull to brilliant: the aesthetics of spiritual power among the Yolngu.' In J. Coote and A. Shelton (eds), *Anthropology, Art and Aesthetics*. pp. 181–208. London and New York: Routledge.

Moser, S. and Gamble, C. 1996. (this volume).

Rudwick, M.J.S. 1976. 'The emergence of a visual language for geological science, 1760–1840.' *History of Science* 14:149–95.

Rudwick, M.J.S. 1985. *The Great Devonian Controversy: The Shaping of Scientific Knowledge among Gentlemanly Specialists*. Chicago: University of Chicago Press.

Rudwick, M.J.S. 1992. *Scenes from Deep Time. Early Pictorial Representations of the Prehistoric World*. Chicago and London: University of Chicago Press.

Russell, L. 1996. (this volume).

Salmond, A. 1982. 'Theoretical landscapes. On cross-cultural conceptions of knowledge.' In D. Parkin (ed.), *Semantic Anthropology*. pp. 65–87. London: Academic Press.

Shanks, M. 1996. (this volume).

Sparkes, B. 1996. (this volume).

Stoczkowski, W. 1996. (this volume).

Trant, C. 1996. (this volume).

Tufte, E.R. 1990. *Envisioning Information*. Cheshire, CT: Graphics Press.

Vinograd, R. 1991. 'Private art and public knowledge in later Chinese painting.' In S. Küchler and W. Melion (eds), *Images of Memory. On Remembering and Representation*, pp. 176–202. Washington and London: Smithsonian Institution Press.

Wiessner, P. 1984. 'Reconsidering the behavioural basis for style. A case study among the Kalahari San.' *Journal of Anthropological Archaeology* 3:190–234.

Wobst, H.M. 1977. 'Stylistic behaviour and information exchange.' In C. E. Cleland (ed.), *For the Director: Research Essays in Honor of James B. Griffen*, pp. 317–42. Anthropological Papers, University of Michigan, No. 61.

Wollheim, R. 1991. 'What the spectator sees.' In N. Bryson, M.A. Holly and K. Moxey (eds), *Visual Theory. Painting and Interpretation*, pp. 101–50. New York: Harper Collins.

CHAPTER ONE

ART, LANDSCAPE, AND THE PAST

An artist's view

CAROLYN TRANT

When I was an art student I often travelled from my home in London to paint landscapes in the Sussex Downs. It was like travelling back in time to Paradise – the low sunlight on the hills resembled the tiny landscape backgrounds of the Gothic and early Renaissance paintings I had seen in museums and galleries. I painted in egg tempera, the medium of early religious art: pure ground pigment, usually coloured earths, mixed with eggyolk. In some of my earliest pictures I went so far as to paint an angel in a field or garden, but soon I found that this was unnecessary; it was the way this paint radiated from the bright, white gesso ground that gave the landscapes their special character. I was linked to artists removed in time and space by this association between paint, light and land. By choosing to work when the sun was low, I was conforming unwittingly to the hermetic vision of the Renaissance, in which nature and landscape were considered most permeated with sacred meaning at dawn and dusk – when humans could 'touch the deepest rhythms of creation and achieve unity between their own spirit and that of the living universe' (Cosgrove 1988:271). Piero della Francesca, Simone Martini, and Sassetta made their landscapes epiphanies of sacred moments.

  This aspect of landscape presents a rich terrain of imaginative and symbolic thought that helps me to relate to the space and time in which I find myself. In this I agree with David Jones, one of a few twentieth-century painters interested in keeping alive a visual language of symbolic reference, a rich tradition in Europe that has roots in Classical, Celtic, Christian and Renaissance sources. Modernism broke with this tradition and now many people in England, including painters, look for their spir-itual symbols in far away places – the Far East, India, among North American Indians – rather than mining the rich cultural seam in their own back gardens. This is because of a dislocation in our cultural chain. I think we need to look for ways of healing this break with our cultural past while retaining our modernist questioning spirit, and my way is to look at the shape and form and skin of the land itself, the result of man's past activity, history that was once a working present – accretions of deposits, records of relocations, each stratum of civilization growing on the next, and like layers of tree rings, increasing with age.

The poet Kathleen Raine said of Jones, 'History was the space in which he lived'. He could paint a tree, as in *Vexilla Regis*, with many explicit allusions to the Tree of Life, the Cross of Crucifixion, or the column of Roman imperial occupation. But much more simply, and to my mind more effectively, he could also make his historical references implicitly. His watercolour *Roland's Tree*, referring to the medieval *Song of Roland*, seems to suggest that the tree pictured might be the very one that Roland sat against. Now the actual tree happens to be an object existing in the material world of twentieth-century France, but historical 'fact' does not matter here – what is important is that Jones had to make this historical connection before he was able to find the inspiration to make a successful drawing. By bringing the past and present together in this way, Jones connects this living tree to all the trees that have ever been and invests it with a stature beyond time and space. This is what I interpret William Blake to mean when he wrote that paintings should be done from the imagination and not from nature.

This cumulative sense of here and now, linked to the past in a direct confrontation with the landscape is all-important to me. I like to work outside where there are plenty of physical and logistical problems to battle with. There is a tension between the inner and outer vision: what I know about a place affects my vision, at the same time as a stream of information through my eyes makes me reappraise what I know.

This relationship was difficult to achieve and express in images. When I completed my formal art training I moved into the heart of the countryside and made paintings that were a record, a diary, a catalogue of my immediate surroundings in all seasons, and of the livestock I now kept, vegetables I grew, and grass that I cut, spread and dried as hay. I knew every weed and patch of scrub that I fed to my goats. But after ten years and a summer spent by my pond minutely observing and recording the frogs emerging and submerging in the water plants, I realized I had gone too far. I identified with this land too much. When anyone disturbed a part of it in a way I felt was uncalled for – cut down a hedge or a piece of grass – it felt like a physical pain and I became unreasonably upset. Conversely, when the late afternoon sun shone on the tussocks of grass I wanted to roll in it and stuff it into my mouth in bliss. I painted a picture of a large bare field entitled *All Flesh is Grass* (a biblical quotation and the title of Brahms's *German Requiem*). I was surprised when people commented on the lack of content in the picture. I stopped

Figure 1.1 *Erosion on Black Cap Escarpment,* pastel on paper.

painting and, eventually, moved back into town. My inactivity continued until I saw and applied for a commission advertised by South East Arts and the local County Council to study *Earthworks on the Downs*. The Downs in East Sussex represent a totally manmade and culturally defined landscape, from the sheep cropped turf and smooth deforested slopes to the palimpsest of chalk scars – tracks, hillocks, flint mines and quarries – that represent agricultural and protoindustrial activity. I saw the chance to record this dynamic landscape, as 'Artist in Residence on the Downs' working for eighteen months between 1988 and 1990 to prepare an exhibition called *Rituals and Relics*, as a way to rework and clarify what I had been trying to communicate about our relation to the land in my earlier paintings.

An important aim of the project was to produce a body of work with wide public appeal – not limited to the conventional art lover or confined to art galleries – which would be shown in public places such as libraries and museums. I therefore decided to depict the Downs as we walk on them today, rather than producing imaginative illustrations of the sites and artifacts as they might have been when they were used. Archaeology gives us at best only a brief and partial impression of the past, and I was determined to record what was still with us in the land, rather than trying to imagine a past by creating reconstructions of events with people

Figure 1.2 *Towards Firle Beacon from Site of Neolithic Enclosure, Offham, pastel on paper.*

in exotic costumes. By working this way I would also question any preconceptions of 'landscape' as a separate entity divorced from a working countryside and its people.

Since I had tried to live off the land as people in agricultural communities had done in the past I was sensitive to the intertwined physical/historical/social world we inhabit, as well as very conscious of the physicality of the land. I walked miles along the Downs every day making notes and drawings of anything I found interesting and then consulted the archaeological maps and records provided by the County Archaeologist. Sometimes I pored over the maps first, asking about the history of sites before looking for them to see if I wanted to draw them. The time of day was very important to me and it was when the sun was low that the pattern of the past under the skin was best revealed. For speed I abandoned egg tempera and drew with chalk pastels – pure compressed pigment – and charcoal, both elements of the earth which became the landscape again by an almost alchemical process of transformation.

My drawings pictured a land long used – a deep trackway caused by erosion on a medieval cart track already worn by feet and wheels – the swirling white graffiti of scored chalkpaths at an old chalkpit, the result of motor bikes scrambling over the spoil of a quarry, itself a desecration of a neolithic causewayed camp. I intended these images to challenge the assumption that old paths are 'good' and modern trackmaking necessarily 'bad', that medieval feet were somehow more hallowed than ours. On the site of a line of ploughed out barrows I found some fossil sea urchins, damp and crisply marked as if it was the first time they had been exposed for hundreds of years; I painted them against a moonlit sky to show how the moon itself is a kind of fossil and the land is continually turning itself over in a process of upheaval and change.

Many of my images showed a seductively green and pleasant land, but sometimes the juxtaposition of elements challenged that interpretation. I explicitly drew a half eaten and bloody rabbit on the site of the now gently rolling greensward of a hillfort, to show that this site was once a bleak white scar on the landscape, a place of fierce human emotions, death and destruction, devastation under siege and war.

Paul Thompson, in *Oral History* writes about 'bland contemporary tourism which exploits the past as if it were another country to escape to, a heritage of buildings and landscape so lovingly cared for that it is almost inhumanly comfortable, purged of suffering, cruelty and conflict' (Thompson 1988:1). I made an image of a neolithic woman's skeleton, ritually buried at Whitehawk Camp in Brighton, aware that there were few precedents or traditions for this image in a culture that prefers death

Figure 1.3 *Rabbit Remains at Caburn Hillfort,* pastel on paper.

Figure 1.4 *Whitehawk Skeleton*, lithograph.

to be out of sight and out of mind, unlike a previous time when the scoured white barrow mounds were a constant reminder of death and decay as well as of man's appropriation of the landscape.

Often I would set out to draw one site, well documented and sounding interesting, only to be attracted by quite a different landscape feature. I turned my back on Itford Hill Bronze Age Village and drew a land-fill site nearby – obviously an old chalk quarry. A well established clump of trees remained on a small elevation in the middle of the dust of bulldozers refilling the chasm with rubbish. When I showed the drawing to an archaeologist he said the site had once been a hillfort. To make a drawing of this dynamic process seemed more in the spirit of the project than drawing the gentle slopes that are all that remains of most hillforts (structures that would be unlikely to be given planning permission today).

The picturesque settings of so many ancient sites, removed from their original working or ritual purpose, have been routinely depicted by artists and photographers so that, like Constable paintings on biscuit tins, it is

Figure 1.5 *Barrow*, lithograph.

hard to see them afresh. I have made two drawings of the chalk figure of the Long Man of Wilmington trying to challenge the stereotype of this image. He is an enigma, so in one I moved him to the edge of the picture and tried to focus on all the pockmarks around him – flint mines, barrows, trackways old and new – that tell us so much more about the landscape of which he is but a part. In another I literally turned the image on its head, drew him from the top down in order to see a different rhythm and pattern of the land below.

Stonehenge is barricaded against New Age Druids but snapped by innumerable tourists. If we are not to become a society of voyeurs but participants it is important to have a clear idea of the nature of the landscape. By focusing our interest towards only one aspect of the land and its past, we may ignore other histories it contains. At the site of the landfill opposite Itford Hill Bronze Age Village, the remaining small grove of trees had contained Asham House, associated with Virginia Woolf and the Bloomsbury group. For the loss of their 'sacred site', Bloomsbury

Figure 1.6 *Beddingham Land Fill Site,* pastel on paper.

devotees have demanded reparation in the form of a financial donation to creative arts in the area, from the industrial company who have demolished the house.

We seem to have broken the threads of our connections with the past almost beyond repair and are left only with fragments or 'relics' – usually cleaned up and adjusted for the edification of a heritage market which seems to want to preserve static images of the past in aspic. In societies where change is gradual the patterns of the past are meshed into everyday ritual activity and sometimes objects are deliberately destroyed, such as pottery ritually smashed at long barrows, perhaps to free the spirit of the dead. My art teacher told me how the Balinese were quite happy to burn or break vast quantities of beautifully sculpted effigies in the course of rituals and ceremonies, objects that we would rush to salvage for museums, because they had supreme confidence that they could and would make more. Of course I am fascinated by objects in museums but I am also an artist who works here and now and I should hate our own culture to be fossilized too soon. I have made images of objects in museums that were being exhibited in isolation and returned them visually to the landscape from which they were removed. I have, for example, 'reconstructed' the large Hove Barrow, destroyed for a Victorian housing development, and 're-interred' the amber cup, dagger

Figure 1.7 *Long Man of Wilmington,* pastel on paper.

and axes from the Brighton museum. And when my landscape drawings went on tour they were exhibited in museums alongside cases of relevant artifacts.

What we choose to value about our surroundings is a difficult problem as we attempt to reconcile a need to remember and preserve the past with the practical demands of contemporary life. I have tried to look at the landscape as a cumulation of life of all kinds. Overlooked, 'unimportant' places and objects are as exciting to me as the major ones – the fragments of an ancient field system, a lynchet running across a field, a patch of disturbed land left fallow year after year – for they all signify our continuous working relationship with the land. Where their origin is obscure I find a kind of comfort in the reminder that we cannot know everything. While drawing I have seen such places serve as part of the modern rituals of walking and dog exercising, and they seem precious in ways hard to express verbally in the language of a preservation or conservation order. I have drawn the rusting remains of old cars in a dry dewpond that perhaps one day will be excavated and put in a museum of the twenty-first century.

By drawing an image of these ambiguous areas of landscape it is good to think that an artist could give them an identity or legitimacy that could be proffered against the developer or Department of Transport's

Figure 1.8 *Long Man of Wilmington*, charcoal on paper.

barrage of paper work and glossy pamphlets. Drawing and documenting these places is one way of lodging them in community memory and celebrating their various uses. This is important because although some of these places have survived undisturbed for centuries, many have succumbed, some even since I drew them: a pagan Saxon burial ground reduced to a slurry pit, outlying ditches of an important hillfort lost to a housing estate, barrows nibbled away year by year by the plough. Inspired by a picture – *The Nest of Wild Stones* by Paul Nash, himself working at a time when the landscape was under threat of sudden change – I made a very red image, *The Nest of Outraged Stones*. The stones are stripped bare – perhaps from under a ploughed out barrow – a reflection of the anger and powerlessness of individuals and communities over the control of their landscape.

REFERENCES

Cosgrove, D. 1988. 'The geometry of landscape. Practical and speculative arts in sixteenth-century Venetian land territories.' In D. Cosgrove and S. Daniels (eds), *The Iconography of Landscape*. pp. 254–76. Oxford: Oxford University Press.

Thompson, P. 1988. *The Voice of the Past. Oral History*. Second edition. Oxford: Oxford University Press.

CHAPTER TWO

DRAWING INFERENCES

Visual reconstructions in theory and practice

SIMON JAMES

INTRODUCTION

Think back: what originally inspired your interest in the past? Pictures are likely to have been a key factor, depictions of people living in remote times. When I was about 8 years old, my parents gave me some historical picture books, including the *Ladybird Book of Julius Caesar and Roman Britain*. It contained colour scenes of Iron Age and Roman life (Peach 1959). This and other illustrated books, along with the influence of some inspirational teachers, fired my imagination and led to a career studying past human cultures.

Although not trained as an illustrator, I have drawn since childhood, and when I came into archaeology I soon specialized in site drawings. Since then, as an archaeologist, sometime illustrator, and latterly a museum educator, I have created and employed visual reconstructions to study and to teach about the human past, and in consequence have developed strong views on their use and value.

Except in rare cases, we are not actually reconstructing the true appearance of people or places in the past, since most of the evidence is missing and what remains has been altered by time. As Brian Hobley has said, we should perhaps call these simulations, not reconstructions (in Adkins and Adkins 1989:131), but the term 'reconstruction' is established and we are stuck with it.

The effectiveness of reconstruction illustrations depends on how far the archaeologist understands their use in communication and research. Reconstructions for academic purposes and for communication to non-specialists are closely related, but each has its own particular characteristics. I will examine this issue and also look at the obstacles which may interfere with the achievement of our aims – especially in communication to the public.

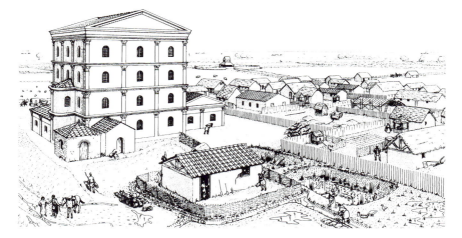

Figure 2.1 The Romano-British fenland settlement at Stonea Grange, Cambridgeshire, England. The purpose of the drawing was mainly to show the layout and probable appearance of the site (dominated by the large Classical masonry building) in its landscape; hence the choice of elevated viewpoint. Drawn by Simon James (from Longworth and Cherry 1986, Illustration 57).

'BUT IS IT *ART*?'
AIMS, AESTHETICS, AND MECHANICS

Alan Sorrel, a pioneer of reconstruction illustration in Britain, wrote that reconstructions are 'potentially art' (Sorrel 1981:21). I do not understand what he meant by this, although reconstruction may require more 'artistic ability' than other aspects of archaeological illustration (Adkins and Adkins 1989:132). The purpose of making a reconstruction illustration is to convey information and ideas; the aesthetic element is essential, but secondary. The illustration should be good enough to please both illustrator and viewer, but the main point is the message it conveys.

The mechanics of projection or other aspects of technique are therefore not relevant here, unless they affect the impact of the drawing. Take, for example, the choice of viewpoint: seeing from eye-level, the viewer feels included in the space, and almost the action, of the scene (e.g. Fig. 2.8); in contrast a bird's-eye view feels emotionally, as well as spatially, more distant (Fig. 2.1).

PARTICIPANTS AND INTERACTIONS

We need to look at the various components and stages in creating and using an illustration. The psychology of the participants, from the commissioning archaeologist to the illustrator to the people who will use the image, strongly affects the execution, valuation, and impact of reconstructions.

It is important, therefore, to discuss the interaction of people (particularly the archaeologist and the illustrator) with evidence and ideas, the aim of the drawing, and – which is too often neglected – the intended audience.

Since few of us spend much time considering *how* we communicate ideas and information, it is not surprising that we also neglect how viewers *use* visual media. Understanding use is critical when we are deciding how to transmit data and ideas. Outside academia (and, more often than we care to admit, inside it too), many readers may look at the pictures, perhaps read the captions, but may not read the main text at all. Conversely, many academics are hostile to any use of pictures.

Reconstructions may also serve different uses. Within academia, they may be created for the research purposes of the commissioning archaeologist and then directed to the wider audience of archaeologists in the published version. And in popular publishing especially, the process has other layers, such as sometimes unwelcome input from publishers, editors, and designers in which commercial considerations override academic content.

ACADEMIC ATTITUDES

In scholarly publications, illustrations are commonly seen as auxiliaries to written text – even though they may be critical for effective communication. As Gould has said: 'Since primates are visual animals, we must never omit (though historians often do) the role played by scientific illustrations in the formation of concepts and support of arguments' (Gould 1985:272). Moser has effectively shown how reconstructions have expressed and shaped arguments about the human past (Moser 1992). Yet there is a widespread 'logocentrism' and 'iconophobia' among academics, based on the notion that the more pictures a work has, the less seriously it is taken, a prejudice currently worsened by the fashion for the textual metaphor in British archaeology. The idea that reconstructions in particular are unscholarly seems almost instinctive. The attitude seems to be that such pictures, especially in colour, might be all right for children and for the general public, but not for serious scholars; to include them would imperil one's academic credibility. Put simply, the use of images is subject to academic prejudice. This attitude is misguided, to say the least.

Images as a means of expression and communication are not inferior to text; they are fundamentally different in kind and mode of operation. Miller has highlighted Langer's distinction between 'discursive' and 'presentational' forms:

Language and thought are discursive processes from which a series of independent component parts derive their overall meaning through sequential articulation. The rules of grammar are intended to analyse the structure underlying this discursive order. A presentational form such as a picture, on the other hand, has no natural divisions. . . . In assimilating a presentational form we have to take it in all at once, rather than sequentially, and there is nothing equivalent to grammatical structure underlying it. . . . Langer sees presentational symbolism as the major vehicle of objectifying feelings, and argues that these are thereby under-represented in our philosophies.

(Miller 1987:95)

Pictures and texts present information in unique and often mutually untranslatable ways. We need to exploit both modes much more even-handedly.

Of course reconstructions *can* be unscholarly and misleading. My original inspiration, the *Ladybird* book, for example, is wildly inaccurate. Queen Boudica is shown black-haired, and looks like a young Joan Collins rather than the powerful red-haired, middle-aged woman plausibly described by Dio (Peach 1959:21; Cassius Dio 1914–27). Even if Dio was an unreliable witness (he lived AD 155 to 235, generations after Boudica's death), the contemporary objects in the scene are demonstrably inaccurately depicted. Still, reconstructions remain a vital medium of communication and an invaluable research tool, although they are still too often a 'bolt-on' afterthought, merely a nice frontispiece to the serious report.

RULES AND GUIDELINES

A reconstruction should obey certain basic rules, which, though apparently obvious, are nonetheless frequently broken. It must not contradict the available evidence and should aim to account for as much of it as possible; selecting certain aspects may lead to temptation to 'cheat' by omitting awkward data. It should also respect the physical properties of the materials and structures depicted (see below).

Even if you follow the rules, the only certain thing about any reconstruction drawing is that it is wrong. The only real question is, how wrong is it? Demonstrable accuracy is inversely proportional to the complexity of the scene: so, for example, I feel confident that my painting of the Kirkburn sword (Fig. 2.7) is much closer to a true representation of ancient visual reality than my drawing of the Roman settlement at Stonea Grange, Cambridgeshire, which contains very many more inferences (Fig. 2.1). For this reason I disagree with Sorrell's views about labelling reconstructions with 'bold certainty' (Sorrell 1981:25); the caption should emphasize the tentative nature of such works.

AIMS, PROCESSES, AND LIMITATIONS

Before starting, illustrators must have a clear idea of the *aim* of the work – this is the fundamental question 'we never ask' (Schadla-Hall and Davidson 1982:171, Illustration 102). In general, a reconstruction is intended to give the viewer a perception of what something, someone, and/or somewhere looked like in the past, with the maximum effective impact and the minimum of misleading content.

Reconstruction may sometimes be inappropriate. For example, very fragmentary evidence does not provide enough information for a complex scene (you can build many different things on a few postholes or foundations running across an excavated trench). I have declined to produce drawings from such limited data, because the result would be utterly speculative, wholly misleading, and in effect, dishonest.

If a drawing is appropriate, we need to know how detailed it *needs* to be. A schematic approach using simple diagrams might serve better than an elaborate scene. On the other hand complex reconstructions have a positive value, as they force you to commit yourself on, and therefore to think hard about, various issues to be seen in the drawing. But this is a two-edged sword: such works also inevitably convey a tangle of ideological messages, assumptions, inferences, and pure guesswork.

Archaeologists deal with probabilistic arguments, but they are often expected – especially by the public – to make unequivocal statements of 'truth'. In a drawing particularly, there is no room for the 'ifs', 'buts', and 'maybes' beloved of scholars. Unless you draw impressionistically or, like Alan Sorrell, opt for strategic clouds of smoke to obscure guesswork, you must make definite visual statements about what was happening, who was doing it, how and where, even when evidence is lacking – and risk misleading the viewer. Single reconstructions appear to give the certainty people crave, freezing a view of 'truth' ('oh, so *that's* what it was like'). But how do you 'flag' to the viewer what we know, and where we are guessing? Generally, the more precise and detailed the drawing, the more convincing it is – but the more unflagged guesses it contains. A misleading image may become the kind of *idée fixe* which inhibits re-interpretation and new perspectives.

This raises another important psychological consideration. People often subconsciously assume that the more impressively finished something is, the greater the authority it carries. Just as typeset text is generally more impressive than that bashed out on an old typewriter with a faded ribbon, so a realistic-looking gouache that contradicts the evidence seems more convincing than a faithful but crude pencil sketch. An illustrator's talent can lend credibility to a demonstrably false message; conversely lack of talent can destroy or obscure a valid one. People are put off by bad drawings. Clearly, archaeologists may knowingly or subconsciously use this human response to claim false authority for dubious interpretations (for an example of this from biology, see Gould 1985, especially pp. 270–80).

These issues are not easy to resolve, but possible solutions to at least some of them are discussed below.

RECONSTRUCTION AS AN ARCHAEOLOGICAL RESEARCH TOOL

Reconstruction drawings should often be an integral part of the research into the site or assemblage even, perhaps especially, during the fieldwork, not something done at the end of the process (*contra* Sorrell 1981:22,26). A good understanding of the functional aspects of ancient life is essential to the creation of good reconstructions, or indeed good archaeology in general. Archaeologists still often show prejudice against the practical and apparently uncerebral, and many betray ignorance – sometimes scandalous – of the physical properties of materials. For example, it was once common to see illustrations of shallow-pitched roofs of straw or reed thatch in spite of the fact that such roofs must have a minimum pitch of about forty-five degrees to be watertight (Reynolds 1979:33).

The value of hands-on experience and knowledge of materials is seen in the following example of the reconstruction of the Roman saddle. Sometimes practicalities allow only exercises on paper, as in the second example, that of interpreting early medieval buildings at Cowdery's Down.

Reconstructing the Roman saddle

Good two-dimensional reconstructions are often best achieved via a three-dimensional stage, as in Peter Connolly's brilliant elucidation of the structure of the Romano-Celtic four-pommel saddle (Connolly 1986,1987; Connolly and Van Driel–Murray 1991). The stirrup was not introduced to Europe until post-Roman times, and so it was widely assumed that the seat of horsemen in earlier periods must have been precarious. Scholars believed that cavalry had been less effective in warfare, since without stirrups horsemen 'obviously' could not charge home with a lance, or wield a sword with full force, without falling off. No complete Roman saddle exists, but fragments of both metal reinforcements and leather covers have long been known, and there are some reasonably informative sculptural depictions.

Connolly is highly unusual in combining the roles of researcher, illustrator, and craftsman. Using fragmentary evidence he demonstrated the true and unsuspected shape of the saddle. He carefully examined details

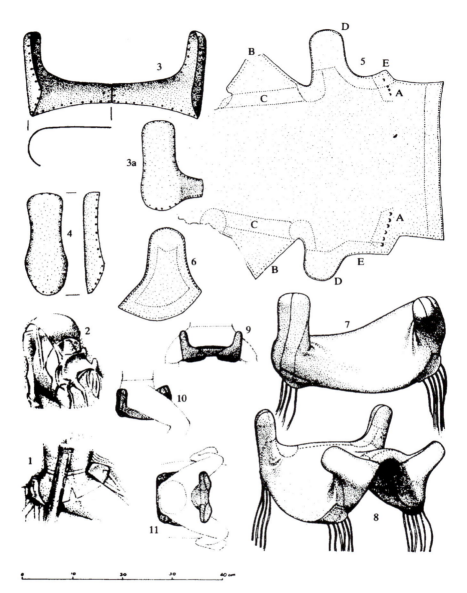

Figure 2.2 Connolly's drawing of the evidence for, and reconstruction of, the Roman cavalry saddle. The original caption reads: '1: A detail of the gravestone of Gaius Romanius showing the lozenge-shaped four-pommelled saddle; 2: A fallen horse with four-pommelled saddle shown on the Julii monument from St Remy in southern France; 3: A pair of bronze pommel stiffeners for the back of a saddle from Rottweil in southern

such as stretch marks on the leather and signs of stress and sewing direction in the stitching holes. Crucially, he combined this with dogged experimentation to create a model saddle that uniquely matched the evidence – and one that worked (Fig. 2.2).

The resulting saddle is very comfortable and gives a far firmer seat than had been assumed by armchair 'experts'. In fact the seat is as firm as that of a saddle with stirrups (the main problem is not falling off, but the skill needed to mount and dismount cleanly when desired!). This elegant piece of work, produced via two- and three-dimensional experiment and published in fine two-dimensional illustrations, has changed our understanding of a key aspect of ancient technology, transportation and warfare. And it has begun a chain of further research, resulting in, for example, the discovery that the Partho-Sassanian world had a similar saddle (Herrmann 1989). Connolly's findings were also swiftly made available to the general public in an excellent full-colour book (one of the original main aims of the exercise) (Connolly 1988: 10–11,30–1).

As this example clearly shows, two-dimensional reconstruction is part of a feedback process between archaeology, other evidence (e.g. depictional and textual) and, ideally, three-dimensional experimentation.

Reconstructing complex timber buildings. Cowdery's Down

Working on reconstructions during research and excavation provokes questions which would otherwise go unasked. I first encountered this as site draughtsman and excavator on the early medieval settlement at Cowdery's Down, Hampshire, England, under the direction of Martin Millett (Millett with James 1983; James, Marshall, and Millett 1984). The regular and complex foundations of massive timber buildings there demanded attempts at detailed reconstructions, to provide hypotheses that might be tested on future excavations. We did not, however, develop visual interpretations after excavation finished; we did much of this work on site. As we dug I created interpretive sketches of the buildings, based on the groundplans, the form of the foundations, and the properties of the timber (identified as oak from charcoal samples) and other materials

---

Figure 2.2 continued   Germany; 3a: The right-hand stiffener seen from the side; 4: One of the front pommel stiffeners seen from front and side; 5: The fragmentary leather saddle covering from Valkenburg in Holland: the left side was presumably a mirror image of the right; 6: A pommel cover from Valkenburg; 7 and 8: Side and three-quarter front views of the reconstructed saddle: 9, 10, 11: Back, side and top views of the saddle showing the rider's position.' (From Connolly 1986, Fig. 11).

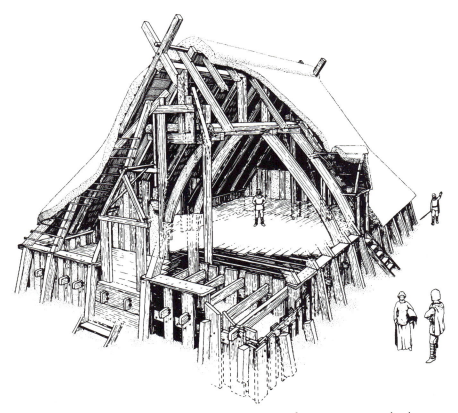

Figure 2.3 The (then) preferred reconstruction of Structure C12, the largest of the early medieval buildings in the settlement at Cowdery's Down, Hampshire, England. This perspective cutaway, with some human figures for scale, is part way between a straightforward technical illustration and a full 'scene showing life at the time' (From Millett with James 1983, Fig. 70).

known or expected to have been used. From these we generated hypotheses that fed questions back into the strategy of the continuing excavation.

We also looked at comparable sites of the period, notably Hope-Taylor's excavations of the huge timber buildings at the famous early medieval royal site of Yeavering, Northumbria, and later medieval building traditions, to see how similar structural evidence had been addressed by other archaeologists.

There has been a major problem in previously published building reconstructions, especially of elaborate structures, such as some timber roofs, which are often inadequately researched or thought through, or

Figure 2.4 The second alternative reconstruction of structure C12, the 'Heorot option', showing a more elaborately embellished building, with carved panels and other decoration, a steeper roof-pitch and an alternative roofing material – wooden shingles (From Millett with James 1983, Fig. 71, top).

at best insufficiently explained in print. Hope-Taylor's reconstructions of the Yeavering buildings, for example, published as we dug our site, either dodge the issue entirely or offer interpretations which are unexplained (Hope-Taylor 1977, Fig. 59, Plates 105–7). Learning from this, Martin Millett insisted that our workings be published, to show how and why we came up with the interpretations we proposed (Millett with James 1983:227–50; James, Marshall, and Millett 1984). Clearly the working out of the reconstructions was a major aspect of the excavation and analysis of the site, not an afterthought.

We faced the problem of representing the varying degrees of knowledge and conjecture in a single drawing while working on the final

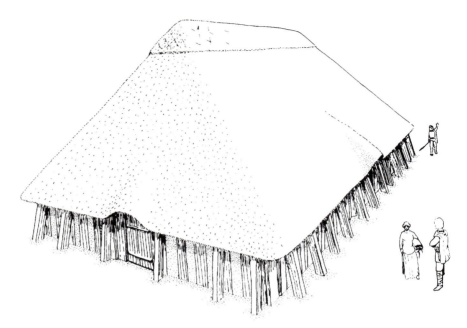

Figure 2.5 The third alternative reconstruction of Structure C12, the 'barn option', representing the other end of the plausibility scale from Fig. 4, constructed as simply as possible (From Millett with James 1983, Fig. 71, bottom).

publication reconstruction of the largest building, the massive but un-romantically named Structure C12 (Fig. 2.3). The component parts of the image appeared equally solid and precise, but they were more and more conjectural the further they were from the ground. How could we indicate what we knew, and where we were guessing? Our solution was to produce three drawings, the preferred option (Fig. 2.3) plus two others, to try to express the range of plausible variation possible on the same evidence. One, which I call the 'Heorot option' (Fig. 2.4), after the legendary royal hall in the Anglo-Saxon poem *Beowulf*, was very elaborate, with decorative carvings and a towering roof with wooden shingles instead of thatch. The other, the 'barn option' (Fig. 2.5), was as simple as possible. I thought of these alternative drawings as crudely analogous to the standard deviation on a radiocarbon date, as a rough expression of the degree of uncertainty.

We had hoped that this approach would encourage discussion of these alternatives in print, but we were disappointed; perhaps response was muted because no similar sites with such finely detailed evidence have yet been found (although see Alcock and Walsh 1993 for some critique). There were verbal objections, however, especially about the raised timber floor shown in the preferred reconstruction – and rightly so, I now think. I still believe there was a floor, perhaps suspended, but how could you build it as shown? The roof structure is probably right in principle (see the detailed arguments in Millett with James 1983 and James, Marshall, and Millett 1984), even if the detail of the timbering is dubious.

Despite (or perhaps because of) the lack of effective critique, these drawings have been much reproduced, sometimes without the variants, and ironically are in danger of becoming exactly the *idées fixes* we tried to avoid.

RECONSTRUCTING SOCIAL RELATIONS

Complex illustrations will betray aspects of the views, prejudices, preferences, and habits of the commissioning archaeologist and illustrator, and will be influenced by their expectations of what the audience will understand. Similarly, viewers will apply their own prejudices in (mis)interpreting the subtle ideological messages conveyed by the images. These issues are especially complex when not only static structures and material processes but also social relations are depicted.

Reconstruction works best for material aspects, for the appearance of portable artifacts, buildings, even landscapes, and in this they can be a great help in both thinking about and presenting the evidence. When they involve human figures interacting within an environment, however, they inevitably raise questions about social structures and relationships. We may find archaeological evidence that allows us with some confidence to reconstruct how people interacted with artifacts, and to some extent with buildings and other spaces, but how did they interact with each other? Unless they are just depicted standing around, their interactions will convey messages about aspects of social organization such as gender, age, and class.

Depictions of humans together speak powerfully to the emotions of the viewer, so this is perhaps the most difficult aspect of all in creating reconstructions, being particularly open to emotive misreading of the archaeologist's intentions. It is where people are most able, and most likely, to project their own preoccupations about human relations, especially where these seem to have implications for wider contemporary debates, such as gender roles and stereotypes (on the largely unacknowledged role of personal emotional makeup in predisposing our attitudes towards archaeological theory and practice, and the projection of our own emotions and preoccupations onto our conception of the past, see James 1993b).

RECONSTRUCTION AS A MEDIUM OF COMMUNICATION WITH THE PUBLIC(S)

Communication with the non-specialist public might appear simple, but we have to consider the cultural conventions and degree of prior knowledge of target audiences. Each will have different sets of assumptions and will lack background knowledge and ideas that academics take for granted. Audiences are also likely to be accustomed to particular sets of visual conventions. Western audiences have long been influenced by television and the cinema and Western children, according to age, by these and comic books. These conventions are now changing at a great rate, however, with the increasing visual sophistication and expectations arising from video and computer-graphic effects.

Conversely, non-Western audiences may not understand conventions familiar to Western archaeologists, such as three-dimensional cutaways; their own traditions may be different (on the question of visual grammars and learning, see Hartley 1978:44–5). So, we must ask what intellectual equipment (which helps understanding) and what baggage (which may promote misinterpretation) will the intended viewers bring? We need to think about the visual conventions familiar to, and the prejudices, preoccupations and stereotypes we expect to find among our target audience. You cannot expect to please everyone, and this makes people fear taking risks.

As reconstructions are inherently subliminal in the way they operate, they can reinforce or even help to create stereotypes; but they can also challenge them. In the past there was a tendency to depict other cultures as inferior; as many people now react consciously to the prejudices of our imperial past, they may make images of earlier cultures that emphasize sophistication. Each alternative, however, may suppress inconvenient evidence. There is also the question of that which is considered 'not suitable for children'. Iron Age Gauls, for example, practised headhunting and human sacrifice. Should you show this or suppress it? How do you judge the appropriate degree of emphasis? It is hard to avoid being either pusillanimous or prurient about aspects of the past which our audiences would consider bizarre. There is a tension between emphasizing 'otherness' and maintaining comprehensibility: attempts to show otherness could be misread as showing 'savageness' or some other message that academics would find undesirable and uncomfortable. On these grounds archaeologists and illustrators may feel pressure to sanitize drawings, or make them look more 'Western', more familiar and so more accessible – so that they represent little more than ourselves in fancy dress.

The examples that follow, primarily intended for non-specialists, show some of these issues in action.

IRON AGE NOBLES. A RECONSTRUCTION FOR THE GENERAL PUBLIC

In 1987 I created a British Museum travelling exhibition, *Celtic Britain; Life and Death in the Iron Age 500 BC–AD 50*; for several years it toured a number of provincial museums across England. It specifically (and literally) drew an analogy between the process of archaeological interpretation and reconstruction illustration. Using image rather than text as the metaphor for how we study the past, it ended with a section entitled 'a picture of the Iron Age', and a painting of an ancient British couple, by Peter Connolly (Fig. 2.6). Connolly worked hard to get a convincing result, photographing costumed models (in this case, my wife Patricia and me) to get realistic poses, fabric draping, and so on. The image was not primarily intended to be experienced in isolation (although it appeared on the poster and later as a postcard). It was intended to be interpreted with accompanying texts: one on an adjacent panel and one on a free handout with an outline of the evidence for the reconstruction on one side and a copy of the image on the other (Fig. 2.6).

The following is the explanatory text for the image, written in 1987, from the handout which accompanied the exhibition.

Peters Connolly's painting of two British nobles . . . shows how we use current knowledge to build up a picture of the Iron Age, in this case quite literally. These figures give an impression of the appearance of a British warrior noble and his wife about 200 BC, drawing on the full range of available evidence.

The woman's jewellery, and the man's sword and iron mail shirt were found in graves in Yorkshire. His shield is based on a mixture of evidence from Britain and the continent. As fabrics rarely survive in Britain, his clothes are based on depictions and continental descriptions. The textiles and cut of the woman's clothes are taken from Iron Age clothing found in peat bogs in Denmark; literature also refers to the Celts wearing multicoloured checked and striped fabrics. The colours used are derived from vegetable dyes used, or at least available, at the time.

The best known of these is the blue dye from the Woad plant, which according to Caesar, was used by the Britons for painting their bodies. It has seemed reasonable to suggest that this was applied in the swirling patterns of Celtic art. The woman's braided hair style is copied from a North European bog body. The man's moustache, and spiky limewashed hair, were fashions recorded throughout the Celtic world. Torcs, or neckrings, were also widely used, but none are known in Yorkshire, so they have been omitted even though they may have been commonplace.

Such attempts at reconstructions can raise new questions. Most Celtic warriors wore their swords on the right. Was this true in Britain in 200 BC? What sort of house would these people have lived in? They are depicted in front of the reconstructed house from Pimperne in Dorset. Were such houses known in Yorkshire in 200 BC? On present evidence we cannot say.

This example shows how diverse sources of evidence can be brought together to form an image of Iron Age Britons. But it is not a definitive

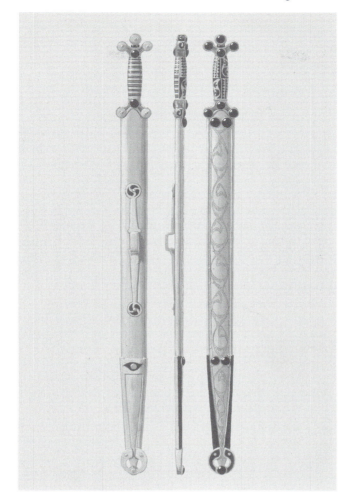

Figure 2.7 The third-century BC La Tène sword from Kirkburn, East Yorkshire (from James 1993a:112). It is a reconstruction, but mainly a technical illustration, in which damage and corrosion have been 'repaired'. Here there were relatively few variables, or (beyond the decision to create the illustration at all) ideological subtexts (there being no figures and therefore no implied roles nor relationships).

Figure 2.6 Gouache of an Iron Age British couple, painted by Peter Connolly for the British Museum's travelling exhibition, *Celtic Britain; Life and Death in the Iron Age 500 BC–AD50.*

picture. If the overall impression is about right, many of the details are informed guesses. New evidence will certainly add new details, and will show that other points are wrong. By constantly modifying our ideas, we hope to improve our picture of the Iron Age.

The text did not discuss gender relations or other social questions, such as why the subject is nobles (the reason is that the archaeological remains of dress and personal equipment belonged mainly to the privileged). This was partly due to lack of space, and to the metaphor being pursued, i.e. a *picture* of what people may have *looked* like in the Iron Age. Undoubtedly it was also because I did not concentrate on such issues at the time.

This example provides several lessons about illustration. Even within its limited and, with hindsight, unsatisfactory terms of reference, some aspects are implausible. The house is both geographically wrong and anachronistic. Other aspects have been overtaken by research, notably the appearance of the Kirkburn sword he is wearing (Fig. 2.7). Also, after studying the sources I now doubt that limewashed hair is so likely in Britain, while the woman's skirt is probably too long, given the muddy conditions.

Reaction to this image has been varied. Barbara Wood of the Museum of London reports that comments, by men and women, vary from: 'she looks like she's about to nag him' to 'why has he got all that gear and she hasn't?', and 'why is she looking up adoringly into his eyes?' (Barbara Wood, personal communication).

The last question is especially interesting, as it contains two components: the difference in stature of the figures and their visual engagement. A woman once confronted me and demanded to know why the woman in the picture was not shown the same height as the man. The answer is that the painting reflects the true difference in physical stature between the models who posed for the original photograph. Such sexual dimorphism is, and was, a fact of life (for data on the stature of Iron Age East Yorkshire populations, see Stead 1991:128, Table 12), and it is instructive that such details can be read as if they were *intended* to be politically threatening.

The interpretation of the mutual engagement of the figures is more complex. First there was my decision to feature, centre stage, a couple in close proximity. Then there was the influence of the models – in this case my wife Patricia and myself. I think the resulting image, based on photographs of us, incorporates aspects of our individual personalities and our relationship at the time – in fact, the emotional communication between the figures startled me when I first saw the result. This was articulated by the illustrator, Peter Connolly, who applied his own particular interpretation to the task. And the viewers have their own responses, conditioned by their life-experiences and attitudes to gender and relationships.

PRODUCING A DRAWING

Reconstruction is an interaction between archaeologist and illustrator. Illustrators often know little of the material culture or technology of the time, and so need close guidance and supervision. Archaeologists need a basic understanding of how drawings are produced; it is not easy, at advanced pencil rough stage, to change the view 'thirty degrees to the left'. The best artwork is usually expensive. A reconstruction may require considerable research and preparation, time and labour, and include photography or model-making. For the book *Archaeology in Britain Since 1945* (Longworth and Cherry 1986) I was asked to produce eighty drawings, many in perspective or axonometric/isometric projection, in six months – a rate of 1.5 working days per drawing! For the Museum this was a substantial financial commitment for one book; academically, the time was inadequate, and I had to use short cuts, such as tracing existing drawings.

Cost and production goals also affect choice of medium. Computer graphics can be stunning, but they remain an expensive option for most purposes. Line drawing is generally cheapest, but has less visual impact than full colour.

In commercial publishing, the fact that the commissioning archaeologist and illustrator are usually working within a predetermined framework set by a publisher (such as a series of books to a standard format) introduces its own constraints. In the commercial world quality control is largely out of the hands of the author. It is often a painful lesson when the idealistic first-time author discovers that publishing is driven by commercial, not academic, considerations. Unless this is taken on board, problems are inevitable. Popular books, especially children's books, are often built around reconstructed scenes of life. Until I wrote one, I cursed authors of such books for egregious errors in illustrations – but the blame may really lie elsewhere. Financial stringency and tight deadlines often place extreme pressure on authors to deliver source material for the illustrators quickly, thereby increasing the possibility of error. Haste is also a key reason that so many books look the same: the easiest solution is to photocopy drawings from earlier books to use as models, a problem not confined to historical publications (Gould 1991). As a result, many reconstructions in children's books reveal no clear thought at all, ideological or otherwise; such copying simply perpetuates the old stereotypes inherent in the exemplars. A recent example from a new school textbook on Roman Britain makes the point (Lancaster 1991). Depicting an Ancient Briton, it swallows Roman propaganda, misuses archaeological evidence and ignores generations of scholarship. The figure is shown dressed in a Fred Flintstone-type animal skin and tasteful coat of blue paint, while carrying the Battersea shield (as usual) and wearing the Meyrick helmet (back to front, baseballcap-wise) (Lancaster 1991:28).

As producing a drawing inevitably generates questions about the evidence on which it is based, there must be constant interplay between illustrator and archaeologist to get a good result, especially with complex scenes or elaborate structures. This is glaringly obvious, but failure often happens on both sides with, for example, illustrators not listening to, or even ignoring, information and archaeologists not alert enough to spot errors in time.

Since illustration of entire landscapes precludes the gaps and evasions possible in text, specific decisions have to be made about how things looked. Many archaeologists find this process difficult, as they consider it speculative. The conflict is especially intense in figural scenes, between preserving due academic reticence (in other words covering ourselves against peer criticism) and producing something detailed, interesting and exciting enough to catch attention and convey specific information and messages. For the illustrator, this frustrating process can be like pulling teeth.

The illustrator usually begins by providing pencil roughs for comment and correction. Next these may be inked in, and/or coloured, before being given a final check. Mistakes can be corrected at proof stage, but this is expensive, sometimes clumsy, and is disliked by publishers.

Problems arise because authors may be ignorant of the relevant material, and illustrators may be awkward and uncooperative, or overworked and forgetful. Sometimes the illustrator forgets or ignores requested corrections. In the first children's book I wrote, I asked the illustrator to draw a Roman bath-house, under construction, to give a plausible reason for showing a cutaway. His pencil rough showed what looked like steel scaffolding poles; they were actually supposed to be lead water-pipes. I asked him to remove these misleading details, but they continued to appear at each stage, inked drawing and proof, and, despite repeated demands, actually made it into the publication, to my anger (James 1987:21). More often, the editor will say that there is no time to redraw an inferior rough, and won't some amendments do? On one book project, I never met the illustrator at all! We communicated only via the editors, and I was not very happy with the results (James 1992). Given these potential pitfalls, it is perhaps not surprising that there are so many bad reconstructions.

The following is a specific case study of how and why a drawing was created, one aimed at the 'interested layperson'.

BOXGROVE

I was commissioned to produce line drawings for the book *Archaeology in Britain Since 1945*, prepared by the British Museum to accompany the major exhibition on the subject in 1986. One, to accompany Nick Ashton's text, was to be a full-page landscape reconstruction of

Figure 2.8 The Boxgrove reconstruction (From Longworth and Cherry 1986, Illustration 2).

Boxgrove, Sussex (Fig. 2.8; Longworth and Cherry 1986:16 and Illustration 2). The drawing was to be peopled with a gatherer–hunter group and fauna, representing the interpretation of the then-current excavations at this Lower Palaeolithic site, with its important environmental data and *in situ* evidence of flintworking (Roberts, Stringer, and Parfitt 1994).

The trick was to try to construct a plausible scene, not too obviously posed and choreographed, that incorporated all the geological, topographical, environmental and archaeological evidence and made the necessary points (such as technology, behaviour, activities, landscape, flora and fauna). This difficult task is one biological illustrators also face, trying to show ancient landscapes and their biota unrealistically crowded together, for the sake of visibility (e.g. Gould 1993:8–9).

The excavator, Mark Roberts, gave me ideas and information about the site itself and inferences from the wider context of the period. After going through the evidence, maps, and illustrations he supplied, we developed the broad structure of the scene and I made a crude preliminary sketch (Fig. 2.9). The drawing was projected at eye-level, to bring the viewer into the scene as much as possible. After we discussed this sketch, I produced a more detailed pencil layout, with figures in correct poses and spatial relations, and we made further modifications (Fig. 2.10). We had to decide numerous points, such as how many figures should be depicted, and what they should be doing. We based the group size on anthropological work on gatherer–hunter groups, and group composition on inferences drawn from limited sexual dimorphism among contemporaneous hominid populations; this implied that there was no dominant male, so that groups could contain a number of adult males.

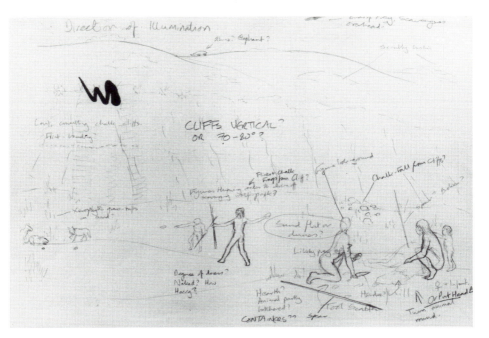

Figure 2.9 The initial rough sketch of the Boxgrove reconstruction.

The scene was to include flint-knappers, placed in the foreground so that their actions were clearly visible.

Here I encountered the problem of gender roles in the Palaeolithic. Did women knap flint? Although no evidence, ethnographic or otherwise, exists for women taking up this task, there are no physical reasons why they should not have done so. Unfortunately, a drawing like this demands specific visual statements on such matters, with no integrated explanation of the reasoning, even if such details are contained in accompanying text. We attempted to make a point about possible gender roles and about cultural transmission; the young boy is learning flintworking from older males. As a deliberate counterbalance to this, to show women also in active roles, I decided to make the pair of figures about to butcher the carcass both female, one with a child. My impression was that such butchery was usually assumed to be a male task, that men used handaxes to butcher their kills, to carry meat to the home base for the women and children; I used female figures to challenge the stereotype. The group driving off the wolves consists of both males and females.

The subject of clothing is entirely speculative; there are no needles or other archaeological correlates so early. We decided that the climate would allow them to be naked, but also that they would use pelts to carry materials.

Figure 2.10 Boxgrove: preparatory sketches for Fig. 2.8, posed photographs as references for the figures, and photos of wolves from London Zoo.

I decided that working from photographs of models for some of the figures would get the best possible results in the limited time available; I worked from the resulting prints to produce plausibly posed, balanced figures. In the final drawing, five of the nine figures were based on models (Fig. 2.8).

The models were Mark Roberts himself and two colleagues from the Museum of London and the British Museum. Although the figures in the drawing were naked, the models kept their clothes on. This was not ideal from the illustrator's point of view, as the conformation of the skeleton and the outline of musculature in the required pose, the main reasons for using live models in this case, were obscured. Archaeologists seem strangely reluctant to strip off, even for the advancement of knowledge, but the fact that the photography took place in a university carpark and a public square may, on reflection, have been factors! (Fig. 2.10).

The archaeological evidence showed that one of the flint-knappers had been left-handed. I achieved this in the drawing by getting the right-handed Mark to pose in an appropriate position and then reversing the negative for printing.

Boxgrove produced skeletal evidence for equid (with clear evidence of butchery), rhinoceros and wolf species. The wolves, drawn from photos of animals at London Zoo, appear as scavengers threatening the kill. I drew the dead equid in the foreground from imagination, hoping that the unusual angle and prone position would hide any anatomical errors from all but keen equestrians and palaeontologists. We inferred the generalized large raptors wheeling overhead from the condition of small mammal bones which had evidently been their prey.

Mark was concerned that we should not be too specific about the figures, as no hominid skeletal remains had yet been found at the site (remains have recently been discovered; see Roberts, Stringer, and Parfitt 1994). Facial morphology is crucial here (post-cranial anatomy at this scale appears generally like that of modern humans), so the scene showed as few faces as possible. I arranged the figures to address Mark's concerns and produced a plausible spatial arrangement: the flint-knappers have their heads down, intent on their work; and some of the foreground figures turn their faces away from the viewer, hiding them as desired. This also helps to draw the eye deep into the scene, where some of the band are driving off wolves with stones.

Another key decision concerned the distribution of body hair on the hominids, a feature that strongly affects one's perception of 'humanness'. As for colour of skin, hair and eyes, no evidence exists, so I chose to show hair distributed like modern humans. This was partly to foster a sense of identification and kinship; these are our ancestors, not something alien or 'inferior'. The wolves, the rhino and the herd of equids are as distant, and therefore as small, as possible. This saved a lot of time in constructing their forms and made them believably far off in the wide, open landscape.

I traced the figures from the photographs, modified them to 'remove' clothes and changed their facial and bodily features, reduced these intermediate pencil drawings to the appropriate scale to fit into the perspective of the scene and then traced through again. I then inserted them into a pencil drawing (not illustrated) from which the final, inked line-drawing would be traced. A last discussion with Mark resulted in further modifications, including a replacement of one of the figures in the foreground. The new figure, based on a photo, had to be further adjusted because the distortion of a wide-angle lens on the camera made his projecting foot far too big.

Illustrators may create artwork the same size as the reproduction or, to get a tighter result through reduction, they may work 'a half up' (150 per cent linear, as Peter Connolly often does) or 'twice up' (200 per cent linear, as I usually do, because of shaky hands!). Boxgrove was drawn at 200 per cent linear, or four times the area, of the printed result. I made the final pencil drawing on paper and traced the inked drawing on plastic film.

As is so often case, the completed drawing was not reproduced as intended: landscape across a full page. Instead it was reduced, to appear across the top half of a single page, with the wheeling birds cropped off. Luckily the line thickness was adequate and the quality of reproduction was good.

In such illustrations there may be unexpected results arising from the composition, or from the model photography, which may not be noticed by illustrator or archaeologist as they are too close to the work. A number of male observers have commented on the unfortunate size, position and orientation of the soft hammer held by one of the flint-knappers!

Palaeolithic archaeology, being relatively 'uninhibited' by data, has maximal scope for speculation, error, controversy, and the projection of one's own prejudices. This may be seen in reactions to the drawing, which was published with negligible explanatory text. For example, feminist criticism, which I recently encountered at the *Women, Heritage and Museums* conference held at the Museum of London in May 1994, provides much insight into the social and political agendas we bring to the perception of pictures.

Not surprisingly, women commented on the gender roles implied by the decision to make the flint-knappers male and the butchery group female. As discussed above, I thought that showing women using handaxes and performing primary butchery was challenging a stereotype; one delegate, however, interpreted it as 'showing women doing the cooking, as usual' (personal comment). The image also provided ammunition for polemic. When Barbara Wood discussed the sexism of the public reporting of the discovery of hominid remains at Boxgrove, she showed a slide of this scene and described the female figure holding the handaxe as a 'sex-kitten'. I find these readings particularly interesting, as the implied gender roles that one may read into this image are actually highly ambivalent. The image makes no statement about who had done the hunting; the kill has been made. Indeed, since the only people who are in proximity to the spears and the kill are female, one might reasonably conclude that the women were the hunters. This visual fact was not remarked upon, and neither was the fact that both males and females drive off the wolves, because these scenarios did not fit with the agenda these delegates applied to the drawing – selecting components to get angry about. The lesson here is that viewers apply their own perceptual biases, conscious or unconscious, to images, just as much as illustrators do in making them. It is impossible, *from the image alone*, to tell whether the various components arose from unthinking sexist assumptions or from carefully thought-out hypotheses.

One picture, it is said, is worth more than ten thousand words; it has taken almost two thousand for but a partial exegesis on this single illustration and its creation, underlining once again the deceptive depths of information hidden in such images.

BUILDING ON EXPERIENCE. VICES INTO VIRTUES

Some archaeologists do not believe in reconstructions, especially for the general public, because of the problems in their use and interpretation. This attitude is surely mistaken, as we alone cannot decide what to present to non-specialists; we have a duty to answer their legitimate questions, of which perhaps the most difficult of all is, 'what did it/they look like?'. Using reconstruction appropriately, we can play up its strengths and even make a virtue of its undoubted weaknesses. Building on approaches discussed above I would argue that reconstruction, either single or, preferably, with multiple alternatives, can be an ideal starting point and centrepiece for a challenging, question-based approach to looking at the past, in live discussion, in books, galleries, or on a computer screen. Did it look like this? How do we know? Where are we guessing? This approach allows the viewer to understand the *process* of archaeology, as well as the 'answers' it produces. Deconstruction of drawings now known or believed to be in error can also be valuable here, for example in highlighting changing assumptions and theoretical fashions.

Where a 'live' interpreter is not available to explain and answer questions arising from such pictures, an integrated text/image approach is a good substitute. In this case, the reconstruction(s) are the framework or matrix for textual arguments and other, supporting, images (photos of objects, site plans). This is an ideal context for the use of multimedia computer technology, with its integration of text and graphic, photographic, and video images. A group of alternative reconstructions would be available on a touch-screen, with the option to zoom into details. The programme would have many routes allowing the viewer to 'click' on points of interest, to bring up explanatory texts and supporting images showing the evidence − if any − and the basis of any inferences. Video clips could show processes like pot-making or flint-knapping, or even show the archaeologist and/or illustrator explaining why they have proposed a particular hypothesis. It allows the viewer to take the argument apart and follow it at will.

Reconstructions created in traditional ways will continue to be used for scholarly research and interpretation by the general public. But if such images are integrated into multimedia programmes in the way advocated here, they will have an even greater potential, as tools at the heart of the dissemination of archaeological knowledge (data, ideas) and knowledge of archaeology (process). The creation and implementation of multimedia reconstructions is more elaborate, and certainly more expensive than traditional images − but not more so than other interpretive display systems used in museums or other educational institutions. Using reconstructions in this way could revolutionize the use and value of such illustrations, changing passive, often enigmatic images into an active means of understanding archaeology, helping the viewer to gain a deeper comprehension of the nature and extent of evidence and the character of academic argument.

ACKNOWLEDGEMENTS

I owe a special debt of gratitude to Brian Molyneaux for encouraging me to write this, and for his patience in awaiting a delayed manuscript.

Particular thanks are also due to Peter Connolly for many enjoyable conversations and much advice and information over the years, and more immediately for permission to reproduce Figs 2.2 and 2.6.

I am grateful to Nick Ashton, Jill Cook, and Mike O'Hanlon for additional information; to Steve Crummy, illustrator, and Karen Hughes, chief illustrator, both of the Department of Prehistoric and Romano-British Antiquities at the British Museum, for references.

I would also like to acknowledge my gratitude to the Trustees of the British Museum for permission to reproduce Figs 2.1 and 2.8, and the Royal Archaeological Institute for permission to reproduce Figs 2.3–2.5.

REFERENCES

Adkins, L. and Adkins, R. 1989. *Archaeological Illustration*. Cambridge: Cambridge University Press.

Alcock, N.W. and Walsh, D. 1993. 'Architecture at Cowdery's Down: a reconsideration.' *Archaeological Journal* 150:403–9.

Connolly, P. 1986. 'A reconstruction of a Roman saddle.' *Britannia* 17:353–5.

Connolly, P. 1987. 'The Roman saddle.' In M. Dawson (ed.), *Roman Military Equipment: The Accoutrements of War*, pp. 7–27. British Archaeological Reports International Series no. 336.

Connolly, P. 1988. *Tiberius Claudius Maximus the Cavalryman*. Oxford: Oxford University Press.

Connolly, P. and Van Driel–Murray, C. 1991. 'The Roman Cavalry Saddle.' *Britannia* 22:33–50 and Plates V–VII.

Dio (Cocceianus), Cassius 1914–27. *Dio's Roman History*. With an English translation by Earnest Cary on the basis of the version of Herbert Baldwin Foster. London: Heinemann.

Gould, S.J. 1985. 'To show an ape.' In *The Flamingo's Smile*, pp. 263–80. London and New York: Norton.

Gould, S.J. 1991. 'The case of the Creeping Fox Terrier Clone.' In *Bully for Brontosaurus*, pp. 155–67. London: Hutchinson Radius.

Gould, S.J. 1993. 'Reconstructing (and deconstructing) the past.' In S.J. Gould (ed.), *The Book of Life*, pp. 6–21. London: Ebury Hutchinson.

Hartley, J. 1978. *Designing instructional text*. London: Kogan Page; and New York: Nichols.

Herrmann, G. 1989. 'Parthian and Sassanian saddlery.' In L. de Mayer and E. Haerinck (eds), *Archaeologia Iranica et Orientalis. Miscellanea in honorem Louis Vanden Berghe, II*, pp. 757–809. Ghent: Peeters Presse.

Hope-Taylor, B. 1977. *Yeavering; An Anglo–British centre of early Northumbria*. London: HMSO.

James, S. 1987. *Rome 700BC–500AD*. London: Franklin Watts.

James, S. 1992. *Ancient Rome*. See Through History series. London: Hamlyn.

James, S. 1993a. *Exploring the World of the Celts*. London: Thames and Hudson.

James, S. 1993b. 'How was it for you? Personal psychology and the perception of the past.' *Archaeological Review from Cambridge* 12(2):85–100.

James, S., Marshall, A., and Millett, M. 1984. An early medieval building tradition. *Archaeological Journal* 141:182–215.

Lancaster, S. 1991. *The Roman Empire*. Ormskirk, Lancs: Causeway Press.

Longworth, I. and Cherry, J. 1986. *Archaeology in Britain Since 1945*. London: British Museum Publications.

Miller, D. 1987. *Material Culture and Mass Consumption*. Oxford: Blackwell.

Millett, M., with James, S. 1983. 'Excavations at Cowdery's Down, Basingstoke, Hampshire, 1978–81.' *Archaeological Journal* 140:151–279.

Moser, S. 1992. 'The visual language of archaeology: a case study of the Neanderthals.' *Antiquity* 66:831–44.

Peach, L.G. 1959. *Julius Caesar and Roman Britain*. No. 561. Loughborough: Ladybird Books.

Reynolds, P. 1979. *Iron Age Farm*. London: British Museum Publications.

Roberts, M.B., Stringer, C.B., and Parfitt, S.A. 1994. 'A hominid tibia from middle pleistocene sediments at Boxgrove, United Kingdom.' *Nature* 369:311–13.

Schadla-Hall, T. and Davidson, J. 1982. 'It's very grand but who's it for? Designing archaeology galleries.' *Museums Journal* 82:171–5.

Sorrell, A. 1981. 'The artist and reconstruction.' In M. Sorrell (ed.), *Reconstructing the Past*, pp. 20–6. London: Batsford.

Stead, I. 1991. *Iron Age Cemeteries of East Yorkshire*. London: English Heritage.

CHAPTER THREE

THINGS, AND THINGS LIKE THEM

ALAN COSTALL

> In a map, squares may represent houses and lines may represent streets, and this can be explained to a child.... Now, it's as though everything on the map represents something . . . but representing is not represented on the map.... Its use is what makes it a map. In the same way it is the use of a sentence which makes it intelligible.
>
> (Wittgenstein, cited in Bouwsma 1986:343)

The inspiration for Wittgenstein's early account of linguistic meaning is supposed to have been a rough sketch of a car accident intended for an insurance claim. Just as the marks on the sketch correspond to the states of affairs depicted, so too, he argued, does language map on to reality. Of course, in his later philosophy, Wittgenstein rejected this 'picture theory of meaning' in favour of an account of language as social practice. Language, he argued, is used in a diversity of ways, and not merely to re-present; in any case, the linguistic act of referring itself presupposes a regular usage, a custom.

Current theories of pictorial meaning divide rather sharply into two main categories: perceptual theories, based on the idea of resemblance, and social theories, which insist upon the essential role of shared practice and convention. These two kinds of theory would appear to be irreconcilable, in terms of both their logic and their empirical implications. Either pictorial meaning is intrinsic and universal, or it is extrinsic and culturally relative.

As the other chapters in this book make clear, visual representations lead a highly active cultural life. Does it follow, therefore, that a 'perceptualist' account must be wrong? In other words, must we reject even the picture theory of pictures? In this chapter, I shall admit to being a psychologist and I will set out the case for what I regard as the most defensible version of resemblance theory. I shall argue that even though resemblance theory has clear limitations, it also has undeniable scope.

THE PLACE OF PICTURES IN PERCEPTUAL THEORY

Pictures could hardly have played a more central role in the history of visual theory. Within traditional theory, the problem of vision has become identified with the question of how we perceive images, and, in particular, perspectival images. This identification stems from two main sources. The first is the traditional analogy between the eye and the camera, proposed in its modern form by Kepler in 1604. The second is much more implicit; it concerns the paradigm of the 'observer', deriving from the practices of perspectival painting.

According to the rationale of linear perspective, a picture should replicate the pattern of light deriving from the depicted scene – a replication unique to a static, monocular station-point adopted by the artist. This 'observer' paradigm has largely structured modern empirical research on perception. Perceptual experiments in effect studied how people 'peer' at things (or more typically pictorial representations of things) when their ability to explore or transform their situation has been prevented. The subjects in such experiments agreed, as it were, to 'lend' their eyes to the experimenter (Merleau-Ponty 1962). Thus, within the confines of the experimental cubicle, at least, the picture theory of vision became true. And, precisely because pictures seemed to be so fundamental to vision in general, they appeared to pose no special problems – except, that is, for that vast range of pictures which never aspired to be in perspective.

However, we are not (usually) the monocular, static creatures presupposed by traditional visual theory. As the psychologist James Gibson observed, our visual system has arms and legs. We get around, and act in and upon the world. Perceiving is part-and-parcel of our activities. The experience of looking at a picture does not, therefore, provide a promising starting point for understanding normal visual perception. After all, 'eyes evolved so as to see the world, not a picture' (Gibson 1967:20).

THE WINDOW THEORY OF PICTURES

But where does this leave pictures? The standard answer within perceptual theory is that an effective picture should replicate the pattern of light which would have emanated from the depicted scene:

> The picture in perspective of a scene or a set of objects is . . . a substitute of the actual objects themselves, so constructed that it sends to the eye a distribution of light similar to that which would be sent by the actual objects, with the result that, for any given eye, the picture produces retinal images similar in shape and dimension to those which would be produced in the same eye by the actual objects.
>
> (Pirenne 1948:15)

On this view, the picture (to use the words of Leon Battista Alberti) can be regarded as 'an open window through which the subject to be painted is seen' (Alberti 1991[1435]:54). Yet there are many problems with this window theory of pictures. Most obviously, there is the problem that many pictures, ranging from outline drawings to extreme caricatures, do not preserve a point-by-point optical equivalence, and they are still highly effective. Furthermore, pictures in perfect linear perspective also pose some serious problems of their own. On the one hand, some pictures in linear perspective – those including extreme foreshortening or involving wide-angle views – appear grossly distorted even to viewers well used to linear perspective. On the other hand, perspective pictures sometimes behave better than they should. Although the point-to-point optical equivalence of a perspective picture to the depicted scene is specific to the proper station-point, observers seldom experience the stark distortions of shear and compression which should arise when the picture is viewed from any other position (Pirenne 1970).

THE INFORMATION THEORY OF PICTURES

An alternative perceptual account of pictures is that they sustain not an optical but an informational relation between the picture and what it depicts. That is to say, the picture selectively 're-presents' not the detailed pattern of light *per se*, but subtle relational structures, available within a normal optic array, which serve to specify the properties of the objects and events depicted (Gibson 1971). Many of these informative structures are not intrinsically perspectival.

Margaret Hagen (1986), an adherent of James Gibson's ecological approach to perception, is widely regarded as having presented the definitive ecological account of pictorial representation. Hagen's account does not privilege linear perspective as the one true mode of depiction. She identifies a range of additional systems of representation which are also geometrically consistent, such as the orthogonal system of Egyptian art and the oblique system of Classical Japanese art. Whereas linear perspective implies a station-point close to the objects depicted, the various additional systems in which no perspectival convergence occurs can be approximated by adopting a relatively distant station-point. The distinctions between these various 'parallel' systems is determined both by the orientation of the object and the picture plane with respect to the line of sight.

Hagen's least contentious point is that many pictures which appear 'out of perspective' are nevertheless projectively consistent, a point, in fact, which had been earlier established by Dubery and Willats (1972,1983). There are indeed a range of traditions of picture making, across a variety of cultures, for which this claim holds. Not all pictures, however, can be assigned to one or other of the possible 'projective systems'. Hagen, unlike Dubery and Willats, fails to acknowledge that drawing systems can only be identified in relation to a scene which happens to include several rectangular objects or surfaces. And even then, the fact that a particular object in a picture happens to correspond to oblique perspective, for example, does not in itself imply that the artist intended to apply any general system to the entire scene. Instead, the particular mode of depiction may simply reflect a preferred solution for representing that kind of object, a so-called 'canonical form' (see Costall 1993). (By this term, I mean a depiction especially informative about the characteristics of the object represented (Katz 1906; Arnheim 1974:108 et seq.; Palmer, Rosch, and Chase 1981), not simply an institutionalized, standardized representation, as in Davis's sense (Davis 1989)).

Hagen also sought to establish the following, more basic claim, that there are good perceptual reasons why any effective picture has to conform to a possible projection:

> My position is that representational pictures, all representational pictures from any culture or period in history, exploit the fact of natural perspective, the geometry of the light that strikes the eye. They succeed as representations because they provide structured visual information equivalent to that provided by the real scene represented.
>
> (Hagen 1986:8)

As it stands, the above quotation could be taken as a restatement of Gibson's definition of a picture. Yet because Hagen's analysis concentrates upon geometrical projection, and has remarkably little to say about information, it precisely misses Gibson's important point – a questioning of the centrality of projection as the basis of pictorial information. By insisting upon the point-to-point consistency of projection, Hagen's account, far from providing an alternative to the traditional window theory of pictures, proves hardly more than a reformulation. She simply relaxes the exclusive emphasis upon linear perspective to include other forms of perspective. And the basic objection to the window theory still applies. There are plenty of pictures which are highly effective, and yet which do not correspond to any consistent projection system, caricatures providing one striking example.

Gibson himself grappled with the problems of pictures throughout his long career (see Reed and Jones 1982). Yet his treatment of pictures remained highly ambivalent. When rejecting the picture theory of vision, he stressed the unreliability of pictures as conveyors of 'frozen' optical structure; when he sought to incorporate pictures within his own alternative account of vision he was happy to acknowledge their remarkable effectiveness. In short, Gibson found himself in a quandary. On the one hand, he wished to stress the rich informative resources of the flowing optical structures available to an active perceiver, in contrast to the static, ambiguous structures identified by the traditional picture-based theories of vision. On the other hand, he could hardly deny the basic fact to be explained by any theory of picture perception, that a static pictorial array can work remarkably well. Indeed, Gibson's texts on visual perception, including his 1979 text in which he most strongly argues for the importance of optic flow, are profusely illustrated – by static pictures.

In his theory of formless invariants, Gibson came to propose that the relevant structures underlying even perspective pictures may not be, after all, the perspectival shapes projected onto the picture plane – shapes which are indeed unique to a particular station-point – but rather more general structures common to (invariant across) various locations. And he provided some suggestions of what these structures might be:

> The information-bearing features are things like the following: alignment or straightness (being 'in line' but not necessarily a line as such) as against bentness or curvature; perpendicularity or rectangularity; parallelity as against convergence; intersections; closures and symmetries. These features are present in an unchanging array but they are best revealed in a changing array, one kind of change being transformation.
>
> (Gibson 1973:45)

Gibson's suggestions are admittedly sketchy, yet in their motivation and specific proposals they bear some interesting relations to Biederman's recent work on recognition-by-components (Biederman 1987). Biederman's purpose, too, was to identify what he terms 'nonaccidental properties' of the array, that is to say structures that are not tied to a particular station-point, and hence generally unaffected by slight variations in viewpoint. And, although Biederman makes no reference to Gibson, there is an interesting overlap between 'the non-accidental two-dimensional relations' he adopts from Lowe and those sketched out by Gibson: collinearity of points or lines, curvilinearity, symmetry, parallel curves, and vertices (see Lowe 1985:77 et seq., Binford 1981).

On this alternative view, vision is not a unitary process of *inverse perspective* (i.e. the reconstruction of the original scene from a perspective image), but a resourceful exploitation of a limitless diversity of informative structures. Such informative structures, unlike the 'pictorial depth cues' of traditional theory, are essentially relational and specific (rather than probabilistically related) to environmental properties and events. Even though a perspective picture can incorporate some of these structures, the structures themselves are not tied to any one view – they are not inherently 'perspectival'. The majority, if not all, of these structures can as easily occur in a non-perspective picture, such as a child's drawing or a highly accomplished caricature. In this way, resemblance theory has broken its exclusive linkage to linear perspective, whilst continuing to maintain that pictures function by re-presenting some of the optical structures which support normal vision.

THE EVIDENCE FOR RESEMBLANCE THEORY

The outright dismissal of 'perceptualist' theories of representation by cultural theorists is astonishing (e.g. Bryson 1983). One has to concede with such critics that anything can become a representation in so far as it can be co-opted within a representational activity. A salt cellar and pepper pot may indeed serve to represent opposing armies during the reminiscences of a general even though they bear no striking resemblances to the entities they are supposed to re-present. But it would be a serious mistake to suppose that pictures normally represent in such an *ad hoc* fashion. There is a substantial body of evidence to suggest that pictures can be 'understood' without the requirement for any sustained prior experience of pictures.

Young babies, and even animals, are able to perceive the similarity between pictures and the objects they depict (e.g. Dirks and Gibson 1977). In one heroic 'deprivation' study, Hochberg and Brooks (1962) did their best to prevent their baby son from seeing any pictures, and, with the exception of occasional glimpses of advertisements in the street, largely succeeded. When their child was two (and sufficiently mobile to threaten intruding upon their furtive television viewing), they tested his recognition of photographs and even line drawings of everyday objects. And he performed remarkably well.

Until quite recently, the cross-cultural research seemed to present quite a different story, of how people from cultures with no tradition of picture-making would be effectively blind to the content of even good quality photographs. Much was made of the apparently foolish way in which these people would turn the pictures over to inspect the other side. Yet, as Kennedy (1974) noted, the people being tested would hardly have been puzzled by the images if they could see them as nothing but meaningless patches of light and dark. Indeed, it was a peculiar assumption on the part of the investigators that the people they were investigating might be unable to make sense of the pictures they were shown, and yet be perfectly *au fait* with the social institution of the psychology experiment! In an impressive and trenchant reassessment of the cross-cultural research, Jones and Hagen (1980) exposed the incompetence and (it has to be said) prejudice of some of the major researchers in this field. Jones and Hagen convincingly argued that much of the existing research was flawed by the use of poorly designed materials; failure to present the material in such a way as to help the observers attend to the pictorial display in the proper way; confusions, on the part of those tested, about the true purpose of the 'test'; and selective reporting of the results. Reassessing the available cross-cultural research, they reached a more positive conclusion, that it is possible to recognize objects, and appreciate the spatial relations between them, without any extensive experience with pictures.

Psychologists have primarily been fascinated by the problem of how the two-dimensional surface of a picture can depict 'depth', and have largely neglected the perhaps more remarkable fact that picture can also represent 'time' – that is, events and actions (Valenti and Costall 1995,1997). Yet the depiction of events and narrative progression is not an invention of modern Western art, but a characteristic of art from many cultures (e.g. ancient Egypt and the Sioux of the nineteenth century in North America, as shown in Chapters 6 and 8 by Molyneaux and Fox). Although there has been little research on the perception of depicted events, the available developmental evidence suggests that recognition is relatively immediate (e.g. Beilin 1991).

The psychological research, then, certainly challenges any theories which formulate the problem of pictorial meaning in terms of a corre-spondence between the picture and what it depicts, but then insist that this relation of correspondence is essentially arbitrary. The 'contents' of pictures are not totally unrecognizable to the uninitiated.

Perceptual accounts do not necessarily predict that pictures should pose *no* problems for the initiated. After all, pictures, being static, cannot display all of the available optic information available, and their presence as objects in their own right is typically conspicuous to the spectator; consequently, there might be a need for the perceiver to learn to deal with these discrepancies.

One variant of perceptual theory has been very influential in the devel-opmental and cross-cultural literature yet has been based upon entirely illogical deduction. According to such an account, pictures should pose *special* problems to the perceiver, precisely because they contain ambig-uous and arbitrary cues *of the same kind* as those supposedly available in the normal environment. Clearly, if the cues available in pictures indeed provide only impoverished information, then picture perception will be difficult. Yet so too would be normal perception. In so far as picture perception shares the same cues as normal perception, no matter how reliable or unreliable these cues might be, then pictures percep-tion has to pose the same problem as normal perception, not a special problem.

Indeed, it is very curious that this form of the conventionalist account could have gained any serious currency among anthropologists and archaeologists, of all people, given their everyday practical experience of dealing with pictorial materials from a wide range of different cultures. What should have impressed them is the remarkable accessibility of such alien images (Molyneaux 1980).

As Kennedy has put it:

> The modern eye can often tell what the lines and contours stand for without instruction or prompts. There are sites on every continent where the flora and fauna of the cave artist's time are plainly available.
>
> (Kennedy 1993:269)

Resemblance theory – the claim that there are fundamental perceptual commonalities between a picture and what it depicts – cannot be
easily rejected. In some important respects, pictures work more effectively than the critics of the theory have claimed, and many of the
relevant informational structures have been identified by researchers. For
many psychologists and other writers as well (e.g. Gibson 1973, Hagen
1986, Kemp 1990, Kennedy 1993), the case for resemblance theory is
secure. But is resemblance theory enough?

DOING THINGS WITH PICTURES

There is more to the understanding of pictures than the 'recognition' of
the depicted objects, the spatial relations among them, or even the events
and actions they enter into. Indeed, as some recent lines of research in
psychology help to reveal, there are important limits to the resemblance
theory of pictures.

Developmental studies prove particularly instructive, in two contrasting
ways. On the one hand, young children fail adequately to grasp how
pictures relate to what they depict, and hence are unable to use pictures
in all of the ways adults take for granted. On the other hand, in their
own art work, they can prove to be refreshingly open to many representational possibilities of painting neglected by adults. Either way, the
developmental studies serve to alert us to the diversity of ways in which
pictures can be used.

In considering the various functions of pictures, Gibson's concept
of affordances is helpful since it challenges the unworldly outlook of
much psychological theory, by stressing the material conditions of human
action (Gibson 1979). But it is also an attempt to avoid the dualisms of
traditional theory, by defining action-possibilities with reference to an
agent. As Gibson put it, affordances cut across the old dichotomy of the
objective and subjective, or of the material and the 'psychological'.
Edibility, for example, a very real property, is not intrinsic to an object
but to an object with respect to an animal. The concept of affordance
is particularly relevant to the study of pictures, given the temptation, in
psychological theorizing, to treat pictures as somehow existing 'outside'
the world within which they represent. Pictures are admittedly unusual
kinds of things, but they are nonetheless things like everything else.

CHILDREN'S (MIS)UNDERSTANDINGS OF PICTURES

A number of recent experimental studies have revealed surprising limitations upon the child's understanding of pictures. Young children can
be very confused about how pictures relate to the world, even when
they are perfectly able to identify the actual contents of the picture. They
may suppose that a photograph of a certain situation should itself change

when that situation undergoes change (Zaitchik 1990). On the other hand, they may prove incapable of using a photograph of a room as a 'map' for telling where in that room something, such as a doll, may have been hidden (see DeLoache and Burns 1993, Nye, Thomas, and Robinson 1995). The difficulty the child has in these tasks is especially perplexing in the light of traditional resemblance theory, since the 'mapping' – the projective relation – between the scene and its depiction was supposed to be 'transparent', the self-evident consequence of the rectilinear propagation of light.

Yet if children fail to appreciate some of the representational affordances of pictures, they also, in their own art work, reveal remarkable insights. A standard assumption in the perceptual approaches to picture making has been the idea that what counts as the representation is the finished artifact. The activity of drawing, painting, or carving is supposed to be merely the means to this end. Theories of children's earliest drawings have typically followed this line of reasoning, assuming that the child's scribbles are entirely meaningless, at best a pretend attempt to produce a drawing 'of something'. It has been supposed that the child enjoys scribbling simply for its own sake, only discovering by accident, as it were, that the traces might create a resemblance (Gibson and Yonas 1968; Luquet 1927; Piaget and Inhelder 1969). Yet this disregards the rich representational significance of early scribbling. It is true that the child sometimes does scribble simply for its own sake, and may indeed become somewhat indignant when asked 'what it is'. At other times, however, as John Matthews' research has shown so well (Matthews 1984), the activity of scribbling proves to be highly representational. For example, what (after the event) appears to be a chaotic tangle of lines may have been the outcome of an energetic enactment by the child of airplanes circling around a target, accompanied by appropriate commentary and sound effects.

Pascale van Dort and I recently studied the painting activities of four-year-olds, during their 'art sessions' at a university nursery (Dort and Costall 1995). We obtained no examples of meaningless scribbling. To a remarkable extent, the children's painting was part-and-parcel of a wider 'performance', where the child would add, or point out, details of the painting as their narrative progressed. Disappearance was often very effectively represented by slapping layers of paint over the depicted person or object to show that they had gone away. The meaning of the paintings would have been impossible to discover in the final, multi-layered product that was left behind. The only example where there was no ongoing narrative proved to have an unexpected twist. One of the girls took an orange pencil in each hand and carefully covered the paper with large overlapping loops; then all of a sudden she turned the pencils around, scooped at the traces, and announced that she was eating noodles!

It is a revelation to observe young children, in action on their own paintings, taking as perfectly 'natural' many of the affordances of trace making which adults often disregard. Of course, even within our society, this kind of 'situated' representation is not completely exclusive to young children's art. Adults, too, sometimes engage in drawing in this way, when trying to convey something to another person. And, when presenting existing images to a child, such as a picture book or the family photographs, adults typically provide a rich narrative context (DeLoache and DeMendoza 1987; Edwards and Middleton 1988). The neglect of the wider affordances of pictures – of picturing – occurs, in its most extreme form within our theories, which take the picture to be a 'finished' object, encountered by a solitary observer (see Costall 1985 and 1995).

THE SOCIAL LIFE OF PICTURES

The developmental research points to important limitations to resemblance theory. It indicates the need for a broader view of what constitutes pictorial representation, and a wider conception of the problem of picture perception. My reason for wishing to locate the debate about the nature of pictorial meaning within psychology, however, is to try to take this debate beyond the territorial wrangle it has largely become. The perceptionists downplay the importance of convention, whilst the sociologists and semioticians question the relevance of resemblance. Yet, resemblance theory and the more social accounts of pictorial meaning are not necessarily mutually exclusive. Indeed, they may indeed be 'symbiotic' (cf. Bryson 1983:64). Both are more or less right in what they affirm, though largely wrong in what they deny.

Although resemblance does not in itself explain representation, it is not beside the point. Many of the social practices which surround pictures depend on resemblance. But it is not the case that usage alone is a social, indeed moral, matter, whilst resemblance is not. The effectiveness and reliability of pictures also depend on the competence and honesty of the picture maker (Costall 1985).

Furthermore, there is a limitless variety of forms and styles of pictures, each with its open-ended possibilities. It is only with the benefit of hindsight that the perceptual theorist pretends to 'predict' the particularities of a tradition from natural laws. The information available in the natural array is inexhaustible, and the structures deployed within any artistic tradition are not just a selection, but, of necessity, a finely judged resolution of competing demands. If, for example, relative size is used to denote the social status of the various people depicted (e.g. Molyneaux 1991), then it cannot easily be deployed within the same picture to represent distance. The lawfulness of a particular pictorial practice does not pre-exist that practice. It emerges, or, more exactly, becomes 'crystallized' in the development of a representational style (see Helmholtz 1954:234–5).

Within the theory of pictorial representation, the appeal to resemblance, mimesis, or 'perceptualism' has been severely challenged. It has been dismissed as politically suspect, an attempt to 'privatize' the problem of pictorial meaning by treating it as a matter of nature rather than culture (e.g. Bryson 1983). Or, as in Goodman's influential criticism of resemblance theory, resemblance has been rightly denied status as a sufficient condition of pictorial representation, only to be relegated, less convincingly, as an entirely incidental matter (Goodman 1976). I wish to defend the obvious, that pictures do more or less look like what they depict, and that this fact about pictures must play some part in explaining how they 'work'.

It is true that there is no 'essential copy' (Bryson 1983). Resemblance is not replication. It takes many forms. 'Likeness' depends upon the intelligent, selective deployment of informative structures, and therein lies part of the 'art' of pictorial representation. It is also true, as Goodman (1976:4) claims, that the relation of resemblance is symmetrical, whereas that of representation is not – a portrait and its subject resemble one another, yet only the portrait, not the subject, serves as the representation. This does not, however, imply the irrelevance of resemblance to representation, nor that resemblance is a matter internal to a particular style of depiction. Pictures can educate our attention by alerting us to likeness. Turneresque sunsets really do exist. Turner's contribution was to help us notice them, and, in the process, to impress us by just how much they resemble his paintings.

REFERENCES

Alberti, L.B. 1991[1435]. *On Painting*. Translated by Cecil Grayson with an introduction and notes by Martin Kemp. London: Penguin.

Arnheim, R. 1974. *Art and Visual Perception: a Psychology of the Creative Eye.* New Edition. Berkeley, CA: University of California Press. [First edition published 1954.]

Beilin, H. 1991. 'Developmental aesthetics and the psychology of photography.' In R. Downs, L.S. Liben, and D.S. Palermo (eds), *Visions of Aesthetics, the Environment, and Development*, pp. 45–86. Hillsdale, NJ: Erlbaum.

Biederman, I. 1987. 'Recognition-by-components: A theory of human image understanding.' *Psychological Review* 94:115–47.

Binford, T.O. 1981. 'Inferring surfaces from images.' *Artificial Intelligence* 17:205–44.

Bouwsma, O.K. 1986. *Wittgenstein: Conversations 1949–1951*. J.L. Craft and R.E. Hustwit, eds. Indianapolis, IN: Hackett Publishing.

Bryson, N. 1983. *Vision and Painting: the Logic of the Gaze*. London: Macmillan.

Costall, A.P. 1985. 'How meaning covers the traces.' In N.H. Freeman and M.V. Cox (eds), *Visual Order*, pp. 17–30. Cambridge: Cambridge University Press.

Costall, A.P. 1993. 'Beyond linear perspective: a cubist manifesto for visual science.' *Image and Vision Computing* 11:334–41.

Costall, A.P. 1995. 'The myth of the sensory core: the traditional and ecological approach to children's drawings.' In C. Lange–Küttner and G.V. Thomas (eds), *Drawing and Looking*, pp. 16–26. London: Harvester–Wheatsheaf.

Davis, W. 1989. *The Canonical Tradition in Ancient Egyptian Art*. Cambridge: Cambridge University Press.

DeLoache, J.S. and Burns, N.M. 1993. 'Symbolic development in young children: understanding models and pictures.' In C. Pratt and A.F. Garton (eds), *Systems of Representation in Children*, pp. 91–113. London: Wiley.

DeLoache, J.S. and DeMendoza, O.P. 1987. 'Joint picturebook interactions of mothers and 1-year-old children.' *British Journal of Developmental Psychology* 5:111–24.

Dirks, J. and Gibson, F. 1977. 'Infants' perception of similarity between live people and their photographs.' *Child Development* 48:124–30.

Dort, P. van and Costall, A.P. 1995. '"I'm eating my noodles with crayons": The drawing activities of pre-schoolers.' Unpublished report.

Dubery, F. and Willats, J. 1972. *Drawing Systems*. London: Studio Vista.

Dubery, F. and Willats, J. 1983. *Perspective and Other Drawing Systems*. London: Herbert Press.

Edwards, D. and Middleton, D. 1988. 'Conversational remembering and family relationships: how children learn to remember.' *Journal of Social and Personal Relationships* 5:3–25.

Gibson, J.J. 1967. 'Autobiography.' In E.G. Boring and G. Linzey (eds), *A History of Psychology in Autobiography*, Vol. 5, pp. 127–43. New York: Appleton–Century–Crofts.

Gibson, J.J. 1971. 'The information available in pictures.' *Leonardo* 4:27–35.

Gibson, J.J. 1973. 'On the concept of "formless invariants" in visual perception.' *Leonardo* 6:43–5.

Gibson, J.J. 1979. *The Ecological Approach to Visual Perception*. Boston, MA: Houghton–Mifflin.

Gibson, J.J. and Yonas, P.M. 1968. 'A new theory of scribbling and drawing in children.' In H. Levin, E.J. Gibson, and J.J. Gibson (eds), *The Analysis of Reading Skill*, pp. 356–66. Final Report, 5–1213. Washington, DC: US Department of Health, Education and Welfare, Office of Education.

Goodman, N. 1976. *Languages of Art. Second Edition*. Indianapolis, IN: Hackett.

Hagen, M.A. 1986. *Varieties of Realism: Geometries of Representational Art*. Cambridge: Cambridge University Press.

Hagen, M.A. and Jones, R.K. 1978. 'Cultural effects on pictorial perception.' In R.D. Walk and H.L. Pick (eds), *Perception and Experience*. New York: Plenum.

Helmholtz, H. von 1954. *On the Sensations of Tone as a Physiological Basis for the Theory of Music*. Translated by A.J. Ellis. New York: Dover Publications. [Based on fourth German edition of 1877; first edition 1862.]

Hochberg, J. and Brooks, V. 1962. 'Pictorial recognition as an unlearned ability: a study of one child's performance.' *American Journal of Psychology* 75:624–8.

Jones, R.K. and Hagen, M.A. 1980. 'A perspective on cross-cultural perception.' In M.A. Hagen (ed.), *The Perception of Pictures*. Vol. 1, pp. 193–226. New York: Academic Press.

Katz, D. 1906. 'Fin Beitrag zur Kenntnis der Kinderzeichnungen.' *Zeitschrift für Psychologie* 41:241–56.

Kemp, M. 1990. *The Science of Art: Optical Theories in Western Art from Brunelleschi to Seurat*. New Haven: Yale University Press.

Kennedy, J.M. 1974. *A Psychology of Picture Perception: Images and Information*. San Francisco: Jossey-Bass.

Kennedy, J.M. 1993. *Drawing and the Blind*. New Haven: Yale University Press.

Lowe, D.G. 1985. *Perceptual Organization and Visual Recognition*. Boston, MA: Kluwer.

Luquet, G.-H. 1927. *Le Dessin Enfantin* Paris: Alcan. [Third edition republished by Delachaux and Niestle, Lausanne and Paris, 1977.]

Matthews, J. 1984. 'Children drawing: are young children really scribbling?' *Early Child Development and Care* 18:1–39.

Merleau-Ponty, M. 1962. *The Phenomenology of Perception*. London: Routledge and Kegan Paul.

Molyneaux, B. 1980. 'Cave art.' Videotaped interview, Scarborough College, University of Toronto.

Molyneaux, B. 1991. 'Perception and situation in the analysis of representations.' Unpublished PhD thesis, Department of Archaeology, University of Southampton.

Nye, R., Thomas, G., and Robinson, F. 1995. 'Children's understanding about pictures.' In C. Lang–Küttner and G.V. Thomas (eds), *Drawing and Looking*, pp. 123–34. London: Harvester-Wheatsheaf.

Palmer, S., Rosch, F., and Chase, P. 1981. 'Canonical perspective and the perception of objects.' In J. Long and A. Baddeley (eds), *Attention and Performance*. Vol. 9, pp. 135–51. Hillsdale, NJ: Lawrence Erlbaum.

Piaget, J. and Inhelder, B. 1969. *The Psychology of the Child*. London: Routledge and Kegan Paul.

Pirenne, M.H. 1948. *Vision and the Eye*. London: Chapman and Hall.

Pirenne, M.H. 1970. *Optics, Painting, and Photography*. London: Cambridge University Press.

Reed, F.S. and Jones, R.K. (eds) 1982. *Reasons for Realism: Selected Essays of James J. Gibson*. Hillsdale, NJ: Lawrence Erlbaum.

Valenti, S.S. and Costall, A.P. 1995. 'Perception of lifted weight in photographs.' In B. Bardy, R.J. Bootsma, and Y. Guiard (eds), *Studies in Perception and Action*. Vol. 3, Mahwah, NJ: Lawrence Erlbaum.

Valenti, S.S. and Costall, A.P. 1997. 'Visual perception of lifted weight from kinematic and static (photographic) displays.' *Journal of Experimental Psychology: Human Perception and Performance*. (Forthcoming).

Zaitchik, D. 1990. 'When representations conflict with reality: the preschooler's problem with false beliefs and "false" photographs.' *Cognition* 35:41–68.

CHAPTER FOUR

'TO SEE IS TO HAVE SEEN'

Craft traditions in British field archaeology

RICHARD BRADLEY

ON LEARNING TO SEE

Clive Gamble (1992) has observed an interesting tendency in the archaeological literature. The more theoretical the contents of any book or paper, the fewer the illustrations. Radical archaeology, it seems, is a specifically verbal medium, and drawings or photographs have little place amidst so much abstraction. The emphasis is on the problems of writing and on the possibilities of 'reading' the past. Yet the textual metaphor is actually applied less to the writings of archaeologists than to the study of material culture. Thus Christopher Tilley's book *Material Culture and Text* is actually a study of visual images, the prehistoric rock art of Scandinavia (Tilley 1991).

Even that statement over-simplifies the issues, for Tilley's book is based only partly on his fieldwork. Its chief source is a comprehensive corpus of these carvings compiled by an earlier investigator (Hallström 1960). The main data used in Tilley's study are not the rock carvings of Namforsen at all, but the depictions of those carvings published many years before. Tilley is good at identifying structures amongst the prehistoric images, but he has little to say about the character of the representations through which he views them. That is because archaeologists take the process of illustration for granted. Yet depicting the 'archaeological record' is very far from straightforward, for first it must involve a process of learning to see it.

The history of art is the history of particular ways of seeing, and very often it illustrates a common pattern. At first, new styles are received with incomprehension, even hostility. As they become more familiar, they start to seem inevitable and are imitated by lesser artists until they lose their vitality. What had once appeared strange and incoherent eventually looks quite ordinary. A perfect example is the English reception of Post-Impressionist painting (Bullen 1988). The work of Cézanne was derided as clumsy and ill-conceived, but within a few years his work was being imitated widely. The unfamiliar came to be immediately recognizable and his paintings were no longer curiosities. Rather, they were commodities traded on an international market.

Like painting, field archaeology is all about ways of seeing, and its development goes through a similar cycle to the history of art. This is not fully acknowledged because the process of seeing takes place in a special context. Our perceptions are closely monitored and the process of undertaking fieldwork is dominated by a stance of objectivity. We transcribe the past as if that process posed no problems at all. Too many people are content to assume an agnostic position. Not for them to interpret what they see; that can be left to later users of their records.

The limitations of such a stance become apparent once we recognize that some of the most influential field archaeologists have been deeply involved with the visual arts, many of them those excavators who have had the strongest influence over the adoption of new techniques. There is the famous case of Heywood Sumner, whose pictures are exhibited today, and in Britain there are archaeologists who are also art collectors: Grahame Clark, Stuart Piggott, Martyn Jope, and Colin Renfrew. Far more important are those excavators whose careers began in the visual arts: Mortimer Wheeler was once an art student, and so was Philip Barker. Chris Musson trained as an architect. Brian Hope-Taylor worked as a commercial artist and Philip Rahtz as a photographer. That is no coincidence, for those same people were among the first to discover particular ways of seeing. It is my contention that we overlook this because now everyone has adopted their ways of seeing.

For example, Mortimer Wheeler and Philip Rahtz have both had a major influence on our ability to discern stratigraphic relationships in the field. Brian Hope-Taylor and Philip Barker have done more than anyone else to improve our ability to recognize the remains of ancient buildings. This is especially clear where they excavated on sites that had been studied before. At Bokerley Dyke, Rahtz was able to unravel a stratigraphic sequence left unresolved by General Pitt Rivers (Rahtz 1960). Philip Barker has identified buildings at Wroxeter which were not recognized by his predecessors on the site (Barker 1993, Chapter 10). Such archaeologists have set an example that has been emulated, and Barker has written extensively about his methods of excavation and illustration (Barker 1993). Both Barker and Rahtz have developed new ways of seeing and have made it possible for other people to see in the same fashion. That is the same as the process that we have identified in the visual arts.

CRAFT TRADITIONS IN FIELD ARCHAEOLOGY

So far I have explained what I mean by 'learning to see' – but what is the significance of my reference to 'craft traditions'? Excavation reports make very dull reading, and some parts we skip altogether. I have become an aficionado of Acknowledgements, for these often explain much of the main text. Reading the Acknowledgements is an under-valued skill, yet it can be employed as a source of evidence in its own right. It tells us which field archaeologists worked together at different times, and sometimes it indicates the tasks that they performed. How did those professional relationships work in the field? What would those people have been able to see during their time on particular sites? And how did that experience influence what they were able to see in later life? By charting the interaction of a number of significant figures, we can trace the ways in which observations and ideas are transferred from one project to another. To put it another way, we can identify different networks and their consequences for field archaeology.

To illustrate this point I would like to consider two important excavations in Britain during the 1960s and 1970s – Hen Domen, dug by Philip Barker and Robert Higham (1982), and South Cadbury, dug by Leslie Alcock (1972). What was new on these particular sites? South Cadbury saw the excavation of ephemeral timber buildings inside a hillfort. Here the Cadbury team were able to identify for the first time the remains of stake-built round houses (Alcock 1972, Chapter 4). Barker and Higham's achievement at Hen Domen was really rather similar. Through patient observation, combined with large-scale stripping, they succeeded in identifying the fugitive traces of very slight timber buildings, concealed amidst a wider spread of rubble (Barker and Higham 1982).

The same kinds of observations were made at other sites. Sometimes the director was the same, but in other cases this happened because the projects were mounted by members of the original teams or their associates. One network links the excavation of Hen Domen to work on the late deposits of two Roman towns – Wroxeter and Dorchester-on-Thames (Barker 1993; Rowley and Brown 1981). Another connects former members of the Cadbury team with work at two other hillforts – the Breiddin and Moel Y Gaer (Musson 1991; Guilbert 1976). Those learning networks also intersect, providing an additional link between the teams working at Hen Domen and Moel Y Gaer, where a final phase of buildings was discovered, very similar in character to those on Philip Barker's site (Figs 4.1 and 4.2). In just the same way, work at Trelystan identified stake-built structures which left traces similar to those in the hillforts I mentioned earlier (Britnell 1982). Again the excavator had worked at South Cadbury earlier in his career (Fig. 4.3).

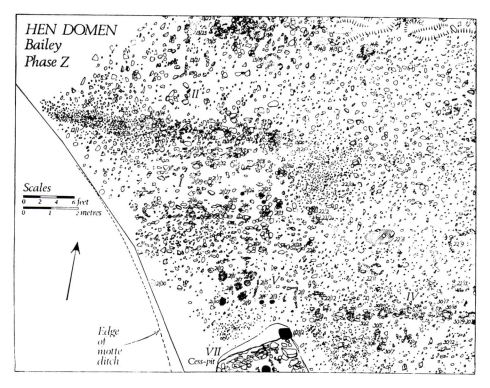

Figure 4.1 Traces of timber buildings at the medieval castle of Hen Domen. Drawn by Philip Barker and reproduced with his permission.

These links are very obvious, and most of them are acknowledged in the literature, but there is another point to consider. Quite often field archaeology leads to the identification of new 'types': types of monument, types of building, even types of artifact. Their initial definition is followed by a period of research concerned with charting their chronology and distribution. But in this case we are concerned with links between features of quite different periods. Thus South Cadbury and the Breiddin contain stake-built houses of Iron Age date, but Trelystan is a Late Neolithic site (Fig. 4.3). In the same way, the buildings at Hen Domen are medieval (Fig. 4.1), but those at Dorchester-on-Thames are probably Anglo-Saxon and those at Wroxeter are Late Roman. The structures attributed to the last phase of activity at Moel Y Gaer (Fig. 4.2) are most likely to date from the Iron Age. In short, we are not tracing the diffusion of particular forms of building as some kind of type fossil; we are tracing the diffusion of particular skills among modern excavators, and, more than anything else, the ability to look at

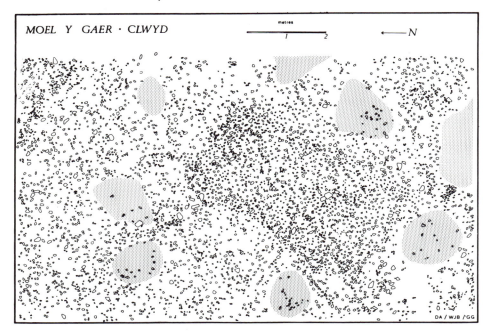

Figure 4.2   The traces of a timber building inside the Iron Age hill fort at Moel Y Gaer. Redrawn by Philip Barker and reproduced with his permission.

excavated surfaces in particular ways. That can best be traced through the careers of individual field archaeologists and their contacts with one another. The outcome of those contacts defines a 'craft tradition'.

I have chosen an example that I know, as a prehistorian, but it is obvious that a similar process could be illustrated taking different points of departure. One well documented tradition can be traced back to Wheeler's excavation at Maiden Castle (Wheeler 1943), where the entire labour force is listed, season by season, in the site notebooks. Another powerful influence was the excavation of the medieval village at Wharram Percy (Beresford and Hurst 1990), and in just the same way the Biddles' work at Winchester developed the range of observations thought possible in urban archaeology (Biddle and Biddle 1969). A more recent example of the same development is Martin Carver's work at Sutton Hoo (Carver 1992). In every case we are concerned with a similar process. Individuals or groups acquire the ability to see hitherto unexpected phenomena, from buildings to body stains. Sometimes their ability to make such observations may be sharpened by a background in the visual arts. There follows a period of re-education in which other people learn how to do the same, and, lastly, a phase of acceptance in which excavators come

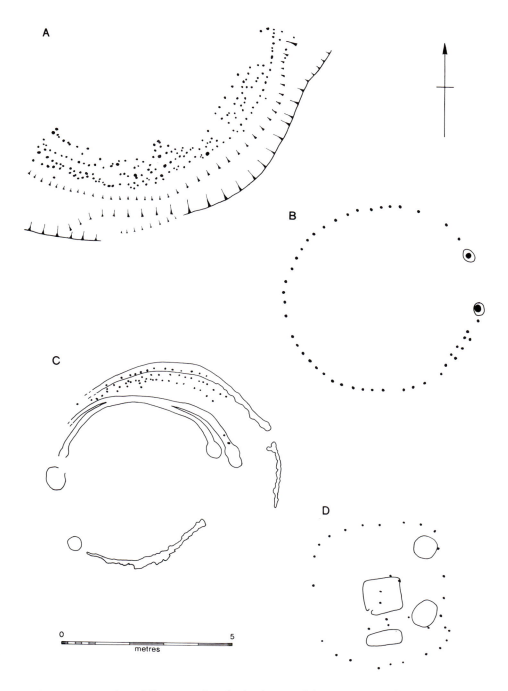

Figure 4.3 The 'diffusion' of stake-built round houses on prehistoric sites in England and Wales. A: South Cadbury; B: Moel Y Gaer; C: The Breiddin; D: Trelystan. Drawing: Margaret Mathews.

to terms with those observations and treat them as straightforward, even commonplace. At that stage certain features are used as conventional equivalents for specific phenomena in the past. But apprehension of those phenomena is visual rather than analytical. Quite simply, people have learned how to look and they know what they expect to see.

But how are those observations to be communicated? The question is especially important as more universities avoid the expense of conducting fieldwork and consign their students to the library. Patterns in the soil may be described in words, but the major emphasis has to be on visual media. Again individual perceptions are absolutely central to the process. All drawings involve fundamental decisions about the manner of representation, even when this is accommodated to a standard 'house style'. Field drawings and printed drawings rarely look alike, and the published illustrations are a very stylized rendition of the records on which they are based.

STYLES OF ILLUSTRATION

If we can trace traditions of seeing, we can also recognize traditions of representation, and again some of the most influential figures have a background in the visual arts. There are styles of archaeological illustration just as there are schools of painting, and underlying them are fundamental disagreements about what is to be shown. One of the most significant disputes was between Wheeler and Bersu, who were digging on the chalk at the same time. Should section drawings mark firm divisions between different contexts and, almost inevitably, fix a particular interpretation? Or should they seek to reproduce the more fuzzy patterning actually seen on the ground (see Wheeler 1954:59–61)? It is no accident that Wheeler became jealous of Bersu's influence and that the two men attracted mutually exclusive teams in the field.

Such differences are not only philosophical. The choice of drawing style conditions what the readers of an excavation report will see on the page, but it will also influence what they may go on to see in the field. It determines their expectations of how archaeological phenomena should look and how they ought to be represented. Again we can talk about learning networks. People who excavate together may share a similar range of observations in the field, and they may also develop similar ways of depicting them in print. Wheeler's style of depicting unambiguous layer divisions was widely imitated by his colleagues and still influences archaeological illustration today. It is worth comparing one of his sections of an Iron Age pit on the chalk with a similar illustration by the equally influential Bersu (Figs 4.4 and 4.5). Not only is this drawn in a quite different way: the latter's field drawings contain quite different types and quantities of information. They epitomize a different style of representation, and they betray a quite different way of seeing.

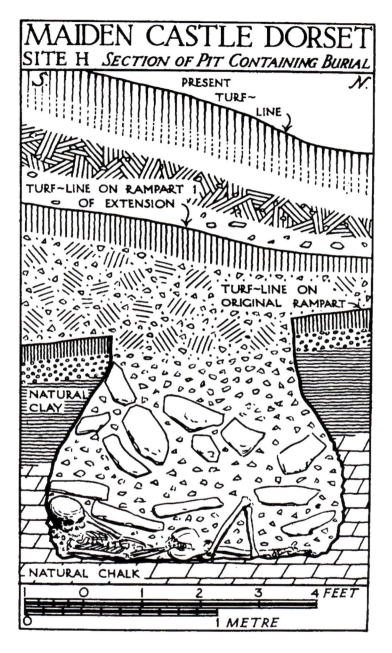

Figure 4.4 Section of a chalk-cut Iron Age storage pit at Maiden Castle. Drawn by Mortimer Wheeler and reproduced by permission of the Society of Antiquaries.

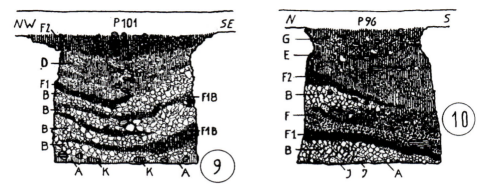

Figure 4.5 Sections of two chalk-cut Iron Age storage pits at Little Woodbury. Drawn by Gerhard Bersu and reproduced by permission of the Prehistoric Society.

One way of learning to draw is by imitating a congenial style: a good example is the work of Dudley Waterman, who taught architectural draughtsmanship before he became an archaeologist. His distinctive way of drawing plans and sections has been widely imitated, and by people who never worked with him in the field. There is no harm in that; archaeological illustrators do not make a virtue of experiment, and those who have done so, notably W.F. Grimes, have attracted very few followers. But such choices inevitably constrain what can actually be shown. They affect the amount of detail in any drawing, and the emphasis placed on different components of the design. Such conventions mean that the results of very different projects may eventually look alike.

CONCLUSION: 'TO SEE IS TO HAVE SEEN'[1]

I have emphasized that field archaeology is a process of learning to see. Field archaeologists may aim for objectivity, but by the very nature of the discipline they can never achieve it. I have also argued that archaeological illustration poses similar problems. The subjective element in fieldwork can be frustrating and even dangerous, but it cannot be avoided. In the case of certain excavators it may be a source of new observations from which the profession as a whole can learn.

Field archaeology is very much a visual discipline and the processes by which observations are made and communicated depend on special skills: skills in seeing and skills in depicting what is seen. What start as individual perceptions may become the common property of those who practise the discipline, but that takes time. It depends partly on the existence of networks of professional contacts and partly on the traditions of representation that we find in the published literature. Both tend to mask the individual consciousness, and over time they can endow the results of archaeological fieldwork with a spurious uniformity and authority. I would ask for a little more humility in the face of the archaeological record, for that 'record' consists of nothing more than what we are able to observe at particular stages in our careers, under the guidance of those who teach us, and within the limits of our own imaginations. Field archaeologists define themselves by looking at things, but what they are able to recognize will often depend on what they have seen before. That is the significance of the quotation which provides the title of this article. Like painters, sculptors, and photographers, archaeologists must spend their working lives in learning how to see.

NOTE

1   The quotation comes from *The Book of Disquiet* by Fernando Pessoa (published in English translation in 1991).

REFERENCES

Alcock, L. 1972. *By South Cadbury that is Camelot*. London: Thames and Hudson.

Barker, P. 1993. *Techniques of Archaeological Excavation*. Third edition. London: Batsford.

Barker, P. and Higham, R. 1982. *Hen Domen, Montgomery. A Timber Castle on the English–Welsh Border*. London: Royal Archaeological Institute.

Beresford, M. and Hurst, J. 1990. *The Wharram Percy Deserted Medieval Village*. London: Batsford.

Bersu, G. 1940. 'Excavations at Little Woodbury.' *Proceedings of the Prehistoric Society* 6:30–111.

Biddle, M. and Biddle, B. 1969. 'Metres, areas and robbing.' *World Archaeology* 1:209–19.

Britnell, W. 1982. 'The excavation of two round barrows at Trelystan, Powys.' *Proceedings of the Prehistoric Society* 48:33–201.

Bullen, J. 1988. *Post-Impressionists in England*. London: Routledge.

Carver, M. 1992. 'The Anglo-Saxon Cemetery at Sutton Hoo: an interim report.' In M. Carver (ed.), *The Age of Sutton Hoo*, 343–71. Woodbridge: Boydell Press.

Gamble, C. 1992. 'Reflections from a darkened room.' *Antiquity* 66:26–31.

Guilbert, G. 1976. 'Moel Y Gaer (Rhosesmor) 1972–3: an area excavation in the interior.' In D. Harding (ed.), *Hillforts: Later Prehistoric Earthworks in Britain and Ireland*, pp. 303–17. London: Academic Press.

Hallström, C. 1960. *Monumental Art of Northern Sweden from the Stone Age: Namforsen and Other Localities*. Stockholm: Almquist and Wiksell.

Musson, C. 1991. *The Breiddin Hillfort*. London: Council for British Archaeology.

Pessoa, F. 1991 [1982]. *The Book of Disquiet*. London: Quartet Books.

Rahtz. P. 1960. 'An excavation on Bokerley Dyke, 1958.' *Archaeological Journal* 117:65–99.

Rowley, T. and Brown, L. 1981. 'Excavations at Beech House Hotel, Dorchester-on-Thames, 1972.' *Oxoniensia* 46:1–55.

Tilley, C. 1991. *Material Culture and Text: the Art of Ambiguity*. London: Routledge.

Wheeler, R.E.M. 1943. *Maiden Castle, Dorset*. London: Society of Antiquaries.

Wheeler, R.E.M. 1954. *Archaeology from the Earth*. Oxford: Clarendon Press.

CHAPTER FIVE

PHOTOGRAPHY AND ARCHAEOLOGY

MICHAEL SHANKS

INTRODUCTION

Photographs are often taken for granted in archaeology. They are treated as technical aids, helping to record or identify features and objects, or they may provide illustrative ambience, landscape backdrop, evocations of setting.

There is little or no questioning of conventional uses of photography. Archaeological photographs are treated as transparent windows to what they are meant to represent. I aim to inspect this apparent clarity. Taking direction from cultural studies (see particularly Hillis Miller 1992) and from the sociology of knowledge (e.g. Fyfe and Law (1988) for visual imagery), my perspective is one of critique, looking within cultural works to reveal sedimented meanings which serve particular interests: it is a negative outlook, aiming, through rational scrutiny, to unveil and debunk neat systems of method and thought, on the grounds that they are always inadequate to reality.[1]

It is proposed that photography, far from being homogeneous, is an unstable category, and that it is better to think less of photographs than of *photoworks*, with emphasis placed upon acts of cultural production: photowork is then one aspect of how the archaeologist may take up the remains of the past and work upon them. This is the positive moment of critique – finding the creative potential within particular modes of cultural production, a potential to express different interests in the material past (Shanks 1992).

In identifying the potential of photowork to relate in different ways to the purpose, interest, and function of archaeological discourses, this chapter is conceived as a contribution to new archaeological methodologies which have been termed *postprocessual*, and which are now better known as *interpretive*, concerned with the interpretation and understanding of the material past.[2] It is considered that the moment is particularly ripe for this because fundamental shifts are taking place in our relationships with (visual) reproductions of 'reality'; the implications of digital technologies will be assessed. The position taken is that the ability to sample, quote, and seamlessly manipulate the visual world offers great scope for presenting pasts of richer texture, more attuned to our contemporary selves, and more edifying.

THE PHOTOGRAPH AS RECORD AND WITNESS

Photographs in archaeology are most often used to record, document, and illustrate what has been found, what is being discussed in a text. Handbooks of archaeological photography are all about how to achieve accurate and full recording (Dorrell 1989 is a recent example). Photography here is a technical issue, to do with means and not ends; the photograph is considered a means to objective recording.

The photograph is demonstrative and pronominal, standing for the thing photographed. A witness says 'I was there'; as a documentary witness, the photograph is held to say 'look and see for yourself'. Thus a photograph may be used to provide authority based upon the notions of presence and seeing.

There are connections with a popular use of photography, the snapshot, which bears witness to a family holiday or the like.[3] Such a photograph shows you have been somewhere. Taking the snapshot of a family occasion is often a response to a desire to capture an objective correlative of an experience or moment, or to capture what will become a memory. Photographs in reports are a way of quoting the material past, attempts to import things directly into text (the objective correlatives) as a support for what is being said; the implication is that material things and looking have primacy over ideas and writing. I will later contrast other modes of quotation.

PHOTOGRAPHS AS NOTES

Excavators and researchers frequently use photographs as notes. A site may be photographed many times in the process of excavation to aid the process of writing up, and as a record. Involved here may be ideologies of *innocent looking*: the idea that a photograph is basically unaffected by the interpreting 'subjectivity' of the looker, once the camera has been pointed. That photography is a mechanical, electronic, and chemical means of reproduction is crucial here. These fields are considered automatic, machinic, and natural (chemical reactions), opposed to the subjective and personal. With care the photographer can be reduced to an operative, minimizing interference in a natural and objective technique. With the camera as automaton, as machinic eye, technology is divorced from social and personal determination.

Figure 5.1 The photograph as technological note: a Korinthian aryballos (perfume jar) of the early seventh century BC. Convenience came with 35mm photography in the 1920s and the Leica camera. Here a hand-held single-lens-reflex camera with close-focussing macro lens, complemented by ringflash and automatic off-the-film metering enables fast and accurate results, which approach those of a studio set-up.

That technique and function are neutral and independent in this way is not a statement of fact but a proposition which is much contested in histories and sociologies of design and technology,[4] as well as in some branches of archaeology.[5] Looking, and the means of its record, are always *situated*. They are from a particular viewpoint, it can be argued, and techniques help constitute particular attitudes to the objects of record and note, particular relations between subject and object positions. This does not invalidate an interest in record and noting, but rather supplies it with motivation and heterogeneity.

GENRES OF PHOTOGRAPHY

Photographs record and also supply *ambience*. Many archaeology books particularly popular publications, are sumptuously illustrated with photographs, and they almost always conform to familiar genres and styles. One genre, the record shot, has already been introduced; two others are the picturesque and the travelogue. Many archaeological photographs are dark and mysterious images of the past: prime subjects of the picturesque. The picturesque is well established as a genre. Many photographs present a 'travelogue past' of sites and artifacts worth visiting and seeing in a cultural itinerary. Generally, the picturesque, the 'important', and the beautiful are the concepts which guide conventional archaeological photography, but these are concepts negotiated or dictated by discourse, being far from pre-ordained.

Various exposure, processing, and printing materials and techniques produce familiar characteristics of colour balance and saturation. Black and white landscape photographs are often taken through coloured filters and printed with contrasty skies, while infra-red film produces an ambience of mystery and otherness. Tonal balance and degree of contrast, in lighting, *mise-en-scène* (see below), and also in developing and printing, are subjects of consideration and regulation. Some standard compositional

Figure 5.2 Bamborough Castle, Northumberland, England and surveyed elevations of the Black Gate, Newcastle-upon-Tyne. Two genres of illustration. Is the picture post-card and picturesque image more subjective and arty (or kitsch?) than the drawing? The photograph records a wealth of empirical information about the moment the camera shutter was released: weather conditions, visibility from camera position, the play of light upon different materials. . . . The drawing represents an alternative (subjective) decision to focus attention simply upon the edges of building stones. The photograph is more naturalistic than the drawing which could be argued to supply more 'useful' information (and so, perhaps, more realistic), but it depends on what we are interested in. The comparison shows that both photo and drawing are constituted by interest and purpose which belong with the photographer, draftsperson, and their discourses.

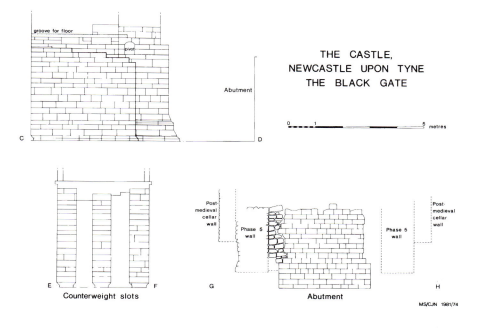

THE CASTLE,
NEWCASTLE UPON TYNE
THE BLACK GATE

0   1   5 metres

MS/CJN 1981/74

rules are evident, having to do with the ratio of sky to foreground, the positioning of central subject matter, and the use, or not, of converging verticals in architectural shots. Focusing conventions require the subject matter to be sharp, perhaps soft-focus for romantic ambience.

Most photography upholds a set of rules around these themes and which can be found outlined explicitly in the standard photographic literatures as well as being so evident simply in the number of photographs which appear merely as variations of the same theme. Histories of photography and illustration are important in understanding these styles and genres. For example, the criteria which apply to the picturesque were explicitly formulated in treatises at the end of the eighteenth century (e.g. Gilpin 1782,1792). Archaeological photography has borrowed its notions of the important and the beautiful as much from photography generally as from within the discipline.[6]

Around notions of the picturesque, beautiful, and important, there is little use of photography other than to praise or document neutrally, little use of photography to awaken consciousness, an aim to be found, for example, in much American documentary photography of the first half of the century.[7] It might also be noted that there is no *art* photography in archaeology – photowork which emphasizes rule, style, and genre, and perhaps questions convention.

We are here beginning to read images, and discourse is a concept central to such reading (Hodder 1989; more generally see Leitch 1983; Shanks 1995; Tilley 1989; for archaeology see Tilley 1990a; Tilley 1990b). The discourse of archaeological photography consists, among other things, of sets of rules which generate photographic images, rules which are the grounds for the acceptance and familiarity of images, for their assessment and for their rejection, if this is considered appropriate. While produced according to sets of rules, photos and photowork confirm and reduplicate dominant subject positions – particular relationships between the viewer and the viewed. I will elaborate on this. A major point is to be that there is no natural relationship between the archaeologist and that which they record in a photograph, no relationship unmediated by discourse and convention.

REALISM AND NATURALISM

A conventional photograph is usually considered to be realistic. What this means is that it reproduces the familiar space of perspective. It is important, however, to distinguish naturalism from realism. Naturalism is an adherence to the appearance of things, a replication of external features. Photography can do this very well, but may not, thereby, provide a *realistic* picture. A realistic representation is not only or necessarily naturalistic. This is clear from the experience of photographs of ourselves – how often they do not resemble us but only duplicate momentary facets.

Figure 5.3   Perspective centred upon the eye of the viewer, and a scene to be photographed: the Stoa of Attalus (reconstructed), Athens. The 'real' centre of ancient Athens a multi-temporal jumble of wall foundations, is a letdown compared with the well known histories of fifth-century BC classical democracy. So here is a reconstructed Hellenistic (!) stoa, from which the ruins may be observed, to show what it was really like.

Realism is a project, not a set of formal conventions. As James Clifford puts it (1988:100) 'realistic portraits, to the extent that they are "convincing" or "rich", are extended metaphors, patterns of associations that point to coherent (theoretical, aesthetic, or moral) additional meanings'. Realism involves allegory. The construction of narrative is but one aspect or possibility here.

So I can say that there is an archaeological reality to be known, but that it is not simply within the material traces of the past. Consider a photograph of some archaeological remains. It is not a watercolour or sketch but a mechanical record and so might be considered more objective or realistic. But to be realistic, I argue, photographs need to be given a past and a future, a context. Let me explain. The photograph merely acknowledges a disconnected instant, but it does often provide some certainty about that instant. Uncertainty and doubt, however, the roots of interpretation, require time for deliberation. Meaning comes from the two, from certainty and doubt, from the *process* of making sense. Meaning comes from making connections and exploring contexts. This is something brought to the photograph by the maker and the viewer and it may involve considerable deviation, temporal, spatial, and conceptual, away from the naturalism of the photograph.[8]

Paul Valery declared that photography freed the writer from describing,[9] but photographs do not describe in the same way as writing: they do not have the same temporality as text. They require duration and interpretation, the contextualization mentioned above. Note also how a photograph may become a reality which is then experienced as a let-down. Visitors may experience the confusion of an excavation, contrasting with the cleaned-up photographed vistas, as a disappointment. Visitors to a site may search for the picturesque view whose photograph has drawn them there, missing other details of the 'real' site.

A photo replicates perspective which is considered the hallmark of a realistic image.[10] But perspective is very much a post-Renaissance convention of realism that has been much questioned in modernist and postmodernist projects, just as the contrast between naturalism and realism has been the focus of much literary experiment and critique. The point is that there is no easy and natural relationship between reality and its depiction. The concept of discourse may be introduced again here. A photograph may be considered realistic because it conforms to the canon of realism laid down by discourse, rather than because it has some special and objective relationship with reality. What is considered photographic realism then becomes a network of mutually referring references which by repetition and cross reference create a generally perceived picture of what may be regarded as real or realistic. This picture is not recognized as a picture, but as what it represents itself as − reality.[11]

THE RHETORIC OF THE IMAGE

The rhetoric of the photograph (Barthes 1977) is to conflate naturalism and realism. The artifact becomes reality. So even when photographs are acknowledged as artifacts, they may also take on something of the status of found objects, harnessing the magic of the real.

There is also an ideology of intimate knowledge gained through seeing. As I mentioned above, the photo may seem to say 'look and believe your eyes'. There is an imaginary plenitude to the photo here: it is supposedly full of meaning. An impulse may be to document an archaeological site with as many photographs as possible; the photo image is considered to be related to knowledge because it presents the real directly to that sense which is imagined to have immediate access to reality − sight. But a multitude of photographs of a site are not so much a means of knowing it as a means of diverting its puzzles and uncertainties. Seeing is not congruent with knowing or understanding, of course, and criticism may justifiably be made of the apparent voyeurism in the will to photograph (Burgin 1982:187f).[12]

This supposed innocence of the photograph-as-analogue is now being corrupted by digitally-based computer technologies, so it is argued by some (see discussion in the journal *Ten-8*, Anon 1991). Digitized images can be manipulated at will without losing the appearance of photographic verisimilitude. Substantial criticism, associated with opposition to the hyperrealities of postmodernism, is being directed against this new sophistry.[13] The fear is that reality itself is being challenged and questioned, replaced instead by information systems, megabitmapped images. We can be presented with a *totally constructed* photographic 'reality'. Made homogeneous by binary encoding, the world appears debased and ready for acquisition, appropriation, and technical control.

But the technologies of photography have *never* been innocent. The will to photograph may involve a desire to grab bits of reality and to own, rather than to understand. Since the early days of photography Reijlander and others have produced compound images, faking pictorial forms. Photographs are constantly used out of 'context', juxtaposed with other images and words in rhetorical forms, backing up particular interests and arguments. Advertising and journalism regularly do this.

Even the technology of photography has often involved manipulation in order 'objectively' to represent: orthochromatic film, for example, a normal emulsion used before panchromatic, cannot do justice to both foreground and sky in an outdoor picture because it is not sensitive to red light; effects have to be manipulated for the final photograph to 'look right'. It might even be argued that the association of objectivity and the photograph is relatively recent (Rosler 1991).

Radical critiques of advertising have made much of the rhetorical function of photography: the objective light–wave image attesting to the truth of an argument to buy a product. The advertising photo says to you 'look, it really could be like this, if you buy' (Williamson 1978 and many after this classic work; see also Haug 1986).

I argue that we should attend to such critiques and be suspicious of the easy identification of objective knowledge with naturalistic representation.

THE RHETORIC OF DISCOURSE

Photographs which seem to represent reality are products of discourse; naturalistic replication does not have a necessary connection with knowledge or understanding of reality. An extension of this argument is that what we take to be objective reality is rhetorically constructed.

Arguments presented in constructivist philosophy of science[14] hold that objectivity is a quality of strength or robustness considered to be held by a statement, but it is not some quality of reality, for example, which exists independently of history and society. Objectivity and truth do not stand up for themselves, but have to be argued for, by people. So the strength of objectivity comes partly from rhetoric. Elements of rhetoric include techniques of persuasion, styles of presentation, forms of argument, and archives for reference and support. Consider archaeology:[15] a statement about or image of the archaeological past is not strong and good because it is true or objective; but because it holds together and makes sense when interrogated it is described as objective. Whence then does a statement or image derive strength, if not from objectivity? There is no necessary answer. It can be many things. An objective image, a true representation of reality, is one connected to anything more solid than itself, so that if it is challenged as being misrepresentative, all to which it is connected threatens also to fall. Rhetoric is the art and science of making these connections and persuading people of their strength. As I have already argued, a photograph has to be lent a past and a future, its disconnected instant reconnected. The multiplicity of the possible connections is the heterogeneity of photowork.

Images can have tremendous rhetorical force because they can gather together so much: information, attitudes, and relationships (Latour 1990). If the image is a photograph, all the more weight is lent to the image by the conception of the photograph as direct replication, or objective correlative. A photograph somehow always seems to attest to some truth; it draws on scientific conceptions of value-free or objective truth, but more importantly upon an ethics of truth-telling rooted in a valuation of sight over words. With observation bound to a moral duty of telling the truth, a hierarchy of experience is erected, with seeing having primacy over telling, and telling possibly involving lies. If the visual is associated with immediacy it seems to avoid the pitfalls of discourse, those rules and conventions which determine expression.

Let us assume that we want objective archaeological accounts and let us define objective as strong, resisting attempts to prove falsity. An archaeological report usually aims to present data as objectively as possible – a strong basis for subsequent inference. Where is the quality of objectivity? Whence the strength of an objective report? It comes, I suggest, from all those diagrams and photographs, the many words of detailed description, the references to comparative sites and materials which give further context to the findings. These all attest to the actual happening of the excavation and to the trustworthiness of the excavation team. The objectivity of the report, its strength, is a rhetorical achievement, but nonetheless real. Because the report is coherent and reads well (no contradictions betraying lies and artifice), and the photographs witness things actually being found, because its style and rhetoric are found acceptable, because it delivers what is required (from format to types of information), it is described as sound. Objectivity is that which holds together. If a report holds together it is considered objective. How, after all, are we to judge a report on an excavation we had no part in? Even if possible, it would be expensive of time and resources, almost certainly unpractical, to go back and re-excavate. Trust and goodness are essential considerations in judging truth. We look for evidence pertaining to these in the report. Photographs may be particularly effective instruments of persuasion, hence the term photo*work* also implies the work 'good' photos do for the author.

If, against this constructivist position, objectivity is conceived to be an abstract quality or principal held by reality, how does it argue for itself, how does it display its strength? It cannot, just as a photograph cannot supply for itself a past and a future, a temporality that makes it sensible. People are needed, and their projects. So gravity, as an objective principle held to describe reality, does not appear to all and everyone on its own. Gravity needed Newton. Microbes needed the likes of Pasteur (Latour 1988). And photowork needs people and discourse.

TEXT AND THE PHOTOGRAPH

My argument is that photographs are powerful rhetorical instruments in establishing objectivity: they work as images, and as products of a technique which apparently captures an objective correlative. This has led me to introduce discourse as a concept vital for understanding the social and historical production of knowledge. Some critiques in archaeology have recently foregrounded truth as an effect of discourse (see Hodder 1989, Tilley 1990b), *a posteriori*, social, and historical. But attention has remained largely with discourse as *text* and *word*: writing archaeology. We should look as well to *imagery* and its particular discursive character.

PHOTOWORK AND THE WORKING OF ILLUSTRATIVE DISCOURSE

To make sense, a photograph needs to have established connections and contexts which work within and beyond the image. This may occur in its subject matter and composition. The viewer may recognize particular social relationships in the photo; the shot may have been set up to make a particular point. *Mise-en-scène* refers to what goes on in front of the camera in cinematography and the term may also be used here. An excavation is cleaned up and prepared for photography, with diggers removed and key features highlighted, ranging pole sited strategically.

The photograph may be given a caption, and is positioned in relation to other images and text (Hillis Miller 1992). The concepts of collage and montage are important (Berger, et al. 1972). Collage is an extension of an artist's palette or a writer's vocabulary, prose, and poetic art, to include actual pieces of reality or fragments of what the artist or writer is referring to. It is direct quotation, literal repetition, or citation of something taken out of its context and placed in another. The photograph, seen as objective correlative, may especially lend itself to collage and quotation. Montage is the cutting and reassembling of fragments of meanings, images, things, quotations, and borrowings, to create new juxtapositions. When recognized for what it is, collage simply questions the notion of representation as finding some *correspondence* with an exterior reality. 'Reality' is instead brought into the picture; collage may be tangible representation without attempting some sort of an illusion. It represents in terms of change – the shift of borrowings from one context to another, from 'reality' to 'representation', and from representation to representation. Indeed the distinction is suspended; reality is actually put in quotation marks, if photography, for example, is recognized as *photowork*.

The aim, whether it is recognized or not, is to construct something new out of old, to connect things that may appear dissimilar in order to achieve new insights and understanding. This emergence of new meaning depends on the perception of instability, of retaining energies of interruption and disruption – the quotation interrupts the smooth surface or text; it is distracting. The interruption of illusion and distraction by collage sets off allusions through the juxtaposed, montaged elements. So the new understanding comes through 'contaminated' representation rather than pure reference to the depicted subject matter. The quotations are cut out of context to create new meanings.

Disruption, cutting, and juxtaposition make of discourse an *unstable* set of links between images, words and concepts, and the material world, between signifiers and signifieds. Things and words and images can always be disengaged from their meanings and inlayed into new combinations. This disassembly *should* be constant. The discovery of *new* insight depends on a nervous novelty which avoids the settling of montages into accepted equations and identities. A certain degree of shock and jolting are necessary, moving on when the juxtaposition becomes too homely. In doing this collage maintains an ambiguity of presence and absence: the presence of fragments of absent items is referenced.

Montage and collage may occur along both syntactic and paradigmatic axes. Discourse may use syntactic sequence and narrative of images and words; paradigmatic connection is a harmony of association within a photo and its reading.[16]

So there is much more to using photographs as a means of quoting the past than is commonly realized. Creative photowork should be aware of the rhetorical potential and subtlety of collage and montage. There is also irony in that instead of bringing in an objective witness, archaeological photographs actually attest to the working of discourse, the practice of heterogeneous association.

FURTHER WORKINGS OF A PHOTOGRAPH

A photograph has a subject matter and pictorial structure which we may read according to discourse — interpreting sense and reference. However, in its attestation to the infinite detail of materiality, in its unwitting record, a photograph sometimes has its transparency clouded. A detail may intrude and indicate that the photograph is in fact only an item of

Figure 5.4   The Rocher Bono, Brittany. This photograph is so much more than an illustration of a megalithic chambered tomb of the type *allée coudée*. The photograph captures the ineffable, translating experiences of dark stone interiors. Photographs also, of course, have different relationships to the creator and the viewer and themselves change with time. Here what began as a snapshot and evokes memories for me of a field trip, can also be interpreted as a genre image of the type 'romantic past', and, should the monument change or be destroyed, this photograph could also become an historical document itself.

discourse. Perhaps we know something of someone or something in a photograph which subverts its apparent message; perhaps an anomaly disturbs the categorization and genre. The photographed world is rarely fully controlled. The heterogeneity of photowork, with all its possible interconnections, may break the predictability of the *mise-en-scène*. Indeed this is part of the working of association and discourse: resistances to the order imposed upon the world are endemic.[17]

TEMPORALITY OF THE PHOTOGRAPH

I have had cause to mention several times the temporality of the photograph as a product of the camera, a clock for making images. For archaeology I think it is something of an instructive irony that photography, the medium which relates most to authenticity in conventional thought, involves the 'truest' image of the past showing its present state of decay. The true picture of the past thus appears ephemeral – the captured moment of the photograph. (I repeat that photographic naturalism is not necessarily realistic, and our models of realism are historical.) There is irony also in that reconstructions of the archaeological past 'as it was' are almost always aiming at visual verisimilitude – a moment arrested before the viewer, or a reconstruction which is a naturalistic *mise-en-scène* ready to be photographed. Consider the number of museum

Figure 5.5 Timeless landscapes? Clennel Street, Northumberland, England. A medieval track *c.* 1990. Timeless as convoluted, folded time.

Figure 5.6 The actuality of the past: Carew Castle, Pembrokeshire, Wales, October 1993. The Feudal Lord riding the land in the hunt was a constituting ideological structure of the Middle Ages. This technology of power, centred upon lifestyle, is transformed here into the Carew hunt.

displays which go to considerable expense and use every technological device to do just this (Shanks and Tilley 1992, Chapter 4).

ACTUALITY

If we consider some issues on the subject of time, photography, and the material artifact, we can begin with three categories of photographic time in archaeology: the moment arrested, date, and continuity from past through present. But consider what I have outlined as photowork and add *actuality* – a return of what is no longer the same. Actuality is the non-arbitrary conjunction of presents: the past's present, the instant of photography, and the time of reading. I contend that actuality so defined is a key concept in understanding photography and the discourse of archaeology.[18]

Compare photowork with memory. Memories live on with us, as do photographs, and as we reinterpret memories and incorporate them into new stories of our life, so photographs change: what was once a holiday shot becomes social document or historical source. Memories sometimes seem to escape time in that they stay with us. We may feel too that photographs sometimes witness that which escapes time, the timeless. The timeless here is not an unbounded infinity, but is convoluted or folded time, a folding or recycling of past moments. As conjuncture between the temporality of person remembering and past event, memory crosses time, just as the photo before you now witnesses a lost instant in time past.

Memory is in fact the *act* of memorizing. The past as memory does not just exist as it was. The past has to be recalled: memory is the act of recalling from the viewpoint of a subsequent time. So too a photograph is meaningless unless lent a past and a future. The captured moment of the photo needs a past and a present to make sense. This is done by the contextualization that takes place in interpretation: we read signs within the photograph (its *mise-en-scène*) and add to these connections made through montage and juxtaposition with text. This too is photowork.

We may add also the idea of rapturous temporality: memory holds onto the past, just as a photograph grabs the moment, potentially missed, now lost. In memory time stands still: there are no clocks (Bauman 1993:52). In the world remembered there is no bottom line, no horizon, no past-as-it-was, no ordained chronology. There are instead only enfoldings. Photowork shares also this art and science of assemblage, while the photograph snatches and attempts to hold onto the connections. Naturalism may require a chronicle: dates and linear chronology. A realistic memory (or indeed history) may need flashbacks, long-term backgrounds, reflexive reinterpretations of past events.

To point out the affinities between memory and photography, and to emphasize the temporality of actuality, is not a call for 'relevance', to recognize simply that archaeology and its photography happens in the present, that this matters above all else and so we should ensure the relevance of

Figure 5.7 Surrealist still-life: 'Nature morte'.

archaeology to present interests. Such an argument simply corresponds (as opposite or negation) to an historicism which denies the present in a self-effacing posture, emphasizing simply what happened in the past as the measure of all archaeology. Instead we should retain the ambiguity and tension which is actuality; actuality is the *primacy*, but not the *superiority*, of the present over the past. This is simply to acknowledge that the soluble present is the medium of knowing the past.[19]

Archaeology has a multiple temporality involving the past, its decay, and the encounter with remains in our future-oriented projects. Photography, with an analogous multiple temporality, thus seems appropriate for the archaeological. Photowork presents us with inventories of mortality, quoting fragments, creating juxtapositions potentially as strange as a fibula, quernstone and ox scapula which may be found together in a typical archaeological report. Photographs turn the now into the past, or more grandly, into history, depending upon the rhetoric. Reality is turned antique, and documented triviality is made memorable.

MELANCHOLY AND RUIN

The last points, about photographs turning the now into the past, bearing witness to the abrasions of time, bring me to melancholy and the romance

Figure 5.9 Moments of ruin, formation processes: old buildings in a forestry plantation in west Wales.

of ruin. The point is the fundamental importance to archaeology of formation processes, yet it is very little theorized as *ruination* (Shanks forthcoming, Shanks 1992). Following this line of argument about the temporality of the past, Michael Schiffer's standard work on formation processes (Schiffer 1987) appears as a sanitization of ruination and an attempt to bring to it an order of formulaic association between an objective past and a separate interpreting present.

NEW TECHNOLOGIES

I have already mentioned the technology dimension: clocks, cameras, light, chemicals, and now digital information. Benjamin (1970) argued that the mechanical reproduction of works of art heralded profound changes in people's relationship with cultural production. The arrival of

Figure 5.8 Archaeological temporalities: a room in Cambridge, England, 28 July 1991, 15.17.48pm. What date or time is this room? There is no one answer, but possible answers are date of original architectural fabric; dates of structural modifications; dates of manufacture of artifacts; dates of their styles; moment of capture on photographic film? (see Olivier 1994).

sophisticated and cheap means of electronic reproduction and storage, of image scanning, of digital camera input into image manipulation computer software, has transformed the darkroom into a computer. With software such as Adobe Systems' *Photoshop*, digitally encoded images can be manipulated instantly at will, then outputted to video screen or printer, the best of which provide photographic quality or higher. The photographic image has lost its link, via light wave and chemical process, with reality. The integrity of the photographic image is questionable, because photographs are now so evidently '*made*'. Any image can be sampled, manipulated, joined with another and the result will still be naturalistic, as this is defined above.

Ideas of the *auteur*, of the body of work and 'consistency' of style, are being further undermined as radical questions of authenticity, which are endemic to the new media, are raised: photographic naturalism need not start with any particular reality at all, but can work with sampled bits and pieces from any source, processed into naturalism upon a desktop. As photography is realized as photowork, the oppositions of fake and authentic, original and reproduction (upon which the conventional fine arts still rely), are challenged, with emphasis placed less on the product than on the *process* of making. And this, as I have sketched above, may be seen as heterogeneous association, the working of discourse.

The new digital technologies hold great potential because they are particularly suited to collage and montage, which are central, I have argued, to photowork. Accepting the distinction between naturalism and realism, accepting that photographs have never been innocent analogues of reality, means that we should embrace the new technologies as a major addition to discursive technique. And what is to stop a digital photowork being more *realistic* than a straight, *naturalistic* photograph of the same subject, if it 'works' better, establishing richer syntactic and paradigmatic networks?

HYPERMEDIA

But the imperative remains, in spite of any emphasis on photowork and discourses of archaeology, to record and make inventories. Here too new storage technologies, recording and retrieval systems are already having effect. Multimedia databases are now cheap and efficient. Videos, still

Figure 5.10 Archaeologies of the ineffable: Sweden, rock carvings and possible lifeworlds. A current research project at the University of Wales, Lampeter, is to combine imagery, soundscapes, reconstructed landscapes, anthropological archaeology, excavation results, and iconographic interpretation in explorations of Bronze Age Bohuslän. Visualization is used as a research tool, and the following images give some idea of the fields being explored. Two of the 'photographs' are computer generated.

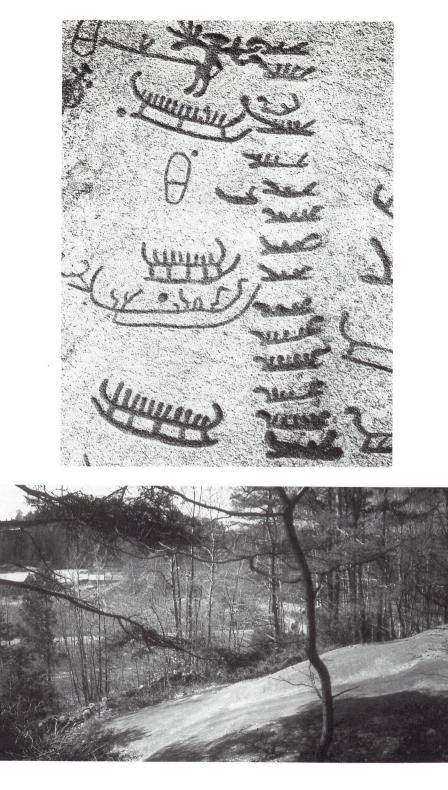

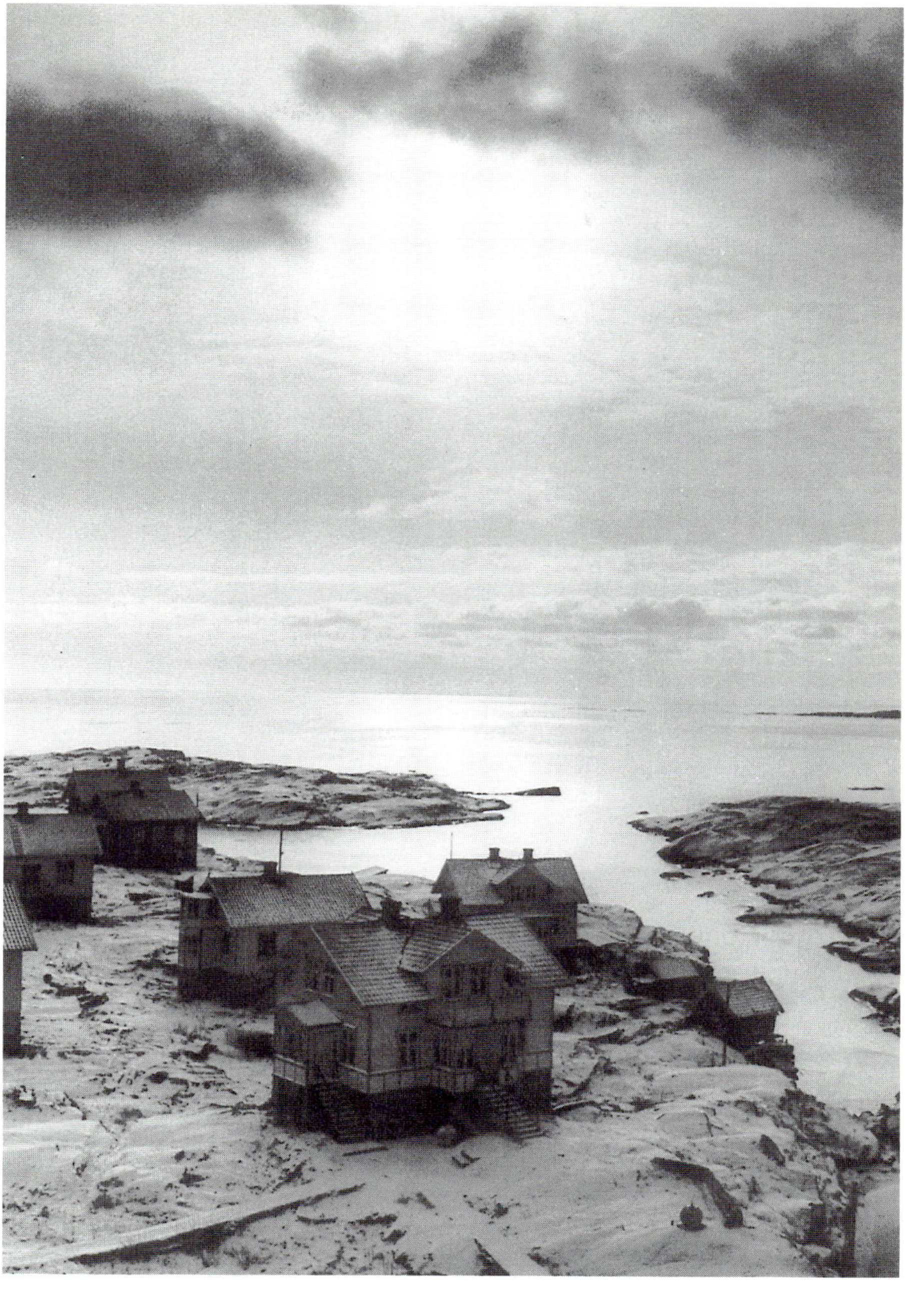

Figure 5.11   Ethnographies and *mise-en-scène*. Excavations on Egine, Greece, 1978 and at the Black Gate, Newcastle-upon-Tyne, England, 1981. The process of mounting projects and reconstructing pasts is archaeology. The standard excavation photograph of site cleaned of debris and people in order to display important features and surveyors' measure, the past as structured in the *mise-en-scène*, omits what makes the past possible now. And stories of forensic work fascinate: a meeting of contemporary interest with the traces of lost lifeworlds. A task is the construction of archaeological ethnographies.

images, text, sound, and graphics can all be combined within the same coordinated recording system. This has been much taken up in archaeology already as an extension of conventional methods.

The boundaries between text, number, sound, images, and graphics are breaking down: they can be combined in digital montage and collage. Pathways through a multimedia database need not be linear: multimedia may be *hypermedia*, where the user defines their own route through the stored information. The potential for creating rich and innovative networks of information and experience relevant to the interests of the user is tremendous. Illustration (the juxtaposition of image and word) is taking on new dimensions.[20]

EXPERIENCE AND THE PHOTOGRAPH

Documenting archaeology has much to do with inventory and databasing, but need not, and arguably should not, end with conventional categories of data. I have made the case elsewhere for ethnographies of archaeological fieldwork that document the life of archaeological projects, just as an ethnographer documents communities (Shanks 1992). Such ethnography would build on the realization that archaeology is not just about the past, but is as much about the people, ideas, and networks which allow the past to be recovered – experience and discourse. There are enormous traditions of documentary photography upon which to draw, and which have hardly been tapped in archaeology.[21] Let it be called a sociology of the discipline if necessary, but let it also be remembered that it is the detective work and experience of doing archaeology which interests so many people, as much as the things found.[22]

VARIETIES OF EXPERIENCE: TOWARDS EMBODIMENT

A range of experiences may be involved in photographs. Photowork may involve estrangement, with the photograph standing for the absence of what is photographed. It may involve making an inventory of inanimate possessions, a fetishism of sorts. An impulse may be to save and celebrate the past, collecting souvenirs. We should be wary here of an ideology that detaches objects from the social relations which give them meaning and bring them to life. The actuality of the archaeological past can easily be denied when the lived experience of the remains of the past is processed according to received categories, genre visions, or with the past locked into its own time and detached from present interest. Photowork may attempt to invoke magical experiences of the past in a re-enchantment of lost times that denies this inventory of meaningless souvenirs. In the texture of their detail photographs provide a partially involuntary record; there is always in every photograph some escape from intentionality and processed experience. That the materiality of the world is ineffable is presented. Finally, temporality, often a melancholy of the past in the present, is invoked throughout photowork.

The fascination of photowork is that it attests to so much sensory experience. Criticism may be made of ocularcentrism (e.g. Taylor 1994, section 3, and Jay 1994), that we are too focused upon sight and have to have other senses and sentiments educated, but realizing the ineffable richness of the empirical is a valuable antidote to one-dimensional or deterministic explanations.

VISUALIZATION AS A RESEARCH TOOL AND ARCHAEOLOGIES OF THE INEFFABLE

The visual is not merely illustrative. Aerial photographs are primary source material for archaeologists. Photographs and drawings of artifacts in a catalogue are there to provide information which cannot be encapsulated in verbal description. Some sociology of science has recognized the vital importance of imagery in scientific research (Lynch and Woolgar 1990). Mention may be made here of descriptive statistics displayed graphically, and of the great potential for summarizing and exploring spatial information offered by Geographical Information Systems.

But consider also the argument that any adequate account of settlement and environment, artifacts, architectures, and space, must consider how these are constituted in social practice, with practice considered multi-dimensionally as embodied, that is rooted in people's senses and sensibility as well as reasoning.[23] Here is to be stressed the importance of the concept of *lifeworld* – environments as lived and constituted in terms of five senses, not just a principle of discursive rationality usually taken to be the basis of understanding.[24]

As a means of exploring such embodiment, the sensory richness of photographs can be a research tool. The challenge for phenomenological archaeologies committed to reconstructing past lifeworlds is to explore sensory as well as conceptual worlds; to be archaeologies of the ineffable, attending to all senses. Photowork can be a means to this end, notwithstanding the valid criticism of ocularcentrism. Increasingly sophisticated and accessible computer rendering software now means that photo–realistic images can be produced of a designed object or environment.

THE POTENTIAL OF PHOTOGRAPHY

The main direction of this chapter has been towards realizing the character of photowork, and away from complacent assumptions of photographic verisimilitude. We would do well to be mindful of what photowork is and is not. Photographs do not provide understanding and are far from innocent analogues. They are made. The key concept here is discourse, a critical attention to the working of which is an essential part of any self-reflective discipline. I suggest that archaeologists should take up the obligation to attend to technique and method, but in a way which recognizes humanistic *possibility*, rather than closing down options with formal rules and procedures. This possibility is inherent in the nervousness and instability of quotation and collage I mentioned above.

The task must surely be to work *with* the medium, and I suggest four main areas for focus.

- The temporality of photowork and its relations with the temporality of archaeological discourse and its objects: I have discussed the analogies between photography and the collections of memory and emphasized the concept of actuality.

- Quotation: here I propose thinking laterally about montage and collage in archaeological texts, devices in the contextualizing practice that is interpretation. The invitation is to experiment with associations that attest to the actuality of the past.
- Embodiment and archaeologies of the ineffable: photographs can introduce the heterogeneous and ineffable into discourse, that richness and detail in every photograph which lies outside the categories and schemes of discourse. I use the term embodiment to introduce bodily sensitivity as a means of suspending our conventional categorizations and a means of achieving a more textured understanding of past social realities. Photographs can help us attend to materiality by saying 'look at what has been omitted', rather than 'look, believe this text'. An imperative here is to keep open things which are passed over in an instant.
- Ethnographies of the discipline: photowork can be part of explaining and documenting archaeological projects.

A RADICAL IMAGING/WRITING

Photowork produced under these headings undoubtedly undermines the present where it feels most secure, in the allegedly once-and-for-all-time recorded past. I extend an invitation to conceive of the dialectical text and image as tangential to the past – a vector (from the present) touching the past at the point of sense and then moving off to explore its own course,[25] partaking of actuality, the temporality of memory. Such texts are part of contextual, interpretive method, lending contexts of all sorts to images, words, and artifacts. Good photography can and does already contribute to such a humanistic discipline which is dialectical because it denies the dualisms of past and present, objective and subjective, real and fictive, with all their pernicious variations. We may work instead upon the continuities which run through our encounters with the remains of the dead.

NOTES

1. For critique and archaeology and for bibliography see Leone and Preucel 1992, Leone and Shackel 1987, Shanks and Tilley 1987, Shanks and Tilley 1992.
2. Hodder et al. 1994. For a wider view of interpretive humanities see Denzin and Lincoln 1994.
3. See John Berger's fascinating discussion of the snapshot and temporality (Berger and Mohr 1982) and its support for elements of my argument later in this chapter.
4. The literature is quite considerable. For introductions and bibliographies see Bijker, Hughes, and Pinch 1987, Bijker and Law 1992, Mackenzie and Wajcman 1985.

5. The journal *Techniques et Culture* is a good place to begin exploring French approaches to the archaeology and anthropology of techniques. See also Anon 1990, Lemonnier 1993.
6. Standard works on the history of photography which are useful here include Freund 1980, Jeffery l981, Lemangny and Rouille 1983, Newhall 1982, Tagg 1988a.
7. See for example, the work of Lewis Hine, Paul Strand, and photographers of the Farm Security Administration of the United States in the 1930s (Rothstein 1986). The history of photography is full of examples of critical photography, as defined in the introduction to this chapter.
8. Berger and Mohr 1982:117–22. For connections and *rhizomatics* see Campbell 1994, Shanks 1992.
9. See the discussion of this point by Sontag 1978:145. I owe a great deal to this insightful book *On Photography*.
10. On perspectivalism as a scopic regime see Jay 1988.
11. Tagg 1988b:99–100. On art photography, modernism, and photography see the work of David Hockney (Hockney 1984, Joyce 1988).
12. On gender, power and the 'gaze' see also Lutz and Collins 1994 and Mulvey 1989.
13. Many issues are raised, for example in the work of Baudrillard (Baudrillard 1988 as an introduction). The debates are too wide-ranging to cite here, but in the context of art and photowork consider Foster 1985.
14. Again there is too much to cite; for introductions to the issues see Holtorf forthcoming, Latour 1987, Lawson and Appignanesi 1989, Schwandt 1994, Shanks 1995.
15. On the rhetoric of archaeological discourse see Shanks 1994.
16. See Berger and Mohr 1982 on such heterogeneous association. Consider also photomontage (Ades 1986).
17. Barthes (1982) introduced the terms *studium* and *punctum* to refer to this effect: studium as the subject matter and structure learned through discourse, punctum as that which punctures the apparently homogeneous surface.
18. Actuality is a concept to be found prominently in the work of Walter Benjamin (Eagleton 1981; Wohlfrath 1993). On such temporality and archaeology see Shanks 1992; Shanks and Tilley 1987, Chapter 5; for related arguments about archaeology and temporality see Lowenthal 1985, Olivier 1994, Schnapp 1993.
19. Michel Foucault answered the question of why he wanted to write the history of the birth of the prison (Foucault 1979:31): 'simply because I am interested in the past? No, if one means by that writing a history of the past in terms of the present. Yes, if one means writing the history of the present.'
20. Much of the literature is ephemeral; a recent book is Cotton and Oliver 1993.
21. See above, note 7. For a critical and subjective documentary consider Braden 1983.
22. Visual anthropology: this mention of ethnographies of the discipline of archaeology brings me to a vital reminder. Interpretive anthropology is associated with critical introspection of the practices of ethnography, the encounter with the anthropological 'other', and its representation. In the

debates of visual anthropology around ethnographic film, for example, can be found insights complementing those made in this chapter, about issues of authority in the relationship between anthropologist and object of interest, viewpoint and perspective in representation, as well as linearity, narrative, and time. The characters of observation, scopic, and haptic fields have been thoroughly covered. And the subject of collage and montage in film, representation, and ethnographic collecting has not gone unnoticed, particularly connections with surrealism. See Clifford 1988, Clifford and Marcus 1986, Edwards 1992, Marcus and Fisher 1986, Taylor 1994.

23. This is one of the main arguments of postprocessual or interpretive social archaeologies.

24. Although located in the reproduced image, consider the photo essays of John Berger and others (Berger et al. 1972, Berger and Mohr 1982). See also Stoller 1989.

25. Consider Paul Ricoeur's analogous argument about sense and reference in texts. An introduction for archaeologists is Moore 1990.

REFERENCES

Anon 1990. 'Technology in the humanities: a commentary.' *Archaeological Review from Cambridge* 9(1).

Anon 1991. 'Digital Dialogues.' *Ten-8* 2:2.

Ades, D. 1986. *Photomontage.* Second edition. London: Thames and Hudson.

Barthes, R. 1977. 'Rhetoric of the image.' In *Image–Music–Text.* London: Fontana.

Barthes, R. 1982. *Camera Lucida.* Translated by R. Howard. London: Jonathan Cape.

Baudrillard, J. 1988. *Selected Writings.* Translated by M. Poster and J. Mourrain and others. Cambridge: Blackwell Polity.

Bauman, Z. 1993. 'Walter Benjamin the intellectual.' *New Formations* 20:47–57.

Benjamin, W. 1970. 'The work of art in the age of mechanical reproduction.' In *Illuminations.* London: Jonathan Cape.

Berger, J., Blomberg, S., Fox, C., Dibb, M., and Hollis, R. 1972. *Ways of Seeing.* London: BBC and Harmondsworth: Penguin.

Berger, J. and Mohr, J. 1982. *Another Way of Telling.* London: Writers and Readers.

Bijker, W., Hughes, T., and Pinch, T. (eds) 1987. *The Social Construction of Technological Systems.* Cambridge, MA: MIT Press.

Bijker, W. and Law, J. (eds) 1992. *Shaping Technology/Building Society.* Cambridge, MA: MIT Press.

Braden, S. 1983. *Committing Photography.* London: Pluto Press.

Burgin, V. 1982. 'Photography, phantasy, function.' In *Thinking Photography.* London: Macmillan.

Campbell, L. 1994. 'Traces of archaeology.' In Ian Mackenzie (ed.), *Archaeological Theory: Process or Posture?* Avebury: Aldershot and Brookfield.

Clifford, J. 1988. *The Predicament of Culture: Twentieth Century Ethnography, Literature and Art.* Cambridge, MA: Harvard University Press.

Clifford, J. and Marcus, G. (eds) 1986. *Writing Culture: the Poetics and Politics of Ethnography.* Berkeley, CA: University of California Press.

Cotton, B. and Oliver, R. 1993. *Understanding Hypermedia*. London: Phaidon.

Denzin, N.K. and Lincoln, Y.S. (eds) 1994. *Handbook of Qualitative Research*. London: Sage.

Dorrell, P. 1989. *Photography in Archaeology and in Conservation*. Cambridge: Cambridge University Press.

Eagleton, T. 1981. *Walter Benjamin: Or Towards a Revolutionary Criticism*. London: Verso.

Edwards, E. (ed.) 1992. *Anthropology and Photography 1860–1920*. New Haven and London: Yale University Press and the Royal Anthropological Institute.

Foster, H. 1985. *Recodings: Art, Spectacle, Cultural Politics*. Seattle: Bay Press.

Foucault, M. 1979. *Discipline and Punish: the Birth of the Prison*. Translated by Alan Sheridan. New York: Vintage.

Freund, G. 1980. *Photography and Society*. London: Fraser.

Fyfe, G. and Law, J. (eds) 1988. *Picturing Power: Visual Depictions and Social Relations*. London: Routledge.

Gilpin, W. 1782. *Observations on the River Wye and Several Parts of South Wales etc. Relative Chiefly to Picturesque Beauty Made in the Summer of the Year 1770*. London.

Gilpin, W. 1792. *Three Essays: On Picturesque Travel; and On Sketching Landscape; To Which is Added a Poem, On Landscape Painting*. London.

Haug, W.F. 1986. *Commodity Aesthetics: Ideology and Culture*. New York: International General.

Hillis Miller, J. 1992. *Illustration*. Cambridge, MA: Harvard University Press.

Hockney, D. 1984. *Cameraworks*. London: Thames and Hudson.

Hodder, I. 1989. 'Writing site reports in context.' *Antiquity* 62: 268–74.

Hodder, I., Shanks, M., Alexandri, A., Buchli, V., Carman, J., Last, J., and Lucas, G. (eds) 1994. *Interpreting Archaeology: Finding Meaning in the Past*. London: Routledge.

Holtorf, C. forthcoming. 'Oral prehistory: radical constructivism in archaeology.' *Current Anthropology*.

Jay, M. 1988. 'Scopic regimes of modernity.' In H. Foster (ed.), *Vision and Visuality*. Seattle, WA: Bay Press.

Jay, M. 1994. 'The disenchantment of the eye: surrealism and the crisis of ocularcentrism.' In L. Taylor (ed.), *Visualizing Theory: Selected Essays from Visual Anthropology Review 1990–1994*. London: Routledge.

Jeffery, I. 1981. *Photography: A Concise History*. London: Thames and Hudson.

Joyce, P. 1988. *Hockney on Photography*. London: Jonathan Cape.

Latour, B. 1987. *Science In Action: How to Follow Scientists and Engineers Through Society*. Milton Keynes: Open University Press.

Latour, B. 1988. *The Pasteurization of France*. Translated by A. Sheridan and J. Law. Cambridge, MA: Harvard University Press.

Latour, B. 1990. 'Drawing things together.' In S. Woolgar and M. Lynch (eds), *Representation in Scientific Practice*. Cambridge, MA: MIT Press.

Lawson, H. and Appignanesi, L. (eds) 1989. *Dismantling Truth: Reality in the Postmodern World*. New York: St Martin's Press.

Leitch, V. 1983. *Deconstructive Criticism*. London: Hutchinson.

Lemangny, J.-C. and Rouille, A. (eds) 1983. *A History of Photography*. Cambridge: Cambridge University Press.

Lemonnier, P. (ed.) 1993. *Technological Choices*. London: Routledge.

Leone, M. and Preucel, R. 1992. 'Archaeology in a democratic society: a critical theory perspective.' In L. Wandsneider (ed.), *Quandries and Quests: Visions of Archeology's Future*. Carbondale, IL: University of Southern Illinois Press.

Leone, M. and Shackel, P. 1987. 'Toward a critical archaeology.' *Current Anthropology* 28:283–302.

Lowenthal, D. 1985. *The Past is a Foreign Country*. Cambridge: Cambridge University Press.

Lutz, C. and Collins, J. 1994. 'The photograph as an intersection of gazes: the example of *National Geographic*.' In L. Taylor (ed.), *Visualizing Theory: Selected Essays from Visual Anthropology Review 1990–1994*. London: Routledge.

Lynch, M. and Woolgar, S. (eds) 1990. *Representation in Scientific Practice*. Cambridge, MA: MIT Press.

Mackenzie, D. and Wajcman, J. (eds) 1985. *The Social Shaping of Technology*. Milton Keynes: Open University Press.

Marcus, G.E. and Fisher, M. (eds) 1986. *Anthropology as Culture Critique: An Experimental Moment in the Human Sciences*. Chicago: University of Chicago Press.

Moore, H. 1990. 'Paul Ricoeur: action, meaning and text.' In C. Tilley (ed.), *Reading Material Culture: Structuralism, Hermeneutics and Poststructuralism*. Oxford: Blackwell.

Mulvey, L. 1989. *Visual and Other Pleasures*. London: Macmillan.

Newhall, B. 1982. *The History of Photography: From 1839 to the present*. London: Secker and Warburg.

Olivier, L. 1994. 'Archaeology as mediation with the past.' Paper delivered at the *European Association of Archaeologists' Annual Meeting*, Ljubljana, Slovenia.

Rosler, M. 1991. 'Image simulations, computer manipulations, some considerations.' *Ten-8* 2: 52–63.

Rothstein, A. 1986. *Documentary Photography*. London: Focal Press.

Schiffer, M. 1987. *Formation Processes of the Archaeological Record*. Albuquerque, NM: University of New Mexico Press.

Schnapp, A. 1993. *La Conquète du Passé: aux Origines de l'Archéologie*. Paris: Carré.

Schwandt, T. 1994. 'Constructivist, interpretivist approaches to human inquiry.' In N.K. Denzin and Y.S. Lincoln (eds), *Handbook of Qualitative Research*. London: Sage.

Shanks, M. 1992. *Experiencing the Past: On the Character of Archaeology*. London: Routledge.

Shanks, M. 1994. 'The archaeological imagination: creativity, rhetoric and archaeological futures.' In M. Kuna and N. Venclova (eds), *Whither Archaeology: Archaeology in the End of the Millennium: Papers Dedicated to Evzen Neustupny*. Prague: Institute of Archaeology.

Shanks, M. 1995. 'The forms of history.' In I. Hodder, M. Shanks, A. Alexandri, V. Buchli, J. Carman, J. Last, and G. Lucas (eds), *Interpreting Archaeology: Finding Meaning in the Past*. London: Routledge.

Shanks, M. forthcoming. 'Archaeological experiences and a critical romanticism.' In A. Siriiainen (ed.), *The Archaeologist and His/Her Reality: Proceedings of the 4th Nordic TAG Conference*. Helsinki: Institute of Archaeology.

Shanks, M. and Tilley, C. 1987. *Social Theory and Archaeology*. Cambridge: Blackwell Polity.

Shanks, M. and Tilley, C. 1992. *ReConstructing Archaeology: Theory and Practice.* Second edition. London: Routledge.

Sontag, S. 1978. *On Photography.* London: Allen Lane.

Stoller, P. 1989. *The Taste of Ethnographic Things: the Senses in Anthropology.* Philadelphia, PA: University of Pennsylvania Press.

Tagg, J. 1988a. *The Burden of Representation.* London: Macmillan.

Tagg, J. 1988b. 'A means of surveillance: the photograph as evidence in law.' In Tagg 1988a.

Taylor, L. (ed.) 1994. *Visualizing Theory: Selected Essays from Visual Anthropology Review 1990–1994.* London: Routledge.

Tilley, C. 1989. 'Discourse and power: the genre of the Cambridge inaugural lecture.' In D. Miller, M. Rowlands, and C. Tilley (eds), *Domination and Resistance.* London: Unwin Hyman.

Tilley, C. 1990a. 'Michel Foucault: towards an archaeology of archaeology.' In C. Tilley (ed.), *Reading Material Culture: Structuralism, Hermeneutics and Poststructuralism.* Oxford: Blackwell.

Tilley, C. 1990b. 'On modernity and archaeological discourse.' In I. Bapty and T. Yates (eds) *Archaeology After Structuralism.* London: Routledge.

Williamson, J. 1978. *Decoding Advertisements: Ideology and Meaning in Advertising.* London: Marion Boyars.

Wohlfrath, I. 1993. 'The measure of the possible, the weight of the real and the heat of the moment: Benjamin's actuality today.' *New Formations* 20:1–20.

CHAPTER SIX

REPRESENTATION AND REALITY IN PRIVATE TOMBS OF THE LATE EIGHTEENTH DYNASTY, EGYPT

An approach to the study of the shape of meaning

BRIAN LEIGH MOLYNEAUX

The meaning of an image from the past is in the eye of the beholder, one individual situated in a particular time and place gazing at the work of another. But meaning, however various and relative, emerges through the physical act of perception within the material environment of the artwork. Using images depicting social situations in paintings from the tombs of high status commoners of the Egyptian eighteenth dynasty, I will briefly examine how meaning takes shape, through the eyes and hands of the artists, and suggest ways that the material and social aspects of representations may be analysed, using quantitative and qualitative methods, to gain information about the society that made them.

REPRESENTATION AND REALITY

The style of ancient Egyptian art changed so little over more than two millennia that it presents great difficulties as a means of understanding the internal dynamics of Egyptian society. The continuity of the culture, especially in its metaphorical landscape, has set the art's majestic, passive face. Images of gods, kings, and humans, architecture and the trappings of material culture are similar enough from the beginning to the end of the dynastic period to give it all an aura of timelessness. The orderly appearance of representations, maintained by an adherence to traditional techniques and bouts of classicizing from earlier dynastic artworks (see Aldred 1980 for examples), further enhanced by the use of grid layouts to standardize the scale and proportion of figures and scenes (Davis 1989; Iverson 1955; Robins 1994), reinforces this sameness.

The impression is of a very conservative, stately, and pious society – but this is an illusion. It arises from what Kemp has described as 'a confusion between form and substance' (Kemp 1989:184). Behind the formality of the art and its reliance on a few standard themes (notwithstanding its obvious beauty, sophistication, and mystery), there was a thriving, dynamic culture, conscious of its great history and more often than not in the throes of change.

Trying to find the social reality in pictures is an especially fascinating problem for works of the New Kingdom period (eighteenth to twentieth dynasties, *c.* 1540–1070BC). Outwardly, society appeared to be 'still firmly in the tradition created in the earlier periods' (Kemp 1989:184). Kings still claimed divine origin and maintained political and economic control, reinforced by ostentatious displays of power. But Egypt was expanding and becoming richer in the process. This growing prosperity encouraged the bureaucratic institutions supporting the kingship – the palace, the military, and the priesthood – and a wealthy elite of individuals, to compete for power and influence. What political turmoil this caused is unclear, but surviving material culture provides abundant evidence of the intensification of ideological reinforcement and control. Temples and palaces moved from the periphery of settlements into their centres and grew to massive proportions, enhanced by more and larger monumental sculpture. And portable religious images became more common, suggesting that worship was becoming more of a public, and hence, political spectacle, as the state replaced 'some of the older bureaucratic control with greater and more overt psychological manipulation' (Kemp 1989:188).

The increasing visibility of these ideological props suggests that the king and state actively adjusted their ideological output in response to changes in the political climate. Whether they acted from a position of weakness or power is not so obvious. O'Connor suggests that kings must have had real power during much of the New Kingdom to organize successfully their massive building projects (O'Connor 1983:205). The state may have also used coercive displays to revive the declining influence of the king – misrepresenting the actual situation. Towards the end of the New Kingdom, for example, the king's actual power and authority evidently declined, but the monumental records still extolled his authority and supremacy (O'Connor 1983:204).

Can an analysis of visual images help to reveal the nature of royal power during the New Kingdom – 'the degree to which the king's political independence was circumscribed by the system of which he was a part' (O'Connor 1983:205)? Art is a logical source for the study of power in a society, as it is essential to the displays that reinforce ideology for the masses. But the benign nature of Egyptian art conveys the same message of order to analysts that it probably did to a diverse and restless population. Indeed, the display of official ideology in the New Kingdom served the purposes of both the state and its elite. It focused on gods and god–kings and confined any real life to the periphery. As Baines has pointed out in a study of ancient Egyptian concepts and uses of the past: 'official ideology presents human action as royal; humanity is almost excluded and its position in the scheme of things poorly understood' (Baines 1989a:132). Such political misrepresentations of cultural life do not allow for the possibility of alternative points of view. This omission is important, as Baines observes, because it should not be assumed 'that state-imposed burdens were universally accepted' (Baines 1989b:11). And yet, finding evidence of resistance to the state in official art seems impossible: both the elite and the rest of the society were, in different ways, 'materially and culturally impoverished by central appropriation' (Baines 1989b:207). How can we then overcome the impression of the 'enduring nature' (Robins 1994:3) of Egyptian art and get at the confusing melange of traditional iconography and contemporary propaganda that was probably its reality?

Traditional stylistic analysis does not allow us to get closer to the actual situation of production of pictures (i.e. the material and social context within which the artists actually worked) and to the individuals and society which produced them. Style subsumes individual differences, and this encourages analysts to generalize about Egyptian art. From this point of view, the putative aims of the artists support the traditional, timeless, canonical viewpoint – as Robins (1994) exemplifies:

> The aim of the artists was to depict the enduring nature of the objects and scenes they portrayed; they were not interested in how these might appear at any one time from a particular viewpoint.
>
> (Robins 1994:3)

The alternative is to look closely at such pictures with the eyes of a field archaeologist, seeing them as material environments containing various material and ideological activity areas, places where individuals infused with the attitudes of their time marked the surfaces of walls (Molyneaux 1991). The pervasive notion of artworks as rare and valuable commodities notwithstanding, pictures are generally, and simply, areas containing information of a different sort (and density) than the walls or other surfaces around them. Each picture records traces of the situation of artistic production, including aspects of an artist's physical and intellectual state, translated through a brush, knife, or other tool into material features on the picture surface. Some aspects of the work are consciously formed, but others emerge through the representational process itself: the artist does not draw or paint first and then look; representation is a task in which the eye and the hand work together, absorbed in the action *within* the image, not *on* the image (cf. Wollheim 1991:101–2, Podro 1991:163–4). Pictures will therefore contain visible evidence of artists' implicit and explicit attitudes, or the positions they take, towards their subjects.

We can identify such positions (without necessarily knowing precisely what they mean – see below) in at least one aspect of art: the form and arrangement of human figures and the depiction of social scenes and events. Representations of social landscapes are very sensitive to contemporary ideological situations (and, of course, susceptible to a variety of modern readings) because they are partly concerned with the recognition and display of individual social status. This may be so even in the staid, canonical art of Egyptian tomb paintings. Grid layouts that traditionally guided proportion and composition show that Egyptian artists (assuming draughtsman, painter, and sculptor) wanted precise formal control, but the grid was only a guide. The draughtsmen 'sketched their outlines with flowing strokes, producing figures that approximated the ideal proportions of the period but often included small variations' (Robins 1994:259).

Such small variations, differences that stylistic analysis obviates, are our primary concern here. The relative size and orientation of individual figures in a scene may be the result of simple variations in sketching. But, as noted above, they may also express the artist's conscious or unconscious attitude towards his subjects. Taking relative size as a means of representing significance, a common technique in non-perspectival paintings (in pre-Renaissance art in western Europe, for example), the artist will probably paint the most important figures, or scenes, larger than others. Even if we are more or less ignorant of the subjects, meanings, or iconographic details of a painting, we may look at such a picture and at least understand the organization of significance within it. And if we find that this pattern occurs over a number of pictures by different artists, we may speculate that it reflects a more prevalent social attitude.

At this point, concepts such as *code, convention, icon,* or *genre* usually weigh in to take the depiction out of its situational context so it can serve as an art historical or semiotic generalization. Our goal is to resist such generalizing tendencies so that we may keep our focus at 'ground level', on the objects themselves in their environments, where the formal details of individual paintings reflect the work of individual artists in specific situations of production. From this position, we may be able to see the hidden dynamism in pictures which on the surface appear so controlled and consistent – formal differences arising from situational variation, reflecting the actuality of artists' representational work as it is influenced by changing psychological and practical circumstances in the workplace.

This is a non-stylistic approach. What is significant is how the artist represents the relation between figures and other elements in a picture, rather than how the rendering as a whole compares to other versions of the same theme (cf. classic definitions of style, such as Shapiro 1953). Content is important, but only at the level of subject matter. We are concerned with the study of the particular form that any specific content (such as the relationship between specific human subjects) takes in a set of pictures – the *shape* of its meaning, how this 'shape' appears and changes over time, and what such variation may signify about the effect of ideology in the situation of production and its social context.

The analysis of the shape of meaning is an analysis of common informational factors that constitute visual expressions of, and adjust-ments to, ideological situations. We used an important example above – relative size, or scale. If we regard picture perception as a scanning process involving selective attention to specific informational elements (artists certainly think this is so, as they use visual means to lead the eye of the spectator to significant information) we can assume that the more visible a feature in a representation (relative to others), the greater the probability that it will be encountered and picked up by the perceiver. It does not take a Native North American or an anthropologist of art, for example, to guess that the largest human figure in a Plains Indian hide painting depicting a battle scene has some special significance (it is most likely the artist himself), or an historian to guess which figure is Custer in 'Custer's Last Stand' paintings (see Fox, Chapter 8). And even people unfamiliar with Christian religious iconography will probably pick out the most important figures in Nativity, Annunciation and other tableaux – as their perception is guided by the manipulation of scale, the arrangement of figures, the sightlines and actions of the people in the scene, light and shadow, colour, and so on. The distribution and relative visibility of the material attributes of the information represented may therefore have some demonstrable relation to their communicative significance.

There seems to be an obvious problem with this premise, as the constraints of cultural relativism seem to limit our ability to measure 'visibility' (and derive meaning from pictures at all – but see Costall, Chapter 3 for a brief, illuminating discussion of the issue of cross-cultural picture perception). Such relativist arguments carry an implicit notion of perceptual relativism as well, the notion that the visible world is, in essence, a social construct, most commonly mediated by language and discourse (see, for example, Wittgenstein's philosophies (e.g. 1958), as discussed by Ackermann 1988, and the work of vast numbers of modern semioticians and critical theorists).

There is an alternative view, however, based on the notion that human activity is a negotiation of situations in an environment of material and social information. According to the psychologist J.J. Gibson (e.g. Gibson

1966), we see the world directly: optical information is retrieved already structured from the material world rather than processed in the brain (Gibson 1966). In this theory of ecological perception (Gibson 1979), humans do not create environments, but live within them. As a result, individual perception is not a myopic, self-centred, and aggressive construction within a chaos of information; it is situated and dynamic, changing as the material and social landscape changes.

A psychological and social complement to this theory of perception is Vygotsky's (1978) notion of a social situation. According to Vygotsky, cognition is not simply a physiological given, but is mediated by the task and the nature of information exchange in the context of that task.

Together, these approaches to perception and action give rise to the idea that the environment of social interaction is a dynamic context of situational relations, where different informational conditions influence activity, communication and production in different ways (see Molyneaux 1991 for further discussion, in particular of Douglas' work (1970, 1975) and the model of information and activity developed by Hillier and Hanson (1984), both of which show how activity may be associated with, and affected by, different forms and intensities of social reinforcement).

Most significantly, this research gives representations a legitimate (theory-backed) claim to reality as environments in which socially-mediated activity takes place, both in production and when perceived.

With regard to the question of the meaning and significance of situational variation in representations, we may refer to Wiessner's (1984, 1989) studies of individual and social attributes in material culture. She shows in the analysis of a variety of material culture types that the ideological balance between individual and social concerns may be identified in the analysis of art styles. It follows that the representation of information itself – outside the constraints of the notion of style – is sensitive to ideological reinforcement in the situation of production.

Following these various leads, we therefore favour the idea that ideological forces in a society affect the position the artist takes (physically, intellectually, emotionally) towards specific subjects and, hence, influence the organization of social significance in representations. If we analyse what may be considered genre scenes in Egyptian art, so that individual variation in the representation of specific social relationships between identifiable persons (e.g. king, god, commoner) can be studied and tracked over time, we can then analyse the patterns and degree of variation in such literal (material) elements of pictures and consider these with respect to social situations and representations, and the distribution of power during New Kingdom times.

THE AKHENATEN PROBLEM

To illustrate the approach, we will briefly examine the nature and distribution of power during a notorious period in the dynastic history of
the New Kingdom, the reign of Amenhetep IV/Akhenaten, *c.* 1350 to
1334BC, near the end of the eighteenth dynasty.

Amenhetep caused a convulsion in the relationship between state and
society by changing some fundamental aspects of Egyptian tradition. Early
in his reign, as Amenhetep IV, he commissioned an official art style radically different from traditional ways of depicting the king (see, for
example, the tomb of the Vizier Ramose (Davies 1941); compare Figures
1 and 2 in Aldred (1973:53)). He then redefined the state religion,
replacing the pantheon of gods with a single god, the Aten, or sun-disc.
The Aten first appeared during the reigns of Amenhetep II and Tuthmosis
IV within the established cult of Amen-Re (Smith 1972:3). Amenhetep
IV appropriated this cult as his own, altering his name to Akhenaten to
reinforce his traditional standing as a divine king. Finally, and most extrav-
agantly, he altered the social fabric by founding a new capital, called
Akhetaten (Amarna hereafter), at a site midway between the primary
cities of the New Kingdom, Memphis and Thebes. He moved there
with his state bureaucracy and a sizeable population (Kemp 1989:267)
and remained until his death, in the seventeenth year of his reign (Petrie
1894). Soon after, the city began to decline (Kemp 1989, cf. Petrie
1894:43). By the time of Tutankhamun's accession several years later,
most people had abandoned Amarna and the ideology. In Thebes, artists
once again reverted (with a very few exceptions) to traditional art forms.

Egyptologists do not agree about why Amenhetep IV deviated so
strongly from tradition (if he did – see, for example, Kemp 1977, Smith
1981, and Robins 1994). O'Connor thinks it was part of a general historical process, 'a tendency to royal absolutism which was inherent in the
political system', as opposed to a more traditional view of a specific
historical incident, 'a conflict between the king and other powerful
sections of government' (O'Connor 1983:220).

The art style and iconography show clearly that major ideological
changes took place. Before Akhenaten's accession (as Amenhetep IV),
kingship scenes were rather lifeless tableaux, stultified by their symbolic
intent. Outside of the main action, however, artists sometimes painted
small vignettes of everyday life, flowing with energy and originality (cf.
Aldred 1973:51). In Aldred's opinion, Akhenaten adopted this less formal
approach as the essence of his official style. The result was 'a wilful
distortion' in images of the royal family and high-status commoners
(Aldred 1973:51).

Akhenaten may have wanted a new style to help distance the new
official ideology from the old. Egyptians used the past to maintain
ideological continuity: 'ancient percepts and beliefs were deliberately

sought out as guides for current policies and behaviour'. During times of change 'their effect was to "reinforce" the traditional world-view' (O'Connor 1983:189). Akhenaten's art symbolizes the opposite, a conceptual break with the past.

Unfortunately, this is as far as style can go into this problem. It cannot give us deeper insight into the actual situation – especially to what extent the population accepted the changes. Aldred's concluding words about the character of Amarna art show how an imagined social consensus can emerge from the generalization of form and content:

> Amarna art in the integration of its compositions betrays the same mental processes that in the sphere of religious thought brought about a simpler eschatology, a more joyous acceptance of the natural world, and a more rational belief in a universal sole god.
>
> (Aldred 1973:79)

The challenge of situational analysis is to see whether this appearance of social integrity and acceptance of Akhenaten's radical ideology reflects the social situation or simply the official style.

As a test case, we will examine the relation between human figures in tomb paintings in Amarna and at Thebes before and after Akhenaten (see Porter, Moss, and Burney 1960). Art in the tombs of high-status commoners is especially appropriate: many paintings depict intensely political scenes, showing interactions between the tomb owner and the king or high officials. Such scenes generally represent the tomb owner in his glory, with all the trappings of power, prestige, and wealth and they proudly display his devotion to gods and the king (e.g. Fig. 6.1). The question is how much these scenes also reveal about the tomb owner as an individual, standing in a negotiative position *vis-à-vis* the state. Indeed, a tomb owner's representations may reveal his status relations with all the other inhabitants of the social landscape: gods, king, his family, and other commoners. In effect, the representations are his (or his family's) putative definition of the ideological situation, interpreted by artists.

The paintings are arranged in a chronology of five periods, depending on kings referred to in scenes or texts. The first period consists of tombs completed during the reign of Amenhetep III (1384–1345BC) but containing scenes or references to his precursor, Tuthmosis IV (1397–1384BC); this period is identified with the early reign of Amenhetep III. The second period contains tombs with references exclusively to Amenhetep III. The third period contains references to Amenhetep III and his successor, Amenhetep IV, and is regarded, therefore, as representing the late reign of Amenhetep III and the Theban reign of Amenhetep IV. The fourth segment represents the tombs of Amarna, constructed during the reign of Amenhetep IV/Akhenaten (1356–1339BC) (see Davies 1903–8). And the fifth segment represents the few private tombs in Thebes dating from the reigns of the last three kings of the eighteenth dynasty, Tutankhamun (1334–1329BC), Ay (1329–1324BC), and Horemheb (1324–1296BC)(see Porter, Moss, and Burney 1960).

The analysis is of the wall painting surface as it appears to modern viewers (i.e. 'literally'), rather than how contemporary spectators might have seen it (given that Egyptian art lays out figures on a flat surface, rather than conveying the illusion of depth through perspective). Therefore, references are to figures being in front of or behind others, rather than beside them. We should also note that although the artist is credited with decision-making in the form and organization of picture elements, each work was probably the creation of draughtsmen and painters, supervised by scribes, with input by the tomb owner or his family.

THE SOCIAL LANDSCAPE OF THE REPRESENTATIONS

The study of social interaction and status relations in the tomb scenes of Amarna is difficult because the artists were preoccupied with constructing images and themes of the royal family. Akhenaten and his wife Nefertiti dwarf all other figures in size, and their activities often take up entire walls. The tomb owner's presence is relatively minor. He is not the highest status nor the most prominent figure in the main register; he may not be in the main register at all. This gives the impression that an all-powerful king truly shattered tradition – at Amarna, it seems that a man could not gain even a little personal prestige in his own tomb!

Still, the tomb owner appears in almost every royal scene, attending the royal family, carrying out official duties honouring the king, or accepting honours and material rewards (Fig. 6.2) and leaving the reception area (palace, pavilion, workplace) to public acclaim and a triumphal homecoming (Fig. 6.3). His participation in all these important state activities shows that he is a high official. How then does the artist manage to communicate the tomb owner's individual status in the overwhelming presence of the king?

We can analyse this problem by looking at how artists used form as a reinforcing device in the metaphorical landscape of the picture, as a means of drawing attention to its significant aspects (see Molyneaux 1991 for a detailed discussion of visibility as it relates to perception and action). The status and power of the king and royal family are evident (to us and undoubtedly to contemporary Egyptians) because these figures are gigantic in relation to others around them. The artist used massive scale as a visibility device, as a means of catching the eye of the spectator. The question is whether he also used more subtle attention-getting devices to lead the eye to the tomb owner.

Figure 6.1   A tomb owner (Tomb 226, Thebes, see Porter, Moss and Burney 1960) presents gold and other wealth to Amenhetep III.

VISIBILITY AND COMPOSITIONAL DEVICES

The tomb owner is most often not the highest status individual in a scene and may not be at the leading edge of the action, so any direction of attention to him required compositional devices other than scale.

The tomb owner is always in open, unobstructed space – and so, entirely visible. When he stands before the king's covered dais, for example, he stands in front of columns, whereas fanbearers or other officials may be obscured by them (Fig. 6.1 is a Theban example).

The flow of action sometimes favoured the tomb owner. In a scene in the tomb of Panehesy (Tomb N6), for example, the king, queen, and four children offer bouquets of flowers at an altar piled with meat and flowers, Panehesy offers another bouquet to the king, and other attendants wait in the background (Fig. 6.4). Panehesy is prominent, almost the same size as the queen and slightly taller than the other attendant. Most significantly, however, he reaches under the hand-tipped rays emanating from the Aten symbol above the king with another bouquet.

Figure 6.2 Ay (a future king), accompanied by his wife, receives gold collars from Akhenaten (Tomb S25, Amarna, Davies 1908).

In no other scene in the Amarna tombs does a commoner violate this most sacred space.

Artists also reinforced the tomb owner's presence by manipulating the narrative structure. Most scenes have a continuous flow of activity around a main event. If time is segmented, however, the tomb owner may appear more than once. A scene of a royal procession to the temple in the tomb of Huya (Tomb N1), for example, has nine images of the tomb owner in adjacent sub-registers. In one he is with the royal party and in eight others he leads various groups of attending servants in praise of the king. Even within a royal family scene, the margins may have a multiple temporal structure. In Mahu's tomb (S9), a scene of the king riding off in his chariot has Mahu simultaneously bidding farewell as head of the force of men left behind, kneeling before the detachment accompanying the king, and greeting the chariot at its destination.

Artists had to be inventive (intentionally or unintentionally) to communicate the status of commoners in Amarna. The metaphorical devices they used to represent the royal family overwhelmed the rest of the social landscape in much the same way as massive buildings and monumental royal statuary loomed over the people of Amarna. Under these circumstances, the use of formal devices to direct the viewer's attention to the tomb owner is significant. Such manoeuvering suggests that although the tombs at Amarna appear at first glance to be entirely devoted to the ideology of the divine kingship, with the royal family as 'the object of

Figure 6.3 Neferhotep is acclaimed after being rewarded by Ay (as king) (Theban tomb 49).

devotion by courtiers and officials' (Kemp 1989:265), the tomb owner was not as selfless or subordinate as Kemp thinks (1989:272). Indeed, Panehesy's intrusion within the sacred space (Fig. 6.4) is matched in northern European art of the Renaissance, when patrons had themselves painted into sacred scenes depicting Jesus, Mary, the Apostles, and angels (see, for example, Jan van Eyck's *Virgin and Child with Chancellor Rolin* (Friedlander 1969); the painters may take pains to show the eyes of the patrons averted from the scene – implying that they do not actually 'see' it – or paint these secular figures separated from the main scene on the altarpiece shutters, as Hugo van der Goes did on the Portinari Altarpiece, but they are still very clearly and intentionally part of the action).

This assertiveness also shows that the artists maintained some continuity with tradition, in spite of Akhenaten's dominance. The link is not obvious. Beyond the differences in style, Theban tomb paintings celebrate the tomb owner's status, not the king's, and it is he who presides over worship, feasting and commerce. Where the king is pictured, he is much nearer to the size of the tomb owner and is passive, more like a picture within a picture (see Figs 6.1 and 6.5). In other respects, however, these styles have much in common – especially the techniques used to direct attention to the tomb owner.

Theban artists sometimes structured the flow of action to favour the tomb owner. In Kha's tomb (Tomb 8, Porter, Moss, and Burney 1960),

Figure 6.4 Panehesy proffers a bouquet to the king during an offering ritual to the Aten. Panehesy's tomb (N6, Amarna, Davies 1905).

in a scene showing Kha and his family offering to Osiris, all face the god, with the exception of one servant, the nearest figure to the god. He faces and attends to the tomb owner.

A similar deflection of action towards the tomb owner occurs in scenes where he is being promoted or rewarded. In the tomb of Huy (Tomb 40, see Davies 1926), the king sits on his dais and presides, but an intermediary carries out the transaction, standing with his back to the king, facing the tomb owner (Fig. 6.5).

Artists also used episodes to increase the frequency of images of the tomb owner. In Haremhab's tomb (Tomb 78, Porter, Moss, and Burney 1960), for example, the main register depicts Tuthmosis IV enthroned, with a goddess standing behind him and the tomb owner offering a large bouquet of papyrus. The focus on the king is diffused, however, by the presence of three adjacent sub-register scenes, showing the tomb owner standing before several ranks of soldiers. The soldiers bow before him – deference which he does not accord the king in the larger scene. And in the tomb of Huy (40, see Davies 1926), there is a row of nine separate images of the tomb owner, in each of which he holds a different object for presentation to the king.

Figure 6.5   Huy is rewarded by a representative of Tutankhamun. Tomb of Huy (40, Thebes) (Davies 1926).

The similar treatment of status in tombs at Thebes and Amarna shows that in Amarna, Akhenaten's omnipotence did not cause artists to stray completely from their traditional path. This has significant ramifications for the assessment of Akhenaten's hold on the population. It does not, however, provide us with a measure of the more general distribution of power and status surrounding Akhenaten's reign. We still need to know whether Akhenaten's ideological excesses were part of an historical trend towards greater emphasis on public displays of power or weapons in his struggle for power with the state.

METRIC ANALYSIS

Given the insights gained through the Amarna analysis, we can expect that differences in ideological relations in the wider realm of Egyptian art will be marked by differences in the visibility of the respective individuals or features. The elements of visibility seen so far in these tombs are all compositional devices designed to direct attention to the tomb owner, and we have interpreted their meaning within the situation as it is represented. We now need an analysis of common informational factors 'outside' meaning (only far enough removed to see its 'shape') so that we can describe visual adjustments in the ideological situation over a longer period of time.

We can analyse and interpret the relative visibility of figures in a more neutral and objective way by simply measuring and comparing various proxemic attributes (i.e. spatial representations of social relations) of the figures (Hall 1969), such as height, distance from other figures, posture, and position within scenes. As the goal here is simply to illustrate the approach, we will examine only height (see Molyneaux 1991 for a full discussion of the theoretical justification, methodology, and results of several proxemic variables).

Height is the most visible formal aspect of status differentiation in the tomb paintings, as the larger-than-life scale of kings suggests. Artists used strategies other than body size as well, differentiating figures by posture, or gesture, by giving them headwear or seating them above ground level. Figures reach their greatest height when their arms are upraised. This position is common in scenes in Amarna where the king rewards the tomb owner. Figures are most diminutive when prostrate – a common posture for foreigners from conquered nations who offer tribute to the king. Headwear increases a person's height, and so gods and kings wear crowns and tomb owners and other figures, festal caps. And seated figures tend to be elevated to maintain physical and social superiority, gods and kings on thrones, and commoners on chairs on low platforms above the floor.

The basic premise in this analysis is that the artist will represent the significance of the various persons and objects in a picture (mediated by the 'habitus' (Bourdieu 1977) and the more specific pressures of ideo-logical reinforcement) by enhancing their visibility in some material way in order to direct the attention of spectators. We can therefore gain some idea of changing ideological significance through visibility – liter-ally by measuring and comparing the amount of information devoted to individuals of different statuses in a given scene.

THE ANALYSIS OF HEIGHT RELATIONS

The size and shape of registers reflects the correspondence of height and status. The focal situation is in the largest register of a scene; subsidiary registers tend to be extensions of the main action or related activities. It follows that the highest status figures occupy the primary register, where they may be most prominently displayed.

The tomb owner is usually at the leading edge of the main action in a register, either heading a group or facing another figure. We can measure his relative visibility by comparing his height to that of other people in the scene (see Molyneaux 1991, Tables 6 and 7). The analysis shows that height is a means of emphasizing primary figures and indi-cating the direction of significance in the activity in the scene: the tomb owner is most often taller than those around him, making him the focal point; where he is shorter than an adjacent figure, he faces them, less prominent but still in the main action. His height actually depends on the status of the persons he is pictured with. The tomb owner is shorter than figures of higher status – king, queen and gods – and taller on average than other commoners, befitting his position as a high official. His stature also varies with social distance: he is nearest in height to his wife, followed by his family, other commoners and the higher status figures.

These results are highly suggestive, given the argument presented in the introduction to this chapter. As pictures are metaphorical landscapes, we can only assume that proxemic variables such as height were socially determined. The tomb owner stands in relation to clearly defined social categories – king, god, wife, family, fellow official, and slave – not actual people. At the same time, the artists (or patrons) worked out the representation of status in a situation of production sensitive to polit-ical or other ideological considerations. Is it possible that changes in attitude concerning the actual people behind the images produced changes in their appearance in the art? Did the artist use visibility as a means of highlighting one figure more than another, to lead the eye of the spectator according to his personal agenda?

The pattern of variation over time in the tomb owner's relative height compared to individuals according to status (see Molyneaux 1991, Table 8) shows that some of these social relations were more or less constant. The height of the tomb owner varies least in relation to his wife. This probably reflects the unambiguous nature of their association. His height also varies little in relation to gods, as befits what is a conven-tional, rather than actual, relation.

Reality seems to intrude in the height relation between the tomb owner and the king, for their representations vary considerably over time. The most striking difference is in the Amarna paintings, yet this phenom-enon is not confined to the Amarna period. Images of the tomb owner begin to decrease in height in relation to the king in the major part of the reign of Amenhetep III and, after reaching their most inequable during the Amarna period, return during the post-Akhenaten period to near the level at which they began (see Molyneaux 1991, Table 8).

This result clashes with normal expectations, as the tomb owner must have occupied as clearly defined a position in relation to the king as to the gods and to his wife. Indeed, the king was divine and, hence, set apart ideologically as well as socially from the rest of society. This suggests that the scenes involving the tomb owner with the king were not subject to the kind of formal conventions that characterized scenes with gods or family. The wife rarely does more than stand or sit behind her husband; and most of the scenes with gods simply show the tomb owner worship-ping in front of the god enthroned.

The dynamic nature of this relation may reflect an increasing rein-forcement of the image and status of the king and the significance of

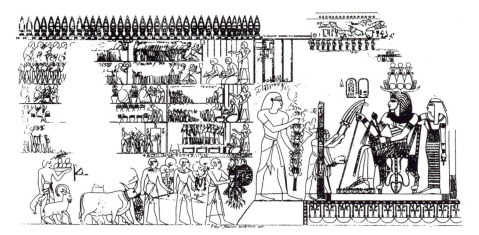

Figure 6.6 Haremhab presents a bouquet to Tuthmosis IV. Haremhab's tomb (78, Thebes) (see Porter, Moss, and Burney 1960).

the state, beginning during the reign of Amenhetep III. In the first encounter of the period, the tomb owner approaches Tuthmosis IV with an offering (Fig. 6.6); the small physical difference between them suggests that it is a relatively equitable relationship. During the reign of Amenhetep III, however, the tomb owner loses direct contact with the king: in scenes of promotion and reward, other officials may act as the king's representatives. The direct relationship is restored and even enhanced by the actions of the king at Amarna, but by this time, the distortion in scale separates the king and tomb owner even further (Fig. 6.2). It is only at the end of the eighteenth dynasty that a measure of equity is restored. In a tomb of the final period (Tomb 50, Neferhotep, see Porter, Moss, and Burney 1960), the tomb owner receives his reward from Horemheb (Fig. 6.7). This king (a former military commander who took over the throne) stands before the tomb owner, larger in size, but not separated by columns, texts, or other barriers, almost as a senior official instead of a monarch.

The increase in the visibility of the king's image before the rise of Akhenaten seems to have affected other proxemic relations. At the end of the reign of Tuthmosis IV and the early part of the reign of Amenhetep III, the tomb owner is much taller than members of his family; in the period up to the move to Amarna, however, the difference becomes less and less – at the same time as the difference from the king becomes greater. And then, in Amarna, there are no references to the family in the display hall at all. The tomb owner is most often with his servants and attendants, as he receives rewards from the king and leaves the palace in triumphal procession, and in tribute scenes, where foreign nobility

Figure 6.7 Horemheb rewards Neferhotep (Tomb 50, see Porter, Moss, and Burney 1960).

prostrate themselves at his feet. It is perhaps not a surprise that he reaches his greatest height in comparison with other commoners at this time.

It is reasonable to expect that the extreme individualism of the king would stimulate similar activity and expression through the social hierarchy. As the tomb owner did exercise status representation in Amarna, it is possible that the decline in the use of his wife and family in the scenes was in fact a pragmatic intensification of his personal status, in response to the climate of ideological reinforcement of the king. According to Kemp, the royal family were the 'sole intermediaries' between the Aten and the human and natural world (Kemp 1989:265), and so piety to the god and service to the king were one and the same. As a result, the depiction of official bureaucratic duties and royal activities in private tombs would have met both religious and political demands.

This emphasis on individual status in the state hierarchy is also evident in another striking feature of the Amarna scenes. Posture relations appear to have been carefully worked out, so that every figure adopts a specific posture and position relative to their status. The resulting variety of postures afforded to the range of figures from high officials to slaves gives the scenes their dynamism and an appearance of 'naturalism' not found in earlier or later times.

CONCLUSION

The evidence of individual, pragmatic responses in the representations supports the notion that there is a significant difference between the ideology of the state and the way that the social milieu reinforces and responds to it – the difference between the representation and the reality.

We can see this difference in the organization of the city of Amarna itself. Akhenaten's official texts, carved on boundary stelae in rock cliffs around the site of the new city (Kees 1961:293–5, Kemp 1989, Petrie 1894) and on Amarna's buildings and monuments, give the impression that the founding of the city achieved an orderly integration of social and spiritual values – the sort of positive idealism that one might find in the words associated with the founding of any settlement or nation (see, for example, Keston 1993:23–6). The archaeological evidence in excavations at Amarna, however, tells a different story. The royal residence, government centre, and officials' residences are organized in a cluster, but the residential parts of the city are arranged haphazardly, with a diversity of house sizes, spacings between residences and neighbourhoods. The exception is a workers' village near the southern tombs; it consists of a block of identically sized houses and one larger, 'presumably for the official in charge' (Kemp 1989:273).

The contrast between the worlds of the text and the settlement, and between parts of the settlement itself, exhibits the difference between an ideal community and the actual situation. The logical organization of the state sector and, outside of Amarna, the workers' village, are consistent with the texts – reflecting the power of the ruling elite and the powerlessness of the lowest sector of society (cf. Kemp 1989:178). The surrounding residential area, on the contrary, occupies the social and spatial middle ground, with its inhabitants holding diverse amounts of status and power.

Apparent order can therefore be deceiving. The absolute power of an Egyptian king was distributed in a highly complex material and social environment with varying degrees of penetration and acceptance. In the rigidly structured workers' village, for example, its grid layout symbolic of the powerlessness of the individuals within, Kemp says that 'the state built the square walled enclosure . . . and laid out the basic house plans' but 'the villagers were left to their own resources to complete their houses' (Kemp 1989:255).

It is important to consider power from such an environmental (i.e. proxemic, or even ecological) point of view; even the weak, living in a situation where behaviour is rigidly controlled, may react pragmatically to ideological reinforcement rather than surrender to it. In the maximum security institutions (e.g. prisons, asylums) and closed communities (e.g. of religious sects) of modern societies, there are always 'damp corners' out of reach, where individualistic activity can 'breed and start to infest the establishment' (Goffman 1984:268).

The relation between official and commonplace beliefs in ancient Amarna shows the uneven impact of ideological control. The excavations in the city (Petrie 1894) and the workers' village (Kees 1961) uncovered a variety of religious images on jewellery moulds, amulets, and rings. Significantly, many were traditional deities supposedly proscribed by Akhenaten. Petrie thought this was simply a sign that production was not limited 'to the fanatically Aten-worshipping times' (Petrie 1894:29), meaning that the city still existed in the reign of Tutankhamun (he discovered rings of Tutankhamun there as well) (Petrie 1894:42–3). Kees interpreted similar artifacts from the workers' village excavation to mean that 'these people were clearly not supporters of the king's religion of the Aten' (Kees 1961:303). Most likely, however, people continued using traditional images in spite of – or simply without regard to – the official cult of the Aten (cf. Samson 1972:81).

These conflicting images of the social order in Amarna suggest at least that the community was not as uniform as the monumental texts claimed. According to Kemp, the differences were minor, most likely the result of 'the transfer to the new site of existing arrangements' (Kemp 1977:126). He therefore accepts that 'no radically different social or economic way of life was being introduced' (Kemp 1977:126). Yet it is difficult to imagine that the state could simply tear out the bureaucratic heart of Thebes and transplant it in Amarna without effect – crucial lines of connection, bureaucratic and personal, were no doubt severed. It is fair to speculate, therefore, that discontinuity existed between the ideology of the state and the situation at ground level, and that conspicuous royal/religious displays were part of the political solution.

The tomb paintings and reliefs incorporate the ideological reinforcement of the kingship and the new ideology, expressing it in themes and images suffused with a dynamism that suggest significant changes in the social landscape. As the analysis of the scenes has shown, however, artists created these images in a subdued, perhaps covert or unconscious, but still visible context of depictions, themes, and activities traditionally used to represent the status of tomb owners.

The scenes of Amarna are no closer to reality, therefore, than their predecessors. By their strategic nature, they are maps of relations, an intense defining and ordering of the world in order to keep everything in its place, fashioned with the fictive naturalism of a state that aspired to control both ideology and social activity.

REFERENCES

Ackermann, R.J. 1988 *Wittgenstein's City*. Amherst, MA: University of Massachusetts Press.

Aldred, C. 1973. *Akhenaten and Nefertiti*. London: Thames and Hudson.

Aldred, C. 1980. *Egyptian Art*. London: Thames and Hudson.

Baines, J. 1989a. 'Ancient Egyptian concepts and uses of the past: 3rd and 2nd millenium BC evidence.' In R. Layton (ed.), *Who Needs the Past?*, pp. 131–49. London: Unwin Hyman.

Baines, J. 1989b. 'Literacy, social organization and the archaeological record: the case of early Egypt.' In J. Gledhill, B. Bender, and M.T. Larsen (eds), *State and Society*, pp. 192–214. London: Unwin Hyman.

Bourdieu, P. 1977. *Outline of a Theory of Practice*. Cambridge: Cambridge University Press.

Davies, N. de G. 1903–8. *The Rock Tombs of el Amarna*. 6 Volumes. London: Archaeological Survey of Egypt, Egypt Exploration Fund.

Davies, N. de G. 1905. *The Rock Tombs of el Amarna. Part 2, The Tombs of Panehesy and Meryra II*. London: Archaeological Survey of Egypt, Egypt Exploration Fund.

Davies, N. de G. 1908. *The Rock Tombs of el Amarna. Part 6, Tombs of Parennefer, Tutu, and Ay*. London: Archaeological Survey of Egypt, Egypt Exploration Fund.

Davies, N. de G. 1926. *The Tomb of Huy, Viceroy of Nubia in the Reign of Tutankhamun (No. 40)*. With explanatory text by A. Gardiner. Memoir 4, The Theban Tombs Series. London, Egypt Exploration Society.

Davies, N. de G. 1941. *The Tomb of the Vizier Ramose*. Mond Excavations at Thebes, 1. London.

Davis, W. 1989. *The Canonical Tradition in Ancient Egyptian Art*. Cambridge and New York: Cambridge University Press.

Douglas, M. 1970. *Natural Symbols, Explorations in Cosmology*. London: Cresset Press.

Douglas, M. 1975. *Implicit Meanings*. London: Routledge and Kegan Paul.

Friedlander, M.J. 1969. *Early Netherlandish Painting*. New York and Washington: Praeger.

Gibson, J.J. 1966. *The Senses Considered as Perceptual Systems*. Boston, MA: Houghton Mifflin.

Gibson, J.J. 1979. *The Ecological Approach to Visual Perception*. Boston, MA: Houghton Mifflin.

Goffman, I. 1984. *Asylums*. London: Penguin Books.

Hall, E.T. 1969. *The Hidden Dimension*. Garden City, NY: Doubleday.

Hillier, B. and Hanson, J. 1984. *The Social Logic of Space*. Cambridge: Cambridge University Press.

Iversen, E. 1955. *Canon and Proportions in Egyptian Art*. London: Sidgwick and Jackson.

Kees, H. 1961. *Ancient Egypt: A Cultural Topography*. London: Faber and Faber.

Kemp, B. 1977. 'The city of el-Amarna as a source for the study of urban society in ancient Egypt.' *World Archaeology* 9:123–39.

Kemp, B. 1989. *Ancient Egypt: Anatomy of a Civilization*. London: Routledge.

Keston, S. 1993. *Utopian Episodes: Daily Life in Experimental Colonies Dedicated to Changing the World*. New York: Syracuse University Press.

Molyneaux, B.L. 1991. 'Perception and situation in the analysis of representations.' Unpublished PhD thesis. Department of Archaeology, University of Southampton.

O'Connor, D. 1983. 'New Kingdom and Third Intermediate Period, 1552–664 BC.' In B.G. Trigger, B.J. Kemp, D. O'Conner, and A.B. Lloyd, *Ancient Egypt: A Social History*, pp. 183–278. Cambridge: Cambridge University Press.

Petrie, W.M.F. 1894. *Tell el Amarna*. London: Methuen.

Podro, M. 1991. 'Depiction and the golden calf.' In N. Bryson, M.A. Holly, and K. Moxey (eds), *Visual Theory. Painting and Interpretation*, pp. 163–89. New York: HarperCollins.

Porter, B., Moss, R., and Burney, E. 1960. *Topographical Bibliography of Ancient*

Egyptian Hieroglyphic Texts, Reliefs, and Paintings. Volume 1, *The Theban Necropolis*. Part 1, *Private Tombs*. Second edition. Oxford: Oxford University Press.

Robins, G. 1994. *Proportion and Style in Ancient Egyptian Art*. Austin, TX: University of Texas Press.

Samson, J. 1972. *Amarna: City of Akhenaten and Nefertiti*. London: University College.

Shapiro, M. 1953. 'Style.' In A.L. Kroeber (ed.), *Anthropology Today*, pp. 287–312. Chicago: University of Chicago Press.

Smith, H.S. 1972. 'Introduction.' In Samson, J., *Amarna: City of Akhenaten and Nefertiti*, pp. 1–13. London: University College.

Smith, W.S. 1981. *The Art and Architecture of Ancient Egypt*, Third edition. Harmondsworth: Penguin Books.

Vygotsky, L.S. 1978. *Mind in Society: The Development of Higher Psychological Processes*. In M. Cole, V. John-Steiner, S. Scribner, and E. Souberman (eds). Cambridge, MA: Harvard University Press.

Wiessner, P. 1984. 'Reconsidering the behavioural basis for style: a case study among the Kalahari San.' *Journal of Anthropological Archaeology* 3:190–234.

Wiessner, P. 1989. 'Style and changing relations between the individual and society.' In I. Hodder (ed.), *The Meanings of Things: Material Culture and Symbolic Expression*, pp. 56–63. London: Unwin Hyman.

Wittgenstein, L. 1958. *Philosophical Transactions*. Oxford: Basil Blackwell.

Wollheim, R. 1991. 'What the spectator sees.' In N. Bryson, M.A. Holly, and K. Moxey (eds), *Visual Theory. Painting and Interpretation*, pp. 101–50. New York: HarperCollins.

CHAPTER SEVEN

SOME GREEK IMAGES OF OTHERS

BRIAN A. SPARKES

INTRODUCTION

Daniel Alain's 1955 cartoon in *The New Yorker* (Fig. 7.1) is well known, as it was used by Ernst Gombrich in 'Psychology and the Riddle of Style', the introductory chapter to his book *Art and Illusion* (Gombrich 1960). It invites us to imagine that, contrary to our presumptions, Egyptian art was not stylized, but was rather a straight transcription of their observable world. Our notion of the Greeks is rather different. In the Archaic and Classical periods of Greek antiquity (*c.* 600–300BC) Greek craftsmen carved, cast, moulded, and painted figures with a naturalism that has seduced us into thinking they represented the 'real world'. Indeed, whereas Egyptian images have been consigned to art and archaeology, Greek images and ideas of nature have had a great influence on the European idea of naturalism.

Just as it is imprudent to accept written evidence as a truthful and unbiased narrative, so it is naive to accept images at what one might call 'face value'. Both written sources and visual evidence are creations of their time. No story in Greek mythology was codified as holy writ, there was no definitive version; the story was a living and developing organism. 'The outcome of a myth may have been generally accepted, but its development could be elaborated at will' (Woodford 1993:63). We are aware that Athenian tragedians dipped into the well of myth and reshaped the stories they drew up, to fit their view of the world and to make comment on the contemporary scene (Podlecki 1966; Meier 1993). Historians also shaped their recounting of events in their own way – 'the historical text as literary artifact' (White 1978) – and what has been recently expressed as a three-stage process in historiography ('myth as history', 'myth in history', and 'myth versus history') indicates the difficulty of entertaining the idea of historians as purveyors of truth (Cartledge 1993:21–33).

Figure 7.1   Cartoon by Daniel Alain from *The New Yorker* 1.10.1955.

Of course it was inevitable that stories and texts would have influenced pictures. But the temptation to demote such images to the status of illustrations must be resisted. 'Illustration, like translation, is never a simple matter of transcription' (Woodford 1993:87), raising questions of method, purpose, and choice. Like speakers and writers, craftsmen drew on myth, history, and everyday life to shape their images, and they did this not only within their artistic traditions and conventions but also with the freedom to adapt to changing circumstances.

We shall be concerned with images that show the complex interplay of past and present that so typified the public and private life of the Greeks. Of primary interest is the way the Greeks saw themselves in relation to others, what traits they considered significant for visual identification, and how miscellaneous the images could be (Lissarrague 1990). We shall concentrate for the most part on Athens in the late sixth and early fifth centuries BC, as this centre at that time provides much the fullest evidence. In carrying out this analysis, we will show what images are, as an information source; where they stand in relation to other metaphorical information sources, i.e. speech and text; and how we can use them in Classical archaeology.

THE DYNAMIC TEXT

In societies that are illiterate or only partially literate (for the degrees of literacy, see Thomas 1992:8–12), visual images have an important role to play. In a centre such as Athens the great creative impulses both in speech and image indicate that listening and looking were in fact more influential in daily life than reading. Some Greeks would have listened to the formal words of orators in the court rooms and to the speeches of politicians in the assembly. Others would have heard leading figures of the day delivering funerary orations over the recently fallen (Loraux 1986), or in the theatres and concert halls they would have appreciated the songs of choirs or solo performers, or the words of actors as they impersonated the figures of myth and took on the characters of contemporary society. They would have observed and inspected the statues by the wayside and at the crossroads, have paid their respects to the images in the cemeteries that lined the roads leading out of town, marvelled at and tried to make sense of the narratives that decorated the temples and treasuries in the sanctuaries of their home town or the national religious centres which they visited as pilgrims (cf. Euripides, *Ion*, ll. 184–218). On a more private level they would have listened to the tales told at the loom and the gossip at the fountain, and would have gazed at the images on the metal and clay objects that they handled at parties or selected for consignment to the tombs of their loved ones.

As myths were therefore mainly oral and visual traditions, they were not frozen in time or text, but varied in popularity and in content. They were linked to times, places, and occasions, both as spoken stories and as visual presentations. The legends of heroes were ancient history or, in modern jargon, 'para-history' (Dowden 1992:11), and as time went by, some of the outstanding events of more recent history passed into the legendary, para-historical realm. Legends could be used to celebrate success, whether of a community or a family; they could reinforce present status or justify a new direction. The past had a practical role in shaping the present; the stories were not fictions, they were living realities that had social and political relevance. They could be moulded and reshaped to persuade the addressees to accept a new version of, or a newly invented episode in, the past. Greek myths and legends do not tell us much about primal truths; what they do best is to teach us of contemporary preoccupations, both of state and of individual.

It is a commonplace that Greek writers and artists often referred to contemporary encounters by reference to mythological and legendary confrontations, and much research has been carried out recently to show how traditional stories were manipulated politically to favour the Greeks, and particularly the Athenians, in the aftermath of the Persian Wars (see recently Castriota 1992). The struggles against the Persians, both at the time of the invasions (490BC and 480–479BC) and in the years of the Greek counter measures led by the Athenian military commander Kimon (470s–460sBC), were heard and seen in the context of myths that were made to act as distant paradigms, often reinterpreted to fit the recent conflicts. As Francis (1990:35) has said:

> At the beginning of the 5th century myth was probably still for most Greeks an extraordinarily potent means of expressing and informing their experience of the world. . . . [There was] a special relationship between myth and history whereby particular myths were selected and at times recast so that they might be perceived as prefigurations of recent and present events.

Our perception of all this myth-handling is reflected in, indeed to a large extent is based on, the evidence of the visual imagery of the time.

Besides the well known public art of monuments and temples, cult statues, and victory monuments, there was much that was privately commissioned. In that private sphere, were, on a major scale, funerary statues and reliefs with gems and terracotta figurines on a smaller. Painted vases, which bulk large in today's evidence, and decorative metalwork, which does not, were mainly produced for private use, at home for parties, as dedications in sanctuaries, or as offerings in the tomb. The painted vases carry a host of narrative scenes, both mythological and contemporary as well as a mixture of the two, and this makes them a storehouse of evidence. Some scenes present stories from epic poems and from mythology, others episodes from everyday life, yet others vignettes from the world of the imagination. Given that the craftsmen had no access to knowledge that would enable them to create an accurate antiquarian setting, scenes are set in the surroundings of the day – there was no 'deep' background. Indeed, no clear distinction could be made then or should be made now between past and present. The created work may, both in subject matter and in aim, refer to the past, but it necessarily responds to the context in which it is produced.

The vases were cheap to produce and were turned out in great numbers; this means that they carried on their surface the popular imagery of the day, and the great quantities in which they survive allow comparisons to be made both amongst the vases themselves and in connection with the major sculptural creations. With this material, we may now take a closer look at the manner in which the Greeks presented themselves and others, whether they were locating the images in the legendary past or in the period contemporary with their production.

IMAGES OF OTHERS

The Greek's image of himself, whether athlete, hero, or deity, is familiar to us all, as it is stamped on the art and history of Western Europe. As an example we may choose one of the recently discovered life-size bronze statues from the sea off Riace (Fig. 7.2) – naked and perfectly shaped.

It was this chauvinistic self-image that was repeated over and over again, whether in archaic, Classical, or later form.

Their view of the 'other', the non-Greeks, the barbarians, was obviously mediated through their own self-image and through this emphasis on the human form that is a hallmark of Greek visual imagery. The Greek image served as a foundation on which specific deviations were built.

Temples and treasuries were expensive constructions, usually commissioned by states, and the choice of their decoration often reflected the state's immediate concerns. The sculptural scenes were not just decorative adjuncts or randomly chosen myths, there was a programme that reflected the interests of the commissioners.

Greeks, whether humans or deities, were shown in mythical, epic combats that spoke of recent struggles against Persians and that projected the superiority of the Greek forces (Hall 1989:68). In fifth-century Athens some of the major architectural constructions of the years after the Persian Wars (the Theseion, the Painted Colonnade, the Parthenon and its cult statue) were decorated with themes that made reference to those recent struggles by reference to legendary combats.

The Persians were cast in different roles, all deviations from the Greek standard: as hostile, uncivilized giants, whether warriors, cavemen, or monsters, that the Olympians had to overcome in order to establish their power (*LIMC* IV: s.v. Gigantes; Arafat 1990, Chapter 8); as hybrids such as the Centaurs who misbehaved in an inhuman fashion; as Amazons, the warlike women who rode horses and wielded the bow, the very antithesis of the masculine Greek warriors and a suitable counterpart for the 'effeminate' Persians (von Bothmer 1957; Tyrrell 1984; *LIMC* I: s.v. Amazones; Hall 1993:114–15; Henderson 1994); and as Trojans, that old enemy to the east, the rich and powerful Asiatic kingdom that had proved no match for the united vigour of the Greek heroes. As Hall (1989:5) says, 'it was the fifth century which invented the notion of the barbarian as the universal anti-Greek against which Hellenic – especially Athenian – culture was defined'.

To enable the legendary conflicts to act as suitable parallels for the new, the shape and emphasis of the myths and legends had to be altered and new episodes inserted. The Amazons, for example, were brought over from their mythical homeland in the east (but see Shapiro 1983) and made to invade Attica, to provide a counterpart to the actual Persian invasion and repulse (Boardman 1982); they were even found a camp on the Areopagus for their assault on the Acropolis (Aeschylus, *Eumenides*, 685–9; Herodotus 8.52 (Persians) and 9.27 (Amazons); Hall 1993:115). Theseus, the Athenian hero whose track record up to this time had not

Figure 7.2   Bronze statue from Riace: Reggio, Museo Nazionale. *c.* 460–450BC (Photo: Museum).

been impressive, became a second Herakles, 'Kimon's heroic template' (Francis 1990:46), acting as an enhanced model for the Athenian military leader of the day, and was given a greater role to play versus Amazons and Centaurs, to magnify Athenian importance in those epic struggles (Boardman 1982). And as for the stories that recounted the sacrilegious conduct of the Greeks at the time of the destruction of the city of Troy, countless generations earlier, they too had to be altered so that they would appear to prefigure the recent encounters. Post-Persian War artists modified the horrors perpetrated by the Greeks so that their now sanitized actions served as exemplars of high moral conduct; the ethical standards of the recent victors were projected back to the destruction of Troy in the Heroic Age (Castriota 1992).

One might assume that contemporary references would be much simpler, as they would be free from the metaphorical burden of myth and legend of the past. And indeed, craftsmen distinguished contemporary non-Greeks by clothing and accessories, facial and bodily differences, colour, contexts and attributes, including names. The characterization was to a large extent perfunctory and was confined to simple indications and easily recognizable aspects of appearance. Familiarity with non-Greeks obviously varied: some may have been met on the battlefield, some brought home as slaves, others glimpsed on a foreign visit, whilst others would have been encountered in the art of other peoples, whether viewed abroad or on goods imported into Greece; yet others would have been conjured out of the descriptions of amazed travellers.

As we shall see, however, the image of otherness was more than a readily identifiable pastiche of symbols. We have only a limited ability to distinguish between the various categories of foreigner. This is partly a result of the Greeks' own incapacity or unwillingness to distinguish their neighbours and their recourse to simple signals, but it is also due to our own misplaced propensity to interpret images in as rudimentary a way as possible.

As Frontisi-Ducroux and Lissarrague (1990) have pointed out, there are three types of ambiguity in the interpretation of images. Two derive from the original artist in his conscious desire to mystify the viewer and in his own unconscious involvement in the varied meanings of a work of art, both 'intrinsic to the thoroughly polysemous nature of the pictorial image' (Frontisi-Ducroux and Lissarrague 1990:211). The third ambiguity arises from a lack of skill on our own part in deciphering the image. None of these ambiguities however should dissuade us from attempting to analyse the images. Our interpretation may reveal more of the social and political background from which the images emerged than about the meaning of the images themselves. From a study of the other, the Greeks' own image of themselves and their relation to others is likely to come into sharper focus than the nature of the others themselves.

THE OTHERS

Let us take a brief look at the four main foreign groups and see the different ways in which Greek craftsmen depicted them and the different problems the images still present to us. The four groups are the Skythians, the Thracians, the Persians, and the Africans (Ethiopians and Egyptians) (Raeck 1981).

The Skythians

A popular image in Athenian vase-painting was the archer in Skythian clothing (Fig. 7.3). The Skythians were nomadic riders in the area north of the Black Sea, an area that the Greeks were coming into contact with more and more through the seventh and sixth centuries BC. To what extent Athenian artists had direct knowledge of them is more difficult to define, as is the problem of differentiating between images of actual Skythians and those in Skythian dress. Certainly, the main method by which painters indicated a Skythian context was clothing. The costume, which admitted great variety, was basically a one-piece or two-piece suit consisting of trousers and a close-fitting top and jacket with long sleeves; the outfit was patterned and edged with decorative strips (Fig. 7.3). It was conspicuously different from normal Greek clothing. The outfit also included a cap of soft material (leather?) with flaps at the sides and back and usually tapering above to a point or curled over (*kurbasia*, Herodotus 7.64; see Miller 1991:62–3). The archers were normally shown barefoot, and their main item of equipment was the composite sigma-shaped bow of wood and horn, with a quiver (*gorytos*) that held both arrows and bow. There are a few images of archers that display un-Greek facial features: mainly a short, sparse beard on the chin, and sometimes a deliberate attempt at a snub nose and bulging forehead (Vos 1963), but it is mainly the clothing that acts as a pointer to Skythian links.

The variety of images makes it difficult to know whether one is looking at a contemporary scene, an epic encounter, or a mixture of the two. Many have seen in these figures, which appear in the art of Athens from the middle of the sixth century to *c*. 480BC, contemporary Skythians who, it is claimed, were recruited by the state under the tyrant Peisistratos as mercenaries in the Athenian army (Vos 1963; Hall 1989:138–9). This view has been shown to be untenable (Welwei 1974:18–22; Lissarrague 1990:125–49; Miller 1991:61), for although we know that Skythians served as policemen in Athens in the fifth century, there is no hard evidence to show that they were recruited in the previous century. Indeed it has been commented that it is odd that their images in popular art should disappear at the very moment when their presence in Athens is properly attested (Pinney 1983:130–1).

Figure 7.3 Archer in Skythian costume: Athenian black-figure amphora (type A) painted by Exekias (Philadelphia, University Museum 4873: Beazley 1956: 145, 16; 1971:60; Carpenter 1989:40). *c.* 540BC (Photo: Museum).

A counter argument shows that they were often set in the context of epic (Pinney 1983), dressed in a costume that the Greeks would have come to know through their increasing contacts with the northern coasts of the Black Sea. Those wearing the outfit were minor characters, squires first to Achilles, it is suggested, and then to other epic heroes, and were the northern counterparts to the Ethiopians of the south (Neils 1980), a contrast that is to be found deeply rooted in Greek history and anthropology (Hartog 1988). Despite their clothes and a certain degree of facial distinctiveness, they have no explicitly contemporary sixth-century significance; modern scholars have given them that significance. The vase-painters have exercised their artistic freedom in combining modern accoutrements and traditional legend. Also, archers in epics (such as Paris on the Trojan side and Teucer on the Greek) as well as the figure of Herakles as archer, were depicted by the painters in the appearance of the archers they knew from their own experience.

This chapter does not cover all the contexts in which Skythian clothing was worn, and Lissarrague (1990:141–9; cf. Miller 1991) has put together those images in which Skythian costume is worn at Athenian banquets where 'faire le Skythe' was a sign of a hard drinker. This is a useful example as it teaches us not to accept corresponding details of appearance as indicators of an exclusive meaning. As Pinney herself (1983:127) rightly comments,

> It is by no means obvious that the realia of legendary scenes on monuments of a given period showing some coherence among themselves are trustworthy representations of men and things of the time. They may be images that begin and end in the realm of the visual arts, and combine in their appearance the true and present with the imaginary and distant.

Just as we must be alert to recognizing that myths were used to prefigure contemporary events, so we must be ready to shed the notions that scenes with contemporary features have no reference back in time and that meanings and contexts cannot expand. Artists must be allowed to have had the freedom to 'pick and mix'.

The Thracians

Of their neighbours, the Thracians of the north were considered to be the Greeks' most savage, stupid, and servile opponents (Hoddinott 1975; Hall 1989:122,137–8; Lissarrague 1990:210–16; Cartledge 1993:138–40). From the middle of the sixth century, we find the clothing that was associated with the Thracians depicted in Athenian vase-paintings (Fig. 7.4; Miller 1991:65): a thick patterned cloak (*zeira*) and a fox-skin cap (*alopekis*) (Herodotus 7.75; Xenophon, *Anabasis* 7.4.4), suitable for the colder climates. The men were also usually shown wearing boots and were depicted as riders. When fighting, the warriors carried a wicker crescent-moon shaped shield (*pelta*) (Best 1969; Cahn 1973; Lissarrague 1990:151–89). Occasionally, as with the Skythians, less than ideal facial features were conferred on them, but this was too restrictive a signal compared with their clothing and equipment, as the artists wanted to represent Greeks as well as Thracians dressed in this way (see below). As with the Skythians, the Thracians form a contrast with the Ethiopians

Figure 7.4 Thracian rider: Athenian red-figure cup potted by Brygos and painted by The Foundry Painter (Rome, Villa Giulia 50407: Beazley 1963: 402, 24, and 1651; 1971: 370; Carpenter 1989: 231). c. 480BC (Photo: Hirmer).

– in Xenophanes' famous comparison (fr. 16): 'The Ethiopians say that their gods are snub–nosed and black, the Thracians that theirs have light blue eyes and red hair'.

Once again we may ask when and how the Athenians had become familiar with the appearance and outfit of the Thracians. Thracian horsemen could have been seen in Athens in the second half of the sixth century when the tyrant Peisistratos who had established connections with Thrace, particularly in the region of the Pangaeum gold mines (Herodotus 1.64: Aristotle, *Athenaion Politeia* 15.2), hired mercenaries from that area. But certainly not all those attired in Thracian outfit were Thracians. The clothing which the artists found fascinating to paint and draw, also attracted the young cavalrymen of Athens for other reasons (riding a horse in standard Greek garments would have been a chilly business). Some riders in Thracian outfit were certainly young Athenian cavalrymen in fashionable garb, some were shown at the annual review known as the *dokimasia* (Cahn 1973,1986; Bugh 1988:14–20; Lissarrague 1990:217–31).

Whereas it was only males who were represented in Skythian costume, besides the Thracian men and the Athenians who are exhibited in Thracian outfit, Thracian women also appear in the repertoire of vase-painting. Many Thracian women were brought back to Greece as slaves and became nurses to Greek children. Their distinguishing mark was not their clothing but the tattoos that they carried (Zimmermann 1980a). Such marks were a boon to the painters who could add a simple and recognizable detail to their nursery scenes (Fig. 7.5) and also to the scenes that had a mythological meaning.

Figure 7.5 Thracian nurse: Apulian red-figure fragment from the Circle of the Sisyphus Painter (London BME 509: Trendall and Cambitoglou 1978:21, no. 1/94). *c.* 420BC (Photo: Museum).

Mention of mythology brings us to another level of Thracian association. Contemporary Thracians (male and female) and their clothing (whether on Thracians or Greeks) were not the only components to engage the attention of artists. There was a rich tradition of mythological Thracians (Zimmermann 1980b:431–41; Dowden 1992:84–5). There were singers such as Orpheus, Mousaios, and Thamyras (Brommer 1971–76: 332–45; 1973:504–9,536–7; Carpenter 1991:81–2). Orpheus was also a member of the crew of the Argo and is shown singing to a Thracian audience in costume, and being done to death by tattooed Thracian women. Kings formed another part of the Thracian imagery, usually in connection with horses: Lycurgus, king of the Edones (Beazley 1928:44–6; Bruneau and Vatin 1966; Brommer 1973:503–4; *LIMC* VI: s.v. Lycourgos I); Rhesus, an ally of the Trojans in the Trojan War (Brommer 1973:440); and Diomedes, king of the Bistones, with his man-eating horses (Brommer 1973:186–7; Kurtz 1975; *LIMC* V: s.v. Herakles J). A Thracian goddess, Bendis, was introduced into Athens for the resident Thracians, and she too, is represented, though rarely, amongst the images (*LIMC* III: s.v. Bendis; Boardman 1989:Fig. 318). Even Zetes and Calais, sons of the North Wind, are appropriately furnished with Thracian uniforms – the north was a cold direction from which to blow (Carpenter 1991:Fig. 276). In all these it is the accoutrements and the context of the myths that mark out the foreign character of the participants, not their actual appearance. Rarely does a Greek painter depart from his traditional manner of representing humanity, to distinguish the appearance of a foreigner (but see 'The Africans' below).

The Persians

The most serious eastern opponents of the Greeks were the Persians. They came out of the east in great numbers but unexpectedly fell to the Greeks at Marathon in 490BC and a decade later at Salamis (480 BC) and Plataea (479BC). Although the Greeks first knew the Medes and Persians when Cyrus moved westwards in the middle of the sixth century, they do not appear in art until after Marathon (Williams 1986) or maybe even until after Plataea (Barrett and Vickers 1978). Given their importance as opponents, the number of representations of them in Greek art is few (Bovon 1963; Hölscher 1973); so important and significant were the victories that the Greeks had won over them that Persian defeat was soon transmuted into myth and mediated through the earlier victories, both divine and heroic (see above).

Like Thracians and Skythians, and unlike Greeks, the Persians were not shown naked – nudity was the major distinguishing feature that marked Greek males from slaves and non-Greek, civilized from barbarian. The Persians' outlandish clothes consisted of trousers, a decorated jacket and a second, sleeveless tunic; they also wore shoes with turned-up toes and a distinguishing soft cap with full top and flaps (*tiara*, Herodotus 7.61) that in Roman times, as the Phrygian cap, became the mark of liberty and at the time of the French Revolution became the famous *bonnet rouge*. The Persians are sometimes shown with cuirasses; some also sport heavy beards. Their weapons comprised a wicker shield (*gerron*), bow and quiver, battle axe, large curved sword (*kopis*), and spear (Herodotus 7.61). It is not surprising that it is difficult to distinguish Skythians and Persians in dress; the artists were giving an impression of the exotic in terms that would be recognizable (Miller 1991:64).

Different artists adopted various ways of representing the Greeks' combat with the Persian opponents who had come so close to defeating them (Bovon 1963). There are some rare instances of Persians depicted defeating Greeks (for a possible explanation, see Kahil 1972:281–2), but naturally the majority underline the Greek victory. Let us compare two sharply contrasting images. On a red–figure cup in Oxford (Fig. 7.6) (Beazley 1963:399), *c.* 480BC, Greek meets Persian, and the Persian, although turning in flight, is shown as a formidable opponent. He is attired in leggings and shoes, sleeved top and cuirass, sports a

Figure 7.6 Greek *v.* Persian (I): Athenian red-figure cup potted by Brygos and painted by The Painter of the Oxford Brygos (Oxford, Ashmolean 1911:615: Beazley 1963:399 below and 1650; Beazley 1971:369; Carpenter 1989:230). *c.* 480BC (Photo: Museum).

Persian bonnet, and carries a spear in his right hand and a large rectangular wicker shield on his left arm. By contrast, another painter
sees this foreign opponent rather differently. After the Greek success in
479BC, the Athenians led the counter attack to rid the Aegean and
beyond of the Persian presence. The naval battle at the mouth of
the river Eurymedon along the southern coast of Asia Minor was the
pinnacle of Greek success under Kimon in the mid-460s. It is hard
therefore to interpret the painting on an Athenian wine-jug of c. 460
BC (Fig. 7.7) that includes the word 'Eurymedon' other than as a reference to that event (Schauenburg 1975; Dover 1978:105; Hall 1993:
111; Kilmer 1993:128–9). A full-bearded Persian, in a one-piece suit
and cap, a quiver swinging uselessly from his left arm, makes a gesture
of fright by placing his open hands on either side of his frontally facing
head (cf. Hölscher 1974). He is bent over and awaits the sexual
attack of a naked Greek who advances towards him, penis in hand.
There are inscriptions in the background. The one near the Greek says
'I am Eurymedon' and the one near the Persian says 'I stand bent over'
(Pinney 1984). The humiliation of the Persian forces at Eurymedon has
been translated into sexual imagery that would be easy for the party-
goer handling the jug to understand. As Kilmer says (1993:128–9),
'the emotions it was meant to arouse in the viewer may be guessed at
least in part: satisfaction, amusement, triumph and, for some at least, a
degree of sexual identification'. Hall (1993:111) comments on the
way in which military victory has turned into sexual conquest and
Greek male domination has unmanned the Persian opponent. This
male superiority explains why the myth of the Amazons is linked to the
Persian conflict.

> The close relationship between the Amazon and the Persian is demonstrated
> by the way in which, after the wars, Persian details creep into the tradi-
> tional type of the Amazonomachy scene, thus turning the mythological
> conflict into an archetype, with profound patriotic significance, of the Greeks'
> subordination of the Persian barbarians.
>
> (Hall 1993:114)

The Africans (Ethiopians and Egyptians)

When we turn to look at the peoples living to the south of Greece,
rather than to the east and north, the picture is different (Snowden 1970;
Vercoutter 1976; Snowden 1983). The Egyptians and other inhabitants
of Africa never acted as policemen in Athens like the Skythians, never
served as mercenaries like the Thracians, and never invaded Greece like
the Persians. Greek contact with Egypt itself was controlled by the
Egyptians, and it was Greek mercenaries and traders, mainly from East
Greece, who had the closest association with, and opportunity to observe,
the different peoples of Africa (Austin 1970). It is not surprising that

Figure 7.7   Greek v. Persian (II): Athenian red-figure oinochoe (Hamburg 1981.173). c. 460BC (Photo: Museum).

Greek visitors were fascinated by what they saw in Africa, nor that Greek artists were confused about the precise origin and location of the different peoples. There would have been little or no understanding of the relationship between Mediterranean Egypt and Ethiopia ('the land of burnt faces') somewhere to the south; as geographic knowledge increased, the location of the Ethiopians was made more precise, but for many wedded to popular geography, the Ethiopians still inhabited an area between the equator, the Red Sea and the Atlantic, and for some they were also to be found in India (*LIMC* I: s.v. Aithiopes). It was also in the interests of the craftsmen to make the meaning of their Egyptian scenes plain by underlining the foreignness of their figures; this would encourage artists to invest any individual connected with Egypt with an Ethiopian appearance.

Amongst Greek writers Herodotus (Book 2) is our most precious early testimony to Egypt, but it does not reveal the reality of Egypt, rather Greek perceptions and misperceptions of it in the middle of the fifth century BC. Similarly the visual images that Greek craftsmen, particularly again the Athenians, created, were indications of their perception; for many this perception would have been at second hand, based on others who visited Egypt and, on their return, described what they had seen, as well as on works of craftsmanship that had reached Greece.

Whereas the recognition of a Skythian, Thracian, or Persian connection was expressed mainly through differences in clothing and accessories, those images that had an African connection deployed greater visual differences, depicted more through skin colour and facial and bodily differences, though accessories were not totally omitted. The technique of Athenian black-figure pottery which exhibited every male as black, forced the painters to concentrate on other distinctions of appearance; the technique of red-figure on a black background prevented the craftsmen from making a sharp distinction between Greeks and blacks, unless by a clever trick (e.g. Boardman 1989:Fig. 75). '. . . from a technical point of view, neither black nor red figure is a particularly happy medium in which to portray a black-skinned person' (Neils 1980:22). It was only on white-ground pottery that the black skin could really be made distinct (Neils 1980). However, the artists' observation of the other contrasts made the differentiation clear: woolly hair, snub nose, and thick lips.

Where the demands of the pottery techniques did not impede them, as in the case of plastic rhyta and head vases, the results can be seen to be masterly and sympathetic studies (Fig. 7.8). Some plastic vases introduce circumstantial local colour such as crocodiles (Boardman 1989:Fig. 104) and painted scenes add camels (Schauenburg 1955–6; Kahil 1972:Fig. 17; Boardman 1975:Fig. 183), palm trees (Neils 1980) and the particularities of dress, such as the royal regalia of Egyptian headdress and beardcase. It is rare to find illustrations of everyday life in Egypt on Greek vases, but a few examples are known, perhaps painted in Egypt (Boardman 1958a; cf. Boardman 1987:147–8 and Strocka 1992:no. 51).

It is mainly through the mythological stories (Hicks 1962) that the Athenian craftsmen's images of Egyptians and Ethiopians can be appreciated. Some, though known in literature, did not attract the artists, e.g. the story of Proteus the king of Egypt who took care of the real Helen whilst her phantom went to Troy, a story known to (invented by?) Stesichorus (Campbell 1991:fragments 192–3) and used by Euripides (*Helen*; see Dale 1967:xvii–xxiv). The story of Io (*LIMC* V: s.v. Io I) was only incidentally an Egyptian story. The myth of Danaos and his fifty daughters who fled from Egypt to escape the fifty sons of Aegyptos, usually centres in art on the daughters and their fate in the Underworld (Brommer 1973:522–3; *LIMC* III: s.vv. Danaides and Danaos; Hall 1989:139–40). In these and other tales that have connections with Egypt and Ethiopia (Hall 1989:140–2), the association is often shown by the presence of Ethiopian subordinates, such as squires, attendants and guards, and allies. The three main stories that are popular in Athenian vase-painting are those of Memnon, Busiris, and Andromeda.

Memnon was king of the Ethiopians, son of Tithonos and Eos (Dawn), and brother of Priam (Brommer 1973:348–52,402; Pinney 1983:131–3; Hall 1989:142–3; Lissarrague 1990:21–29; *LIMC* VI: s.v. Memnon;

Figure 7.8 Black man: Athenian head aryballos (Berlin F 4049). Early fifth century BC (Photo: Museum).

Figure 7.9 Memnon and squire Amasis: Athenian black-figure neck-amphora potted and painted by Exekias (London BM B 209: Beazley 1956:144, 8; 1971:60; Carpenter 1989:39). c. 540BC (Photo: Museum).

Schefold 1992:266–72). It was Dawn who carried Memnon off to Ethiopia; whether east or south, is unclear. He was a Trojan ally who came to Troy after the deaths of Hector and the Amazon Penthesileia (see the prose summary of the epic poem *Aithiopis*) and fell to the spear of Achilles. Iconographically the most popular episode of his career is his fatal duel with Achilles, witnessed by the mothers of the two warriors, Dawn and Thetis (*LIMC* I: s.v. Achilleus XXV). Another popular image shows his soul being weighed in the balance against that of Achilles (*LIMC* I: s.v. Achilleus XXIV), and yet another has his mother (or helpers) lifting his body from the battlefield to carry it home (von Bothmer 1981:74–8). In all these his physical appearance is indistinguishable from his Greek opponents, but by the 460s BC he is given an oriental sleeved and trousered costume (Caskey and Beazley 1954:13–19), perhaps to mark his Trojan/Persian allegiance (Hall 1989: 142–3).

Memnon is on occasion accompanied and aided by black attendants. Their weapon was a club (Herodotus 7.69), and this is what they carry initially in the paintings. Later they are given a bow and quiver (*gorytos*), and are furnished with beards and trousered costumes – like Memnon, they were assimilated by the vase-painters to the Greeks' eastern enemies. In two famous instances painted by the black-figure potter and painter Exekias, an Ethiopian squire of Memnon (Fig. 7.9) is named 'Amasis', the name of a (black) ruler of Egypt and of a contemporary potter in Athens. This is usually seen as a joking reference to the ethnic origin of the potter who was making his pots in Athens at the same time as Exekias. The names of other potters and vase-painters (e.g. Thrax, Skythes) show that the streets of Athens had a cosmopolitan appearance, and representations of blacks in scenes of everyday life are to be seen, though rarely (Boardman 1958b,1987).

A second popular mythological character was Busiris, son of Poseidon and king of Egypt (Brommer 1973:34–6; 1984:42–6; Vollkommer 1988: 22–3; *LIMC* III: s.v. Bousiris; Schefold 1992:143–4). He was notorious in Greek legend for sacrificing strangers who entered his territory (human sacrifice was the sign of a barbarian) and famous for falling to the superior might of the Greek hero Herakles (Fig. 7.10). Many of the images of Busiris' encounter with Herakles are intentionally humorous and in the best known, the Egyptian iconography of the all-powerful Pharaoh trampling on his tiny enemies is caricatured by making Herakles gigantic and the Egyptians puny (Hemelrijk 1984:173–4). In other works there is uncertainty on the part of the artists about whether they are to paint Busiris as a black or not. As with the Memnon story, the henchmen were always shown as black, and one painter shows the figures circumcised (Fig. 7.11), another visually distinguishing difference (Herodotus 3.37).

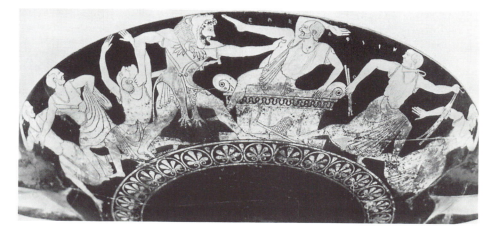

Figure 7.10 Herakles and Busiris: Athenian red-figure cup painted by Epiktetos (Rome, Villa Giulia 57912: Beazley 1963:72, 24 and 1623; Carpenter 1989:167). *c.* 500BC (Photo: Hirmer).

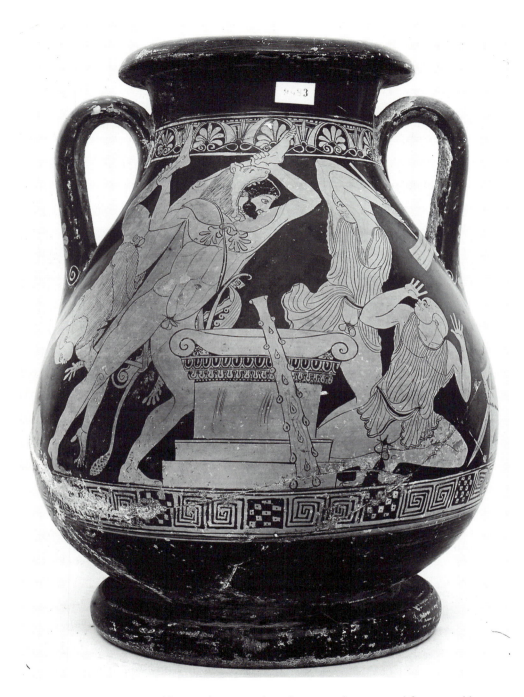

Figure 7.11 Herakles and Busiris' henchmen: Athenian red-figure pelike painted by The Pan Painter (Athens NM 9683: Beazley 1963:554, 82; 1971:386; Carpenter 1989:258). c. 470BC (Photo: Museum).

Figure 7.12 Andromeda and Ethiopian guards: Athenian red-figure hydria from the Group of Polygnotos (London BM E 169: Beazley 1963:1062 and 1681; Carpenter 1989:323). *c.* 440BC (Photo: Museum).

Andromeda, daughter of King Kepheus of Ethiopia and his queen Kassiopeia, also has African connections (Phillips 1968; Brommer 1973: 284–5; *LIMC* I: s.v. Andromeda; Carpenter 1991:106, Figs 160,161), and although she is not given facial features that would link her to Ethiopia, she is shown in foreign dress, again of eastern type. In the episode where she is bound to the rock, she may be seen dressed in oriental costume with Persian headdress, whilst the workers who are chaining her are often shown as Ethiopians (e.g. Fig. 7.12).

This episode is a clear instance of the influence of tragic costume on the vase-paintings (Trendall and Webster 1971:63–5,78–9; Hall 1989: 140–1); in the theatre the alien origin of a hero or heroine would be most easily indicated by outlandish clothing of eastern type, whether appropriate to the story or not; it would appear that masks of Ethiopians were also available, if needed.

There was another, less grand myth that linked Greece with Egypt: the battle of the pygmies and the cranes (Beazley 1951:36–7; Brommer 1971–6:432–3,1973:546–8; Freyer-Schauenburg 1975; Brommer 1984:

Figure 7.13 Pygmy *v.* crane: Athenian red-figure neck-amphora painted by the Epimedes Painter (Brussels Musées Royaux R 302: Beazley 1963: 1044, 7). *c.* 450–440BC (Photo: Museum).

47). When the cranes flew south for the winter, they descended on the fields of Africa and were attacked by the pygmies, to prevent them destroying their crops. This story was usually seen as a humorous one by Greek painters, and pygmies were not given the sympathetic treatment accorded to blacks. They were often represented as manikins but more usually they were later assimilated to dwarfs (Fig. 7.13). Dwarfs were well known in Athens (Dasen 1990, 1993:175–88) and were set in everyday scenes (queuing to see the doctor, following the

Figure 7.14 The Dying Celtic Trumpeter: marble copy of a bronze original at Pergamum (Rome, Museo Capitolino 747). Original *c.* 220BC (Photo: Hirmer).

master or mistress, dancing and tumbling at parties to amuse the guests). The identification of dwarfs and pygmies suggests to Dasen (1990:204) that

> Vase-painters change pathological dwarfs into a race of innocuous, short plump people, conveniently located in a far-away country, who cannot resist the attack of birds. . . . The trouble induced by the genetic anomaly was relieved by laughter, and could be discussed in ethnological and mythological terms.

CONCLUSION

In all the instances discussed the foreigners have to be seen as Greek, mostly Athenian, images pictured in a fundamentally Greek way. They do not tell us what the barbarians looked like or even how they really dressed; they do tell us how Greek craftsmen answered the demands of their customers to provide them with recognizable, even if inaccurate, likenesses.

As mentioned above, antiquarian concerns could not be uppermost in representing mythological and contemporary others. The images arose in the specific circumstances of the time and so were conditioned by the current social and political pressures. They were not fixed and static images that gave any 'true' reflection of the past; they lived, moved, and had their being in the present. The largest quantity of evidence by which we might see how the Greeks viewed non-Greeks comes from Athenian black- and red-figure painted pottery, and this inevitably concentrates attention on Athens in the sixth and fifth centuries BC.

To redress the balance and to show that the Greek artistic treatment of non-Greeks has other perspectives, let us conclude by looking at a later product that belongs to the major art of life-size sculpture. The Greek forces encountered the Celts in Asia Minor when they were harassing the Greek residents there. The Pergamenes defeated them in the later third century BC, and victory monuments were erected at Pergamum (Fig. 7.14 (copy)) and Athens (Pollitt 1986:83–97; Stewart 1990:205–8). These monuments presented the enemy without their Greek opponents but complete with torque, bushy hair, and moustache, and endowed them with a nobility in defeat that had not previously been accorded to real-life adversaries. Whether they fought nude, as was claimed, or not, they were shown so, in the only uniform that the Greeks considered appropriate for a worthy opponent.

REFERENCES

Arafat, K.W. 1990. *Classical Zeus: A Study in Art and Literature*. Oxford: Clarendon.

Austin, M.M. 1970. *Greece and Egypt in the Archaic Age. Proceedings of the Cambridge Philological Society. Supplement 2*.

Barrett, A.A. and Vickers, M.J. 1978. 'The Oxford Brygos Cup reconsidered.' *Journal of Hellenic Studies* 98:17–24.

Beazley, J.D. 1928. *Greek Vases in Poland*. Oxford: Clarendon.

Beazley, J.D. 1951. *The Development of Attic Black-figure*. Revised edition 1986. Berkeley and Los Angeles: University of California.

Beazley, J.D. 1956. *Attic Black-figure Vase-Painters*. Oxford: Clarendon.

Beazley, J.D. 1963. *Attic Red-figure Vase-Painters*. Oxford: Clarendon.

Beazley, J.D. 1971. *Paralipomena*. Oxford: Clarendon.

Best, J.G.P. 1969. *Thracian Peltasts and their Influence on Greek Warfare*. Groningen: Wolters–Noordhof.

Boardman, J. 1958a. 'A Greek vase from Egypt.' *Journal of Hellenistic Studies* 78:4–12.

Boardman, J. 1958b. 'The Amasis painter.' *Journal of Hellenic Studies* 78:1–3.

Boardman, J. 1975. *Athenian Red Figure Vases: The Archaic Period*. London: Thames and Hudson.

Boardman, J. 1982. 'Herakles, Theseus and Amazons.' In D. Kurtz and B. Sparkes (eds), *The Eye of Greece: Studies in the Art of Athens*, pp. 1–28. Cambridge: Cambridge University Press.

Boardman, J. 1987. 'Amasis: the implications of his name.' In M. True (ed.), *Papers on the Amasis Painter and his World*, pp. 141–52. Malibu: J. Paul Getty Museum.

Boardman, J. 1989. *Athenian Red Figure Vases: The Classical Period*. London: Thames and Hudson.

von Bothmer, D. 1957. *Amazons in Greek Art*. Oxford: Clarendon.

von Bothmer, D. 1981. 'The Death of Sarpedon.' In S.L. Hyatt (ed.), *The Greek Vase*, pp. 63–80. Latham, NY: Hudson-Mohawk Association of Colleges and Universities.

von Bothmer, D. 1985. *The Amasis Painter and his World*. Malibu: J. Paul Getty Museum and London: Thames and Hudson.

Bovon, A. 1963. 'La représentation des guerriers perses et la notion de barbare dans la 1re moitié du Ve siècle.' *Bulletin de Correspondance Hellénique* 87:579–602.

Brommer, F. 1971–6. *Denkmälerlisten zur griechischen Heldensage* I–IV. Marburg: N.G. Elwert.

Brommer, F. 1973. *Vasenlisten zur griechischen Heldensage*. Third Edition. Marburg: N.G. Elwert.

Brommer, F. 1984. *Herakles II, die unkanonischen Taten des Helden*. Darmstadt: Wissenschaftliche Buchgesellschaft.

Bruneau, P. and Vatin, C. 1966. 'Lycurgue et Ambrosia sur une nouvelle mosaique de Délos.' *Bulletin de Correspondance Hellénique* 90:391–427.

Bugh, G.R. 1988. *The Horsemen of Athens*. Princeton: Princeton University Press.

Cahn, H. 1973. 'Dokimasia.' *Revue Archéologique* 1972:3–22.

Cahn, H. 1986. 'Dokimasia II.' In E. Böhr and W. Martini (eds), *Studien zur Mythologie und Vasenmalerei. Konrad Schauenburg zum 65. Geburtstag am 16. April 1986*, pp. 91–3. Mainz: von Zabern.

Campbell, D.A. (ed. and trans.) 1991. *Greek Lyric III.* Cambridge, MA: Harvard University Press.

Carpenter, T.H. 1989. *Beazley Addenda.* Oxford: Oxford University Press.

Carpenter, T.H. 1991. *Art and Myth in Ancient Greece.* London: Thames and Hudson.

Cartledge, P. 1993. *The Greeks: A Portrait of Self and Others.* Oxford: Oxford University Press.

Caskey, L.D. and Beazley, J.D. 1954. *Attic Vase-Paintings in the Museum of Fine Arts, Boston, II.* Oxford: Oxford University Press and Boston: Museum of Fine Arts.

Castriota, D. 1992. *Myth, Ethos, and Actuality, Official Art in Fifth Century BC Athens.* Madison, WI: University of Wisconsin Press.

Dale, A.M. (ed.) 1967. *Euripides' Helen.* Oxford: Clarendon.

Dasen, V. 1990. 'Dwarfs in Athens.' *Oxford Journal of Archaeology* 9:191–207.

Dasen, V. 1993. *Dwarfs in Ancient Egypt and Greece.* Oxford: Clarendon.

Dover, K.J. 1978. *Greek Homosexuality.* London: Duckworth.

Dowden, K. 1992. *The Uses of Greek Mythology.* London: Routledge.

Francis, D. 1990. *Image and Idea in Fifth-century Greece: Art and Literature after the Persian Wars.* London: Routledge.

Freyer-Schauenburg, B. 1975. 'Die Geranomachie in der archaischen Vasenmalerei. Zu einem pontischen Kelch in Kiel.' In I. Scheibler and H. Wrede (eds), *Wandlungen: Studien zur antiken und neueren Kunst Ernst Homann-Wedeking gewidmet.* pp. 76–83. Bayern: Stiftland.

Frontisi-Ducroux. F. and Lissarrague, F. 1990. 'From ambiguity to ambivalence: a Dionysiac excursion through the 'Anakreontic' vases.' In D.M. Halperin, J.J. Winkler, and F.I. Zeitlin (eds), *Before Sexuality: The Construction of Erotic Experience in the Ancient Greek World,* pp. 211–56. Princeton, NJ: Princeton University Press.

Gombrich, E. 1960. *Art and Illusion: a Study in the Psychology of Pictorial Representation.* London: Phaidon.

Hall, E. 1989. *Inventing the Barbarian: Greek Self-definition through Tragedy.* Oxford: Clarendon.

Hall, E. 1993. 'Asia unmanned: images of victory in classical Athens.' In J. Rich and G. Shipley (eds), *War and Society in the Greek World,* pp. 108–33. London: Routledge.

Hartog, F. 1988. *The Mirror of Herodotus: The Representation of the Other in the writing of History.* Berkeley and Los Angeles: University of California Press.

Hemelrijk, J.M. 1984. *Caeretan Hydriae.* Mainz: von Zabern.

Henderson, J. 1994. '*Timeo Danaos*: Amazons in early Greek art and pottery.' In S. Goldhill and R. Osborne (eds), *Art and Text in Ancient Greek Culture,* pp. 85–137. Cambridge: Cambridge University Press.

Hicks, R.I. 1962. 'Egyptian Elements in Greek Mythology.' *Transactions of the American Philological Association* 93:90–108.

Hoddinott, R. 1975. *Bulgaria in Antiquity.* London: Benn.

Hölscher, T. 1973. *Griechische Historienbilder des 5. und 4. Jahrhunderts vor Chr.* Würzburg: Konrad Triltsch.

Hölscher, T. 1974. 'Ein Kelchkrater mit Perserkampf.' *Antike Kunst* 17:78–85.

Kahil, L. 1972. 'Un nouveau vase plastique du potier Sotadès du Musée du Louvre.' *Revue Archéologique* 1972:271–84.

Kilmer, M.F. 1993. *Greek Erotica*. London: Duckworth.

Kurtz, D.C. 1975. 'The man-eating horses of Diomedes in poetry and painting.' *Journal of Hellenic Studies* 95:171–2.

LIMC 1981 ongoing. *Lexicon Iconographicum Mythologiae Classicae*. L. Kahil (ed.). Zürich and Munich: Artemis.

Lissarrague, F. 1990. *L'autre guerrier*. Paris: Ecole Française.

Loraux, N. 1986. *The Invention of Athens: The Funeral Oration in the Classical City*. Cambridge, MA: Harvard University Press.

Meier, C. 1993. *The Political Art of Greek Tragedy*. Cambridge: Polity Press.

Miller, M. 1991. 'Foreigners at the Greek symposium?' In W. Slater (ed.), *Dining in a Classical Context*, pp. 59–81. Ann Arbor, MI: University of Michigan Press.

Neils, J. 1980. 'The Group of the Negro Alabastra: a study in motif transferral.' *Antike Kunst* 23:13–23.

Phillips, K.M. 1968. 'Perseus and Andromeda.' *American Journal of Archaeology* 72:1–23.

Pinney, G.F. 1983. 'Achilles Lord of Scythia.' In W.G. Moon (ed.), *Ancient Greek Art and Iconography*, pp. 127–46. Madison, WI: University of Wisconsin Press.

Pinney, G.F. 1984. 'For the heroes are at hand.' *Journal of Hellenic Studies* 104:181–3.

Podlecki, A.J. 1966. *The Political Background of Aeschylean Tragedy*. Ann Arbor, MI: Michigan University Press.

Pollitt, J.J. 1986. *Art in the Hellenistic Age*. Cambridge: Cambridge University Press.

Raeck, W. 1981. *Zum Barbarenbild in der Kunst Athens im 6. und 5. Jahrhundert vor Chr.* Bonn: Habelt.

Schauenburg, K. 1955–6. 'Die Cameliden im Altertum.' *Bonner Jahrbücher* 155–6:59–94.

Schauenburg, K. 1975. 'Eurymedon Eimi.' *Athenische Mitteilungen* 90:97–121.

Schefold, K. 1992. *Gods and Heroes in Late Archaic Greek Art*. Translated by A. Griffiths. Cambridge: Cambridge University Press.

Shapiro, H.A. 1983. 'Amazons, Thracians and Scythians.' *Greek, Roman and Byzantine Studies* 24, 105–14.

Snowden, F.M. 1970. *Blacks in Antiquity: Ethiopians in the Greco–Roman Experience*. Cambridge, MA and London: Harvard University Press.

Snowden, F.M. 1983. *Before Color Prejudice: the Ancient View of Blacks*. Cambridge, MA and London: Harvard University Press.

Stewart. A. 1990. *Greek Sculpture: An Exploration*. New Haven, CT: Yale.

Strocka, V.M. 1992. *Frühe Zeichner 1500–500 vor Chr. Ägyptische, Griechische und Etruskische Vasenfragmente der Sammlung H.A. Cahn Basel*. Berlin: Wasmuth.

Thomas, R. 1992. *Literacy and Orality in Ancient Greece*. Cambridge: Cambridge University Press.

Trendall, A.D. and Cambitoglou, A. 1978. *The Red-figured Vases of Apulia I*. Oxford: Clarendon Press.

Trendall, A.D. and Webster, T.B.L. 1971. *Illustrations of Greek Drama*. London: Phaidon.

Tyrrell, W.B. 1984. *Amazons: A Study in Athenian Mythmaking*. Baltimore, MD: Johns Hopkins University Press.

Vercoutter, J. 1976. *The Image of the Black in Western Art, I: From the Pharaohs to the Fall of the Roman Empire.* New York: William Morrow and Co. Inc.

Vollkommer, R. 1988. *Herakles in the Art of Classical Greece.* Oxford: Oxford University Committee for Archaeology.

Vos, S. 1963. *Skythian Archers in Archaic Attic Vase-painting.* Groningen: J.B. Wolters.

Welwei, K.–W. 1974. *Unfreie im antiken Kriegsdienst, I.* Wiesbaden: Franz Steiner.

White, H. 1978. 'The historical text as literary artifact.' In R.H. Canary and H. Kozicki (eds), *The Writing of History: Literary Form and Historical Understanding*, pp. 41–72. Madison, WI: University of Wisconsin Press.

Williams, D. 1986. 'A cup by the Antiphon Painter and the Battle of Marathon.' In E. Böhr and W. Martini (eds), *Studien zur Mythologie und Vasenmalerei. Konrad Schauenburg zum 65. Geburtstag am 16. April 1986*, pp. 75–81. Mainz: von Zabern.

Woodford, S. 1993. *The Trojan War in Ancient Art.* London: Duckworth.

Zimmermann, K. 1980a. 'Tätowierte Thrakerinnen auf griechischen Vasenbildern.' *Jahrbuch des Deutschen Archäologischen Instituts* 95:163–96.

Zimmermann, K. 1980b. 'Thraker–Darstellungen auf griechischen Vasen.' *Le Monde Thrace, Actes du IIe Congrès International de Thracologie Bucarest 4–10 Septembre 1976* 1:429–46. Bucharest: Editura Academei Republicii Socialiste.

CHAPTER EIGHT

THE ART AND ARCHAEOLOGY OF CUSTER'S LAST BATTLE

RICHARD A. FOX, JR

INTRODUCTION

Eighteen seventy-six – the United States' centennial and the year Alexander Graham Bell patented the telephone – marked the inaugural season of the National League of Baseball Clubs. That year, on 24 June – a Saturday – Cincinnati's baseball team lost to visiting Boston by a run, eight to seven. The National League prohibited contests on Sundays. So no games were being played on the day following Cincinnati's loss, when far away in Montana Territory, Lakota Sioux, Northern Cheyenne, and a few from a handful of other Plains tribes confronted Lieutenant Colonel George Custer and his 7th US Cavalry regiment.

Custer's fate on Little Big Horn River (near Crow Agency and Hardin in south–central Montana) is well known. He and all 210 men in his battalion perished. Less well known are the valley and Reno–Benteen fights, which, with the Custer fight, make up the Little Big Horn battle. Major Marcus Reno, second-in-command of the 7th Cavalry, initiated fighting by attacking the Indian village located in the valley. Ultimately Reno's battalion was driven away. The soldiers scrambled in confusion out of the valley to high bluffs across the river. There the Reno–Benteen fight began; by chance Reno met Captain Frederick Benteen, then returning with his battalion from a scout upriver. The two battalions consolidated on the bluffs where warriors laid siege well into the next day.

Custer's battle took place some four miles north of the Reno–Benteen battlefield. After ordering the attack on the village, Custer, intending to capture the non-combatants, veered to the right and marched north unopposed, as the Indians confronted Reno. Warriors belatedly learned of Custer's battalion as they drove Reno to the bluffs. Many left to meet the new threat and ultimately a numerically superior force of warriors gathered. Most likely it was over in little more than an hour; Custer and all his troops were dead. Indian casualties are difficult to estimate; perhaps forty or fifty warriors died. Though most with Reno and Benteen survived, the Army failed in its objective to move the Sioux to their reservation.

The Little Big Horn battle has generated more treatises, so some say, than any US military event. In any case, its popularity is scarcely restricted to prose. Ever since the gunsmoke wafted from the field, comic books, comic strips, postcards, poems (including one by Walt Whitman, no less), photography, editorial cartoons, songs, film, and videos have helped to perpetuate the memory of the event. Today, there is talk of a software program which will allow aficionados to re-fight the battle. Even a board game exists, and most recently, trading cards like those associated with baseball and bubble gum have appeared. And there is art.

OBJECTIVES

The Custer battle long ago became a symbol of white America's ethos. It remains so to this day, and it is images of the battle created by white artists that are in large part responsible. The problem is, these artworks, principally those I call 'Custer's last stand' images (the genre I examine here), seem to reveal little about the historical nature of Custer's battle. That is what I am seeking in this chapter – an historical perspective. I shall first discuss elements of 'Custer's last stand' imagery, and then argue that the artistic tradition in which these images were produced is ill-suited for portraying history.

But white artists were not the only ones to draw the battle. Sioux and Cheyenne artists created drawings as well. After examining 'last stand' images, I will analyse selected drawings by native artists for their historical content, but only after recapping what others have demonstrated – that there is a strong historical element in Plains Indian art. This includes art produced during the contact and reservation periods, that is, from early contact times (*c.* 1840–50) to about 1930 when, according to John Ewers (1968:14), Plains Indians began to receive formal instruction at art institutes. Though style, form and media have changed since the 1930s, the traditional artistic ways still influence many schooled Plains Indian artists.

The historical element of Plains Indian art doubtless influenced Sioux and Cheyenne drawings of the Custer battle. Thus their depictions should be amenable to historical analysis. I do not simply assume, however, that native drawings are faithful representations of Custer's battle. Independent lines of evidence must be marshalled to evaluate historicity. I use material remains from the Custer battlefield in conjunction with theoretical studies of the behaviour of soldiers in combat. This approach to battlefield studies, presented here in the barest outline, is explicated in my book *Archaeology, History, and Custer's Last Battle* (Fox 1993). The volume is based on professional archaeological investigations conducted at the Custer battlefield (part of the Little Bighorn Battlefield National Monument) during 1983–4 (see also Scott and Fox 1987; Scott, Fox, Connor, and Harmon 1989).

I deduce from native drawings that Custer's battalion suffered defeat through a dysfunctional but common process in warfare, the collapse of tactical unity. Much of the killing took place during panicky flight. This interpretation contrasts markedly with 'Custer's last stand' images, which invariably impart a sense of steadfast valour in the face of insurmountable odds. I end the chapter by contrasting the two artistic traditions within which all Custer battle art has been produced, concluding that one tends to eschew history, while the other emphasizes the past. As a case example, the analyses highlight the analytical complementarity between art and archaeology.

In advancing these ideas, I am not endorsing or criticizing anyone's world view. Rather, I am interested in recovering the past as completely as possible, so I must explore all potential avenues. For the Custer battle, Indian artwork of that event is and must be one of the avenues. So this chapter, in a particularist sense, addresses a long-standing deficiency. Scenes of the Custer fight drawn by Indians, many of whom were there, have not been (as in my book cited above) integrated into interpretations of the battle, virtually all of which are, to one degree or another, formulations that mirror 'last stand' imagery, that is, the gallant, defiant, last stand of history. In principle, exclusion of native pictures of Custer's battle does not necessarily lead to inaccurate interpretations, but I shall show that they simply do not fit conventional wisdom, and so there is really little choice. Indian art is largely ignored.

'CUSTER'S LAST STAND'

Americans are doubtless very familiar with the Budweiser Beer lithograph (Budweiser was first brewed, incidentally, in 1876) – it hung, and hangs, in saloons nationwide. The Anheuser–Busch Brewing Company acquired the original canvas, painted by Cassily Adams, in 1890 and subsequently retained F. Otto Becker to adapt the painting for lithography. Calling it *Custer's Last Fight* (Fig. 8.1), Becker did indeed adapt it, among other things, by borrowing panels from other paintings and even equipping Sioux and Cheyenne warriors with Zulu-like shields (Hutton 1992:404–6). Nethertheless, Becker's composite exemplifies the genre characterized by portrayals of 'Custer's last stand'.

The first 'Custer's last stand' – a drawing by William Cary (not pictured) – appeared in New York's *Daily Graphic* on 19 July 1876, less than two weeks after word of defeat reached the eastern populace (Dippie

Figure 8.1 Otto Becker's *Custer's Last Fight* lithograph (c. 1896), an example of the 'Custer's last stand' genre. Courtesy of Anheuser-Busch Companies, Inc.

1976:34). Cary's was by no means to be the last, and Custer was not confined to the battlefield. Even Auer and Co., a cigar manufacturer, got in on the action, offering the 'General Custer' cigar in colourful artistic packaging (Davidson 1989:94).

In evaluating works by non–native artists, Lane (1973:68) had by 1973 counted nearly a thousand Little Big Horn battle scenes, most depicting 'Custer's last stand'. He encapsulated the relationship between history and this body of artwork, when he noted that 'collectively [the images] reflect the shifting values and attitudes of [Euro]American society more than they establish new truths about the [Little] Big Horn fight' (Lane 1973:67).

Few art historians, it seems, would disagree with Lane. Don Russell (1968:56) asked rhetorically, '. . . who, among the hundreds of artists, has shown The Last Stand exactly as it really happened?' Such works are hardly history according to Brian Dippie (1974:55), who sees them, like Lane, as 'expressions of changing American attitudes and ideals.' Indeed, Dippie (1994:676,680) quite correctly classified 'Custer's last stand' images as cultural creations, part of an American West artistic tradition which, he wrote, 'constitutes its own reality'.

Debates over the social messages each artist intended to convey in his or her painting, lithograph, woodcut, and the like are sharp. The issues are complex. In general, attitudes expressed by artists collectively range broadly from feelings about Indian–white relations to more narrow character statements about Custer. This is true for many Custer battle artworks produced by whites, and especially for the 'Custer's last stand' genre. Whatever the social statement, however, 'Custer's last stand' artworks somehow invariably elicit an heroic image of an epic struggle.

Artists manage this emotion, intentionally or otherwise, by portraying an instant during the battle's climax. Social meaning is largely achieved by placing viewers during this instant at a strategic spot on the battlefield. One may be in a position, for instance, to see warriors clearly, the soldiers only dimly or perhaps not at all, or vice versa. But the technique of freezing time – the 'snapshot' or static image characteristic of the Western-world artistic tradition – adds a telling dimension. Clearly the event is not over. The viewer, wherever located, must conclude the scene. A conclusion can be easily deduced from the composition (chaos, warrior hordes, embattled soldiers, and so on). Whatever the viewer's predispositions, typically what emerges is a doomed yet determined band struggling to the last against fearsome, impossible odds (see Dippie 1976:33 for a similar view).

To be sure, historical detail is not always neglected in 'Custer's last stand' artwork. Largely responding to excesses in artistic licence so well represented by Becker, some white artists have faithfully reproduced landscapes, weaponry, cavalry garb, warrior regalia, and other minutiae (e.g. see von Schmidt 1992:463–72). But in the end, and even if some artists believe they are depicting history, the 'Custer's last stand' genre is clearly ill-suited for understanding the Custer battle as an event. If white artists have not succeeded in writing history with their brushes, and if their 'Custer's last stand' canvases in fact mislead, intentionally or not, what can be said, if anything, about the drawings created by native artists?

PLAINS INDIAN ART

Nearly everyone in Plains Indian societies, children included, participated in artistic expression. Maurer (1992:20) observes that the practice was so integrated into daily life that tribes did not have words for 'art' and 'artist.' Like Western traditions, Plains Indian artistic traditions allowed artists to express their cultural attitudes and those of their societies (Szabo 1994:xv), especially during the later contact period and early reservation era, times of great change (Szabo 1994:xv; Maurer 1992:41). The same traditions also emphasized art as an historical record (e.g. Szabo 1994:xv). Some scenes which recorded important events were strictly historical (Blish 1967:xx–xxi). And, like whites who painted 'last stand' details, Indian artists often faithfully represented equipment, dress, markings on horses, and so on, allowing today's non-native viewers, for example, to identify tribal affinities by comparing artistic details with material culture items from known groups.

Often historical and social aspects of everyday life commingled in Plains Indian art. To Evan Maurer (1992:19), for instance, Plains Indians used visual documentation of their past to mitigate the vicissitudes of the present. Further, attention to historical events during post-contact times seems to derive from earlier artistic traditions. Winter counts are an example, as is biographical art which has pre-contact origins. In biographical art (or heraldic art: see Szabo 1994:10), Plains Indians, usually males, drew important events in which they participated (Maurer 1992:36).

Bound ledger books became an important medium for biographical art during the last half of the nineteenth century. Native artists were able to obtain them from EuroAmerican sources, particularly army personnel, as they could other materials including cloth – muslin was a favourite – sheets of tablet paper, loose sheets of manila paper, and sometimes paper on which government forms were printed. They also used tanned hides, as they had for centuries. Whites also provided watercolours, lead and coloured pencils, and pens and ink. Paints were rarely available.

Numerous Indians drew the Little Big Horn battle. They used nearly all available media, but mostly sheets of paper and ledger books.[1] Art historians analyse these images, commenting on Indian lifeways which might be embedded in a particular drawing, or on what the scene may say about the battle, or both. Native images of the battle, however, have not been integrated in any holistic way into documentary-based studies of the affair. Yet the historical element of Plains Indian artistic traditions suggests such drawings can be considered a highly significant record of what happened on 25 June 1876. They are indeed the only visual records left by eyewitnesses, or by artists who shared in oral histories of the battle compiled by eyewitnesses.

Joyce Szabo (1994:27) has noted that much of the Little Big Horn art was drawn on commission at the behest of white people. She therefore cautioned that native artists, aware of their viewership, might have tempered their scenes to suit white expectations, a point I shall address in concluding. Of course caveats of this sort apply to accounts of any past event, yet historians do not balk at using them. So it should be, as Szabo would agree, with Indian pictures of the Little Big Horn fight.

Indeed, no *a priori* reasons exist to dismiss the notion of a determined last stand. Maybe that is the way it happened. Standing Bear, a Minneconjou Sioux and Custer fight veteran, made a drawing (Fig. 8.2) that might fit into the 'Custer's last stand' genre were not the soldiers all dead. Like 'Custer's last stand' images produced by whites, Standing Bear's scene is static, as are some by other natives, but such treatment is hardly an exclusive feature of Custer battle art drawn by the Cheyenne

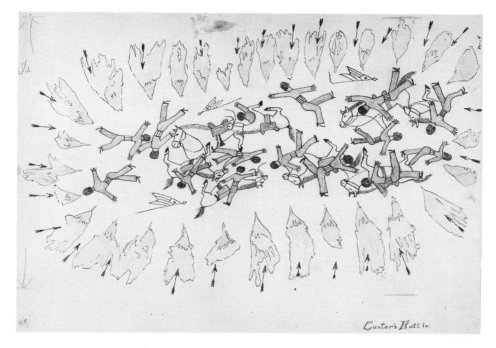

Figure 8.2 Standing Bear's drawing of 7th US Cavalry soldiers killed during the Custer battle (*c.* 1931). Courtesy of the John G. Neihardt Trust and Western Historical Manuscript Collection, Columbia, MO.

and Sioux. They had available conventions by which they could imbue their drawings – and even their maps (e.g. Ewers 1977:37) – with the passage of time.

In some ways, a pre-contact artistic tradition which valued the past – really little more than a graphic manifestation of oral history – flourished with the introduction of new media. Bound ledger books, for example, made it easier to draw multiple scenes, allowing the artist to produce a chronological narrative page by page. The binding preserved the chronology of events. This popular medium became very widespread among native artists, prompting art historians to classify it as ledger art (see Szabo 1994:15–64 for an overview of ledger art). Ledger art contrasts sharply with oils-on-canvas, acrylics, woodcuts, prints, and other types of static scenes so heavily influenced by the American West artistic tradition.

Other media were available to Plains Indian artists who wished to display the passage of time in their art. Frequently they used a number of loose sheets of paper to draw an unfolding narrative. In many instances – art produced on commission is one – the chronological order of these

Figure 8.3   Red Horse drawing no. 17 (NAA INV 08569300), 'Custer's column fighting' (1881). The scene illustrates fleeing soldiers chased closely by warriors. Courtesy of National Anthropological Archives, Smithsonian Institution.

sheets has been preserved. Native artists also developed a quasi-mural technique to convey a sequence of events. In this way, single drawings contain various elements, each sufficiently distinct to set it apart from others, which represent different events in time. Often Indian artists animated an image, whatever the media or convention. They did this by adding to their drawings symbols and other marks – hoofprints are an example – some of which are discussed below.

The most common Little Big Horn battle art genre is ledger art. The best known artist is Red Horse, a Minneconjou who fought in the Custer battle. He drew the valley and Custer fights in 1881 on 41 separate manila sheets; they are the earliest known depictions of the battle by either a Sioux or a Cheyenne.[2] Red Horse's Custer battle is divided into four sets of five drawings each: one set depicting dead Sioux warriors; one dead cavalry horses; one warriors pursuing cavalrymen (Figs 8.3 and 8.4); and one the aftermath – dead and mutilated soldiers (Figs 8.5 and 8.6). Bad Heart Bull (Oglala) drew an even broader sweep. His ledger art includes numerous scenes from each battle phase – the Custer, valley, and Reno–Benteen fights (not illustrated here; see Alexander 1938, Blish 1967). Bad Heart Bull's images of the latter two, while limited in scope compared to

Figure 8.4 Red Horse drawing no. 16 (NAA INV 08569200), 'Custer's column fighting' (1881). The drawing depicts the chaotic and deadly outcome (lower) of panicky flight (upper). Courtesy of National Anthropological Archives, Smithsonian Institution.

written accounts, could easily illustrate stories given by 7th Cavalry survivors. So could Red Horse's depictions of the valley fight (and in fact they have). Mostly, though, Custer battle authors, when they use Sioux and Cheyenne art, do so simply to dress up their works, not for art as history.

Standing Bear, using the quasi-mural technique, drew one of his several Custer battle pictures on muslin (Fig. 8.7). The picture, created on commission sometime between 1889 and 1903 (Powell 1992:82), depicts events over a period of days. First came Sitting Bull's (Hunkpapa) pre-battle vision of victory (sundance, lower right), then the Animal Dreamer's dance just before the fight (lower left), and finally the Custer fight. The fight (upper half) is separated from the former events by Little Big Horn River, which winds through the centre from right to left.

White Bull's (Oglala) ledger is an example of highly personalized biographical art. Produced on commission in 1931, White Bull's eighty-first year, the ledger depicts in chronological order his personal exploits in a number of battles. One Custer battle scene (Fig. 8.8) recalls his daring act of bravado – as the enemy fired at White Bull, he rode up close and then swung away (the arc of U-shaped hoofprints animates

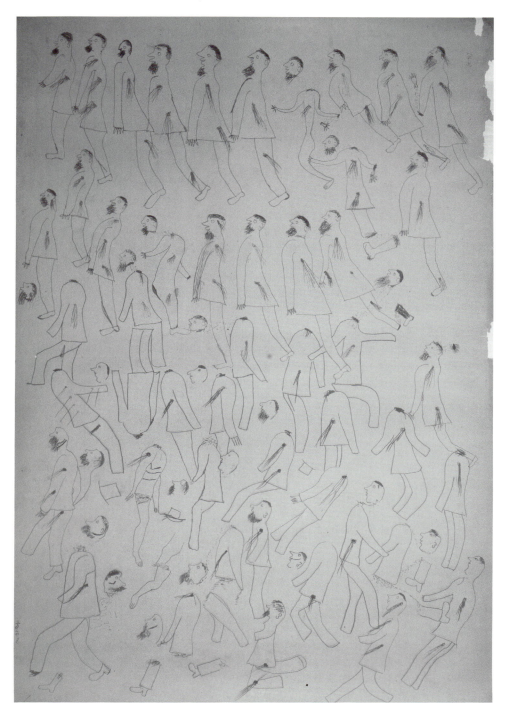

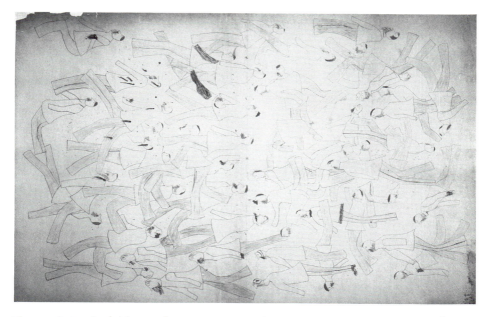

Figure 8.6   Red Horse drawing no. 33 (NAA INV 08583800), 'Dead cavalry – Custer's column' (1881). The scene conveys confusion in death. Courtesy of National Anthropological Archives, Smithsonian Institution.

the act; see Howard 1968:60–1). In another (see Plate 21 in Howard 1968), White Bull is shown looting a dead soldier. Many hoofprints lead away from the dead man, indicating that White Bull killed the soldier as a body of troops passed by him.

Some scenes from the Spotted Wolf–Yellow Nose ledger (compiled before 1889, the year it was collected) also depict time. One depicts a Custer battle event (Fig. 8.9). As soldiers fired (smoke from gunbarrels at right) and missed (flying bullets at upper left), Yellow Nose (a Ute raised as a Cheyenne) daringly charged and counted coup with a cavalry guidon he had captured. Also pictured in the High Bull ledger (Powell 1975:19), Yellow Nose's coup exploit is widely celebrated in Sioux and Cheyenne eyewitness testimony.

Yellow Nose, White Bull, Standing Bear, Red Horse, and others worked within an artistic tradition which valued historical experiences.

Figure 8.5   Red Horse drawing no. 31 (NAA INV 08570300), 'Dead cavalry – Custer's column' (1881). Pictured are the fatal wounds of each cavalryman, some of whom are dismembered. Courtesy of National Anthropological Archives, Smithsonian Institution.

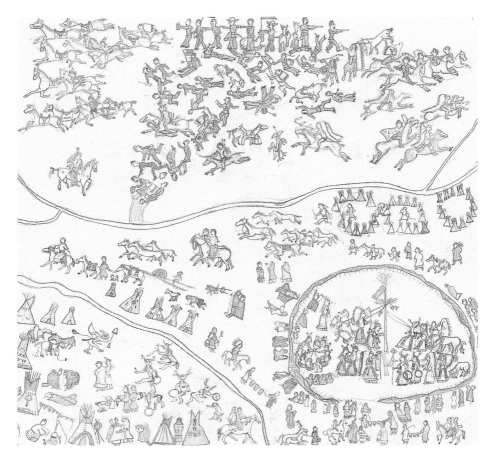

Figure 8.7 Artist's version of Standing Bear's muslin (*c.* 1889–1903). Drawn from a reproduction of the original in Powell (1992:82). Depicted in chronological order are Sitting Bull's sundance (lower right), the Animal Dreamer's dance (lower left), and the Custer fight (upper half). Little Big Horn River separates Custer battle from lower scenes. Father Peter J. Powell, representing the St Augustine Center for American Indians, Inc., would not grant permission to use the original.

That tradition allowed artists to choose their subject matter and render their perspectives according to personal preference. In effect, each artist 'wrote' his remembrances of the Little Big Horn battle in image form. Several warriors favoured recalling personal exploits; others, like Red Horse, took a wider view (see Barrett n.d.). Some focused principally on events during the Custer fight, and a few illustrated each phase of the Little Big Horn battle.

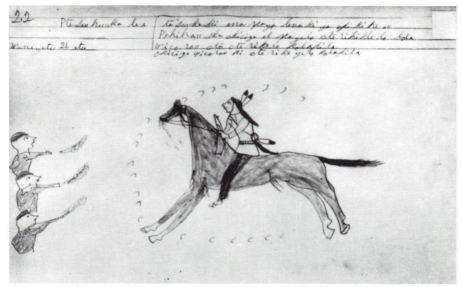

Figure 8.8 White Bull's drawing (1931) of his bravado during the Custer battle. Note soldiers in a battle line. Courtesy of Elwyn B. Robinson, Department of Special Collections, Chester Fritz Library, University of North Dakota.

Why did themes differ between artists? Presumably this variation indicates differing experiences – that is, each artist drew what he saw (or heard about), or chose details from what he or others had seen or heard. If so, Custer battle images may be considered visual narratives in a manner similar to eyewitness testimonies – white or Indian – found in the Little Big Horn documentary record. Thus, various drawings by different Cheyenne and Sioux artists ought to hold clues about the nature of Custer's battle. Like written testimonies, the images may be, and should be, examined collectively in order to extract such clues. This is what I intend to do in the next section, using archaeology and combat behaviour studies.

INDIAN DRAWINGS, ARCHAEOLOGY AND COMBAT BEHAVIOUR

As Ewers (1968:14) noted, Sitting Bull (Hunkpapa), perhaps the most prominent Sioux artist during the early reservation period (he died in 1890), never once drew the Custer battle, a rather notable omission. Why? He did not participate in the fighting (men of status and age customarily did not enter battle); perhaps that is the reason. But that did not dissuade others, some barely children at the time, who later drew

Figure 8.9   Yellow Nose's drawing (NAA INV 08705800) from the Spotted Wolf–Yellow Nose ledger (before 1889) of his daring charge during the Custer battle. Note soldiers in a battle line. Courtesy of National Anthropological Archives, Smithsonian Institution.

from the oral history of the battle. Ewers (1968:14) also suggested that Sitting Bull 'carefully avoided pictorial references' to the battle because of its controversial nature. Perhaps Sitting Bull could not remain faithful to his artistic tradition and still create images of the Custer battle imagined by his white associates, men with whom he, as a leader, interacted regularly. If so, others were not similarly tactful. In this section I analyse some of their images, using archaeology and combat behaviour theory as catalysts to explicate their meaning. Analytical results lend credence to speculation that Sitting Bull avoided depicting a Custer battle that would not sit well with white audiences.

The images drawn by Yellow Nose and White Bull, for reasons soon to become apparent, provide a good starting point for examining the Sioux and Cheyenne drawings. Though both men intended to depict their prowess during the Custer fight, the two images (Figs 8.8 and 8.9) reveal the behaviour of soldiers against whom the personal exploits were directed. Clearly in each the soldiers are ordered in a line of battle (a drawing by Standing Bear depicts the same; see Standing Bear n.d.). White Bull depicts three troopers, and Yellow Nose shows, in addition to two dead or incapacitated soldiers, nine others, eight of whom are in a battle line. In each instance, the soldiers respond by directing a controlled fire at (but missing) their antagonist.

Read literally, one warrior (White Bull) charged three soldiers, the other (Yellow Nose) nine – but perhaps the two warriors meant only to show that they challenged a body of soldiers in a battle line. The latter idea receives support from archaeology: analyses of material remains suggest that two skirmish lines were established as per official cavalry tactics (A–B, C–D, Fig. 8.10). Archaeology further indicates that the two were the only tactical lines established by Custer's troopers during the fight. As archaeological and documentary clues indicate, these lines were occupied early in the engagement, so Yellow Nose and White Bull each evidently recorded an early event, hence a good analytical starting point.

Fig. 8.10 delineates a portion of the battlefield, with symbols illustrating locations of spent cartridge cases from one weapon type, the cavalry carbine. Lines A–B and C–D, both roughly linear distributions of cartridge cases, identify the two skirmish lines. Each case exhibits a mark (signature) imprinted on the base by the carbine firing pin mechanism, or, as it is usually expressed, each case exhibits a firing-pin signature. Firing-pin signatures from one weapon type are quite distinct morphologically from other types. But signatures within a type also vary, usually in microscopic detail, and this unique variation, when analysed in light of provenance, signals positions of individual combatants. In Fig. 8.10, positions of various soldiers are represented in lines A–B and C–D, with length and linearity indicating a company-size unit (c. 30 men) deployed in skirmish formation roughly according to tactical prescription. The unique signatures can also be used to track movements of individuals across the battlefield. In Fig. 8.10, some cartridge-case symbols are connected by lines; the lines, called pathways, connect cartridge cases discharged from the same firearm (they do not necessarily denote actual routes). One pathway indicates that a soldier in skirmish line A–B also participated in line C–D, suggesting that the same cavalry unit formed both lines. Other material remains and certain documentary evidence indicate that line A–B was established first. Pressure from a different sector caused the shift.

Codified tactical prescriptions define skirmish lines (see Upton 1874 for period cavalry tactics); they are formed under conditions of tactical stability. Stability in turn is promoted by cohesion, the willingness to suppress individual concerns and act instead on behalf of the group; to military theoreticians, cohesion is essential to successful operations in battle. Training, drill, and tactics are designed to instill and strengthen cohesion, but in the stress of battle there is never a guarantee: shock effects of battle threaten cohesion. When cohesion is lost, soldiers tend to act individually, and this condition, precipitated by fear, results in tactical disintegration – soldiers lose the will to fight and often flee

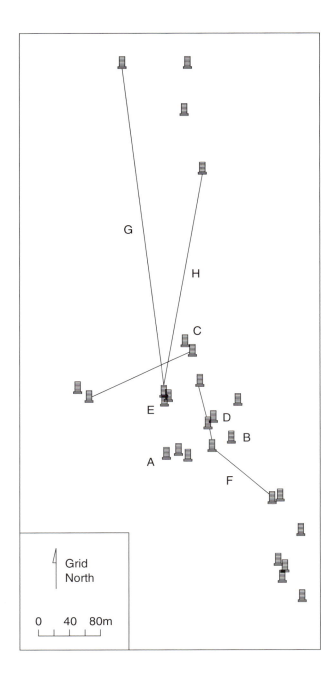

in panic (see, for example, Gabriel 1987:84, Keegan 1978:194 or Wesbrook 1980:244).

Red Horse's drawings depict elements characteristic of flight engendered by disintegration. In two (Figs 8.3 and 8.4), warriors are clearly chasing soldiers, some of whom have already been unhorsed. Warriors are right among the cavalrymen, some close enough to deliver blows or count coup. A few cavalrymen turn to resist; others ride on without using their weapons, seemingly abandoning comrades injured and unhorsed. In both scenes, a fleeing soldier appears to have discarded his carbine, behaviour typical of panicky flight. In Fig. 8.4, Red Horse communicates to his viewers the consequences of flight − death amidst chaos, and a finality complete with mutilation. Two others (not pictured) in this set use the same convention (chase scene juxtaposed with dead soldiers) to convey the results of flight.

Military theoreticians recognize that disintegration not only precipitates flight among the beleaguered, but also 'pitiless bloodlust' in the pursuers. Such behaviour can overtake soldiers when they are themselves released from danger (Keegan and Holmes 1985:24). Heavy casualties usually result − in this case annihilation and mutilation, according to Red Horse, who drew his pictures for Charles McChesney, an Army surgeon. Using sign language, he gave McChesney a narrative account to accompany his drawings. Red Horse thought the soldiers 'made five brave stands', yet noted that warriors 'drove them in confusion . . . [they] became foolish, many throwing away their guns. . . . [They] discharged their guns but little. . . . Once the Sioux charged [into] the soldiers and scattered them all, fighting . . . hand to hand' (Mallery 1972:565).

Bad Heart Bull (1869–1913) was only seven years old in 1876. In later life he developed a deep interest in the history of his people, often recording tribal events using art as visual narrative. Most of his Little Big Horn battle drawings depict the valley fight, but his few images of the Custer fight (see Blish 1967:264,267,268) are noteworthy for their resemblance to Red Horse's themes of confusion and flight. The drawings are very 'busy'; hounded by warriors everywhere, soldiers seem to dash wildly about. Bad Heart Bull drew from an oral history of the battle, one which evidently preserved events very much like those witnessed personally by Red Horse.

Figure 8.10   A portion of Custer battlefield showing locations of cartridge cases discharged from cavalry carbines. Lines A–B and C–D identify two skirmish lines. E depicts a cluster of cases, each with unique firing pin signatures. G and H are pathways suggesting soldiers fled from E. From *Archaeology, History, and Custer's Last Battle: The Little Big Horn Reexamined*, by Richard Allan Fox, Jr. Copyright © 1993 by Richard Allan Fox, Jr. Reprinted with permission of the University of Oklahoma Press.

Disintegration and flight are usual outcomes of the loss of stability. Thus Red Horse's depictions of flight may illustrate an erosion of the stability pictured by Yellow Nose and White Bull. A similar interpretation is available from patterns in material remains: a cluster of cartridge cases, all with unique signatures (E in Fig. 8.10), seems to signal a breakdown in the nearby skirmish line (C–D). Pathways connecting the C–D line and cluster, however, are absent. Nonetheless, a transition from stability to disintegration at this location is, on behavioural grounds, at least plausible.

As combat stresses increase, soldiers seeking safety often tend to cluster together. Such behaviour in modern warfare reduces an officer's ability to control and marshall firepower. Termed crowding or bunching by military theoreticians (see, for example, du Picq 1946:149 or Marshall 1978:144–5), such behaviour is therefore deleterious: if it is left uncorrected, disintegration can ensue. Two pathways (G and H, Fig. 8.10) extending north from the cluster (E) suggest that at least two men fled, and by inference, so did others. Compared to the skirmish line area, fewer government casings in the northerly sector indicates diminished resistance, a predictable consequence of disintegration. Stone memorial tablets (see Fox 1993:73–7,111–13) in the northerly sector indicate that at least a third of the 210-man battalion died during this episode – more than in any other battle sector.

The chaotic and deadly flight so vividly captured by Red Horse (Figs 8.3 and 8.4) is missing from Standing Bear's muslin (Fig. 8.7). Nonetheless, flight is depicted. The scene at top right probably recalls four soldiers who broke away sometime during fighting, as if to escape, only to be chased down and killed. The event was incidental to the battle, but evidently memorable, for a number of Sioux and Cheyenne described it. More importantly, tactical stability is also present in Standing Bear's drawing, as indicated by the line of soldiers (top centre). These troopers, some holding flags erect (as per tactics), are aligned in an orderly fashion as they fire. What appear to be horses being led stand behind the line (as per tactics). This element speaks of the order and discipline characteristic of skirmishing tactics.

Presumably Standing Bear, like White Bull and Yellow Nose, captured one of the earlier moments when cavalry units remained cohesive. But he also illustrated the loss of stability. The dead and maimed soldiers directly below the line of soldiers depict the fatal consequences of unchecked flight: bodies lay strewn about in little semblance of order. To the left, warriors chase cavalry mounts loosed during disintegration. Red Horse seems to have depicted much the same as Standing Bear, but in a different manner: in the top half of Fig. 8.5, soldiers, some mutilated, lie dead (blood and wounds clearly visible) in an orderly fashion, while below the men are scattered helter-skelter as if death came amidst chaos. Red Horse, it appears, indicates that men died not only after disintegration, but earlier as well, while fighting as a cohesive unit.

White Bird (a 15-year-old Northern Cheyenne warrior in the Custer battle), using essentially the same elements, portrayed a scene similar to Standing Bear's (see Tillett 1976:116). In his drawing, created for Captain Richard Livermore in 1894 or 1895 (Meschutt 1994), soldiers in an orderly line fire at encroaching Indians. Directly behind are dead soldiers, and beyond several mounted warriors pursue riderless cavalry horses. Preceding these elements is a chase scene, with warriors nearly upon fleeing soldiers.

The portion of One Bull's sketch (see Stirling 1944:78) which displays the Custer fight lacks chase scenes. But One Bull (Hunkpapa and Little Big Horn battle veteran) illustrated a jumbled mass of bodies adjacent to and in the rear of what seem to be soldiers organized in a battle line. One Bull drew the picture in 1937 for Lieutenant Colonel A.B. Welch. Like Standing Bear, White Bird, and Red Horse, One Bull appears to have used the technique of juxtaposing order (battle line) with chaos (strewn bodies) to encapsulate the transition from stability to disintegration.

The clusters of dead soldiers in One Bull's and White Bird's scenes seem to conclude the confrontation. Standing Bear's image on muslin (Fig. 8.7), on the contrary, suggests that events continued. In his scene, action below the dead men seems to recount another episode of flight: several soldiers chased by warriors flee from the carnage (the cluster of dead) to a location near the river. Four running troopers (one disabled or killed in flight) end up lying dead within a shaded area interpreted as a ravine which joins the river. This element − flight to the ravine − is important. Some warriors stated clearly during interviews that the last fighting took place in and near a deep ravine, not on the hill so prominently displayed in 'Custer's last stand' images (indeed, I know of no Indian account that places the denouement on the hill). According to native accounts, disintegration resulted in the consolidation of survivors with another unit on the so-called Last Stand Hill. This other unit was the left wing, which operated independently of the unit which disintegrated (the right wing). Historical evidence indicates that some measure of control was re-established at this time. Shortly after consolidation, some forty soldiers charged, according to Indian testimony, from the hill towards the river. A heavy attack broke their cohesion, killing some and sending the rest into a deep ravine. Here the soldiers sought to hide, but they were spotted and killed.

About 1931 Standing Bear drew this event in more detail on a single sheet (Fig. 8.11). In this image, warriors give chase to cavalrymen who seem to flee in panic, each discharging a carbine and pistol wildly into the air or ground − a detail remembered, among others, by Lights, a Minneconjou (Camp 1909). Arrows directed toward the soldiers reveal

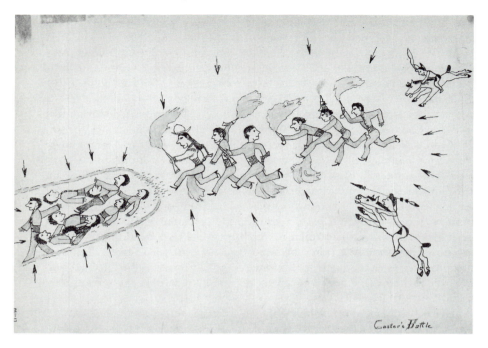

Figure 8.11   Standing Bear's drawing of 7th US Cavalry soldiers fleeing into a ravine during the Custer battle (*c.* 1931). Courtesy of The John G. Neihardt Trust and Western Historical Manuscript Collection, Columbia, MO.

the pressure. Results of the panicky flight are clear: some men made it to the ravine, where they died (most accounts from cavalrymen who survived the Little Big Horn battle put the total dead in the ravine at twenty-eight). Standing Bear's detail of this event finds support in the archaeological record. Remains of soldiers have been found in the sector, and stone markers dot the area, yet few government cartridge cases were found – and those few were scattered among numerous bullets delivered from Indian firearms.

About forty cavalrymen did die on the hillock immortalized in 'Custer's last stand' paintings. The archaeological record (few government cartridge cases, numerous Indian bullets) suggests that resistance there was minimal, and with little semblance of order. Because Indian accounts put the duration of that episode at minutes, however, the material record may be more reflective of time than behaviour. Still, neither option supports the 'last stand' image. Instead, and quite unlike most 'last stand' images, Indian drawings of this episode typically highlight the aftermath, often in grim scenes. Actions culminating in annihilation, however steadfast they might have been, are ignored. Red Horse drew one scene, for example, that clearly conveys confusion in death (Fig. 8.6). In another image, he underlined the sense of chaos by drawing severed heads and limbs (Fig. 8.5, lower half). Two other drawings by Red Horse in this five-image set (not pictured) also portray mutilation amidst disorder. Similarly, Standing Bear drew the scene (Fig. 8.2) complete with fallen battle flags and dead soldiers, who perished while surrounded; the ghost-like symbols represent the gunfire that, along with arrows, brought them down (see also Lame Deer's [Cheyenne] hide painting in Tillett 1976:140).

White Bird's drawing (not pictured; see Tillett 1976:134), which includes a chase scene, also recalls the carnage on 'last stand' hill – clustered bodies, some dismembered, are haphazardly strewn about. The 'last stand' received a similar treatment from Bad Heart Bull (not pictured; see Blish 1967:269): surrounding warriors have dispatched the soldiers, most of whom have collapsed ignobly in a confused heap. Interestingly, in Bad Heart Bull's picture, the warriors are drawn boldly, in contrast to the cavalrymen who are sketched lightly. This technique minimizes the presence – and hence significance – of the latter. The intention, if not the technique, is similar to that of white artists who emphasize the soldiers by strategically positioning the viewer.

In the 'last stand' picture by Kicking Bear (a Minneconjou veteran of the Custer battle), most soldiers are dead, the few alive facing death without resisting (not pictured; see Stewart and Stewart 1957: facing 58). Commissioned by Frederick Remington *c.* 1898, Kicking Bear's drawing identifies Custer's body (as does White Bird's), indicating, as Dippie (1994:678) recognized, the influence of white notions about the battle. Bad Heart Bull seems to have worked under similar influences: his scene shows Crazy Horse (Oglala) striking a mounted Custer. Still, the process of disintegration can be plausibly deduced from the grim, chaotic scenes.

CONCLUSIONS

I have selected scenes reproduced here from a larger body of Custer battle artwork created by Sioux and Cheyenne artists. I consider my selections to be representative of artwork which displays three categories of warrior and soldier behaviour during the battle (there are others, including scenes of the Indian dead; pursuit of cavalry horses; warriors leaving the battlefield, etc.). The categories are: individual prowess against organized soldiers; Indians taking the upper hand among disorganized cavalrymen; and the end of battle and its aftermath. Some drawings include elements of more than one category.

Viewed collectively, I have interpreted art representative of these categories using theoretical combat studies. These studies indicate that tactical stability can erode, resulting in disintegration. Hence, scenes which exhibit soldiers organized in a battle line are interpreted as portraying earlier stages of the fight; those illustrating flight and pursuit (disintegration) a later stage. The final stage – depictions of the aftermath – is predictable on theoretical grounds: unchecked flight will usually result in grim, chaotic deaths.

Cheyenne and Sioux artists also portrayed the valley and Reno–Benteen fights (Bad Heart Bull, Red Horse). Scenes of these fights reflect reasonably well what is generally accepted about the tactics and behaviour displayed (the soldiers and warriors) during these fights. That being the case, there seems little reason to suspect that Sioux and Cheyenne Custer battle scenes miss the mark, even those commissioned by whites. Indeed, their pictures of the Custer fight suggest that dysfunctional processes peculiar to disintegration were in large part responsible for the outcome. Their scenes generally accord well with archaeological interpretations, derived partly from cartridge-case signature patterns viewed in light of combat behaviour (see Fox 1993). Also Cheyenne and Sioux drawings complement a substantial number of Indian eyewitness testimonies which metaphorically describe a transition from stability to disintegration, and finally denouement (see Fox 1993).

Viewed this way, Sioux and Cheyenne depictions of the Custer battle contrast sharply with those by white artists. On the one hand, 'snapshots' by white artists invite viewers to conclude that the soldiers, though knowing they were doomed, fought gallantly to the end. On the other, Indian drawings, as I have shown, collectively form a moving picture of unfolding events. Moreover, and though drawings show that warriors at times faced the dangers of organized firepower, the images contain no elements which might presuppose a gallant resistance.

Why this contrast? To say that only the Indians survived, so only they knew the truth, is too facile. The answer seems to lie in differences between two artistic traditions. White artists created their 'last stands' within an American West artistic tradition that typically represents a single moment of time (as opposed to some modern art that, from cubism onwards, has incorporated time in representation), and which favours dramatic scenes captured in 'freeze frames'. An unfolding history is hardly possible within this canon, making it easier to paint, as Dippie (1994: 676) put it, an invented and repetitive American West. Artistic invention was born of romantic ideals about the exploration and conquest of the West, a sort of 'tribal history for white Americans' (Dippie 1994: 675). Repetitiveness – 'Custer's last stand' is a telling example – tended to validate the romantic view, turning a genre into history for the targeted audiences.

This view of the West had (and has) little to do with reality, and it served (even as now) the doctrine of manifest destiny far more effectively than any reality. In this sense, perhaps it is fair to say that white artists could not have portrayed an historically meaningful Custer battle. For them and their audiences, as Dippie (1994:675) has observed, defeat in the context of an untamed land was victory. There was little need to consult Indian eyewitnesses, either personally or in the documents (a few, like Remington, evidently did, but whatever they might have learned did not influence their paintings, which fit the 'Custer's last stand' mould).

While 'Custer's last stand' images by white Americans invariably play on the romantic ideal of gallantry against all odds, some contain under-currents of unrest about nineteenth-century expansionist policies. I do not suggest, however, that every 'last stand' image is the result of a conscious, deliberate attempt to persuade, or dissuade, as the case may be. Many are, I think, simply products of a tradition, one that subtly influences, rather than one that is always manipulative.

This caution applies also to Custer battle images produced by native artists. Certainly White Bull and Yellow Nose worked within an artistic tradition rich with historical meaning. Yet by drawing the battle they meant to trumpet their exploits – a sort of personal history – and this suggests that egotism may have biased their perspectives. But in spite of their narrow subjectivity they left clues applicable to a larger historical context, a context available to us only in the Sioux and Cheyenne imagery of Custer's battle and indeed the Little Big Horn fight altogether.

Analytical results support the argument made by art historians, some cited above, that Plains Indian art contains a strong historical element. Indeed, it is this artistic tradition, applied by numerous Cheyenne and Sioux to retrospective views of the fight at Little Big Horn, some spon-taneous, some commissioned by whites, that provides an alternative view of this emotive event. Yet it is too simplistic to assume historical accu-racy in the Indian drawings simply because the artists witnessed the battle (or shared in oral history). The archaeology of the Little Big Horn battle-field, however, combined with theoretical combat behaviour studies, provides a strong catalyst for the explication of the events depicted in the Sioux and Cheyenne art of Custer's last battle.

The results of this analysis show that the Indian visual record of events contradicts the long accepted version of the incident and so exposes it as a myth – a myth founded on the romance of a gallant last stand, a myth conveyed as much by brush and palette as by the pen, and a myth which simplifies an event so complex that Sherlock Holmes, who rose to fame barely a decade after the Custer battle, would surely have clas-sified the matter as quite a three-pipe problem.

ACKNOWLEDGEMENTS

I wish to thank James Harwood (National Anthropological Archives, Smithsonian Institution), Michael Moore (Indiana University), Steve Fox (Bozeman High School), Carole Barrett (University of Mary), David Meschutt (West Point Museum), Dan Bennett (National Baseball Library and Archive), and Mary Louise Brown (Anheuser–Busch Corporate

Archives) for providing information for this chapter. I am grateful to Brian Molyneaux (University of South Dakota) for inviting me to contribute to this volume and for his editorial comments. Thanks are also due to the institutions which extended permissions to reproduce the figures.

NOTES

1 One ledger book, the one used by High Bull (Cheyenne) for his drawings, actually came from the battle scene. It belonged to Sergeant Alexander Brown, Company G, 7th US Cavalry, who used it to record various official transactions of his company. High Bull captured it during the Little Big Horn fight, later drawing over Brown's entries (some scenes were drawn by other Cheyennes) (Powell 1975:14–21).
2 Red Horse's drawings have never been published in their entirety. They are curated at the National Anthropological Archives (Smithsonian Institution), Washington, DC.

REFERENCES

Alexander, H.B. (ed.) 1938. *Sioux Indian Painting, Part II: The Art of Amos Bad Heart Bull*. Nice, France: C. Szwedzicki.

Barrett, C. n.d. 'Red Horse.' Unpublished MS. in possession of the author.

Blish, H.H. 1967. *A Pictographic History of the Oglala Sioux*. Lincoln, NE: University of Nebraska Press.

Camp, W.M. 1909. 'Statement of Lights, Spring, 1909.' Walter Camp Collection, A312 C11735, Little Bighorn Battlefield National Monument Archives, Crow Agency, Montana.

Davidson, J. 1989. *The Art of the Cigar Label*. Edison, NJ: Wellfleet Press.

Dippie, B.W. 1974. 'Brush, palette and the Custer battle.' *Montana: The Magazine of Western History* 24(1):55–67.

Dippie, B.W. 1976. *Custer's Last Stand: the Anatomy of an American Myth*. Missoula, MA: University of Montana Press.

Dippie, B.W. 1994. 'The visual West.' In C.A. Milner II, C.A. O'Connor, and M.T. Sandweiss (eds), *The Oxford History of the American West*. pp. 676–705. New York: Oxford University Press.

du Picq, A. 1946. *Battle Studies*. Harrisburg, PA: Military Service Publishing Company.

Ewers, J.C. 1968. 'Plains Indian painting.' In K.D. Petersen (ed.), *Howling Wolf: a Cheyenne Warrior's Graphic Interpretation of his People*, pp. 5–19. Palo Alto, CA: American West Publishing Company.

Ewers, J.C. 1977. 'The making and uses of maps by Plains Indian warriors.' *By Valor and Arms: The Journal of American Military History* 3(1):36–43.

Fox, R.A. 1993. *Archaeology, History, and Custer's Last Battle: the Little Big Horn Reexamined*. Norman, OK: University of Oklahoma Press.

Gabriel, R.A. 1987. *No More Heroes: Madness and Psychiatry in War*. New York: Hill and Wang.

Howard, J.H. 1968. *The Warrior who Killed Custer*. Lincoln, NE: University of Nebraska Press.

Hutton, P.A. 1992. 'From Little Bighorn to Little Big Man: the changing image of a western hero in popular culture.' In P.A. Hutton (ed.), *The Custer Reader*. pp. 395–423. Lincoln, NE: University of Nebraska Press.

Keegan, J. 1978. *The Face of Battle*. Guildford: Biddles.

Keegan, J. and Holmes, R. 1985. *Soldiers*. London: Hamish Hamilton.

Lane, H. 1973. 'Brush, palette and the Little Bighorn.' *Montana: The Magazine of Western History* 23(3):66–80.

Mallery, G. 1972. *Picture Writing of the American Indians* (Vol. 2). New York: Dover Publications. (Originally published in 1893 as the *Tenth Annual Report of the Bureau of Ethnology, 1888–9.*)

Marshall, S.L.A. 1978. *Men against Fire*. Gloucester: Peter Smith.

Maurer, E.M. 1992. 'Visions of the people.' In E.M. Maurer (ed.), *Visions of the People: A Pictorial History of Plains Indian Life*. pp. 15–45. Seattle, WA: The University of Washington Press.

Meschutt, D. 1994. Telephone communication with Meschutt (West Point Museum, United States Military Academy), 2 November 1994.

Powell, P.J. 1975. 'High Bull's victory roster.' *Montana: The Magazine of Western History* 25(1):14–21.

Powell, P.J. 1992. 'Sacrifice transformed into victory: Standing Bear portrays Sitting Bull's sundance and the final summer of Lakota freedom.' In E.M. Maurer (ed.), *Visions of the People: A Pictorial History of Plains Indian Life*, pp. 81–106. Seattle, WA: University of Washington Press.

Russell, D. 1968. *Custer's Last*. Fort Worth, TX: Amon Carter Museum of Western Art.

Scott, D.D. and Fox, R.A.Jr. 1987. *Archaeological Insights into the Custer Battle*. Norman, OK: University of Oklahoma Press.

Scott, D.D., Fox, R.A.Jr., Connor, M., and Harmon, D. 1989. *Archaeological Perspectives on the Battle of the Little Bighorn*. Norman, OK: University of Oklahoma Press.

Standing Bear n.d. 'Standing Bear sketch.' Neihardt Papers, C3716, folder 248, Western Historical Manuscripts Collection, University of Missouri, Columbia.

Stewart, E.I. and Stewart, J.R. 1957. *The Field Diary of Lt. Edward Settle Godfrey*. Portland, OR: The Champoeg Press.

Stirling, M.W. 1944. 'Indians of our western plains.' *National Geographic* 86(1):73–108.

Szabo, J. 1994. *Howling Wolf and the History of Ledger Art*. Albuquerque, NM: University of New Mexico Press.

Tillett, L. 1976. *Wind on the Buffalo Grass: the Indians' own Account of the Battle at Little Big Horn River, and the Death of their Life on the Plains*. New York: Thomas Y. Crowell Company.

Upton, E. 1874. *Cavalry Tactics, United States Army*. New York: D. Appleton and Company.

von Schmidt, E. 1992. 'Sunday at the Little Big Horn with George.' In P.A. Hutton (ed.), *The Custer Reader*, pp. 463–72. Lincoln, NE: University of Nebraska Press.

Wesbrook, S.D. 1980. 'The potential for military disintegration.' In S.C. Sarkesian (ed.), *Combat Effectiveness: Cohesion, Stress and the Volunteer Military*. pp. 244–78. Beverly Hills, CA: Sage Publications.

CHAPTER NINE

REVOLUTIONARY IMAGES

The iconic vocabulary for representing human antiquity

STEPHANIE MOSER AND CLIVE GAMBLE

INTRODUCTION

Archaeological knowledge is represented through a variety of media including scholarly discourse, museum displays, literature, film, television, popular scientific writing, and computerized multimedia. Most of these draw heavily on the use of visual imagery to communicate key points and arguments. In this chapter we will be concerned with the visual representation of archaeological knowledge, and in particular, the role of illustration in the study of the Palaeolithic. While our general aim is to explore the ways in which a visual discourse about the prehistoric past has been constructed, we will be more specifically concerned with the pictorial reconstructions of our earliest ancestors and the sources from which they were derived. We argue that by the end of the nineteenth century, three distinct visual traditions of representing life in the pre-historic past were established: the *Romantic* tradition, the *archaeological* tradition, and the *comic* tradition. All were characterized by a common set or suite of attributes that have been developed and recycled since Classical times. While the archaeological tradition came to prevail as the more authoritative visual discourse on the past, it drew heavily on former traditions of representation. In the following discussion we outline the common attributes or visual icons that characterized images of human antiquity. We then look at the ways in which these icons were used to present distinct visions of the past. Finally, we investigate from where these visual traditions or visions drew their inspiration. We conclude that there is a very restricted iconic vocabulary for depicting the past, and that archaeology has done little in the way of challenging this or in creating a new vocabulary.

ARCHAEOLOGY AND VISUAL REPRESENTATION

The ways in which archaeological knowledge has been represented is a neglected topic. While archaeologists acknowledge that their disciplinary knowledge is represented in many different contexts, we have not really explored the role and impact of this practice on the nature of the subject. Put simply, the representation of archaeological knowledge has been seen as relevant, but not central, to archaeology's analysis and understanding of itself. We challenge this idea of the relevance of representation to mainstream archaeological discourse, where representation is seen as being mainly about how archaeology communicates to the public. It is our contention that the representation of archaeological knowledge has an important impact on the discipline itself because it is a powerful tool for intra-disciplinary communication and disciplinary self-definition.

As archaeology has become increasingly reflective about its nature as a discipline, practitioners have started to deal with issues of representation in studies of archaeological interpretation. Post-processual archaeologists, for instance, have addressed the issue of how the past is presented via discussion of 'archaeological poetics' (e.g. Shanks 1992; Shanks and Hodder 1995; Shanks and Tilley 1989; Tilley 1993). Essentially, an archaeological poetics refers to a concern with the form in which archaeological knowledge is communicated or the style with which archaeology designs and produces its pasts. While it is a positive development that theoretical archaeology has broadened its scope to take into account the representation of disciplinary knowledge, there remains an emphasis on the textuality of archaeological discourse. Current theorizing about the nature of archaeological interpretation, for instance, is primarily concerned with the nature of archaeological *writing* and the production of archaeological *texts*. Sherratt (1993:195) notes the irony in this situation, in that post-processualism is highlighting the significance of the text when text is losing its central place in world culture. While it is important to examine the textual dimension of archaeological interpretation, and to explore how the past is constituted through our 'assemblages' of words, there are other aspects of archaeological representation that warrant attention. Primary among these are the visual or illustrative modes of representation that the discipline has used since its inception.

Archaeology does not yet take its visual language very seriously. Unlike geology, which discovered the importance of its visual language some years ago (Rudwick 1976), it is only now being realized in archaeology just how many of our arguments about the past are presented as images. These range from the convention of the scientific specimen, such as a technical drawing of a flint implement, to the visual jargon of a Harris matrix or a section drawing, to full-blown reconstructions of life as-it-was in the past. Like any tradition of discourse, the visual language developed by archaeologists depends on the repeated association of icons to form interpretative images of its subject matter. Insights on the process by which this is achieved are provided by work in the history and philosophy of science. For instance, the growing interest in understanding non text-based forms of communication in the sciences has led scholars to explore the role images play in the presentation and construction of scientific arguments. Illustration has been shown to be crucial to the articulation of ideas for a whole range of scientific disciplines (see Baigrie 1996; Lynch and Woolgar 1990; Mazzolini 1993). While there now exist a number of studies on aspects of visual representation in archaeology (Gamble 1992; Gifford-Gonzalez 1994; Hurcombe 1995; Moser 1992a, 1992b, 1993a, 1993b, 1996; Nixon 1994; Stringer and Gamble 1993; Trinkaus and Shipman 1993), we still know little about the relationship between our visual language and archaeological knowledge production.

THE VISUAL RECONSTRUCTION

While there are many different types of visual representation in archaeology we have chosen to focus on one particular type. Pictorial or artistic reconstructions of life in the past are the subject of our discussion for a number of reasons. We have already made the case that visual reconstructions are of fundamental importance to archaeology because they constitute theories about what happened in the past (Gamble 1992; Moser 1992a, 1992b). For instance, while such images are simply assumed to illustrate arguments made in the text, they actually represent a distinct form of reasoning in themselves. Another fundamental point to make about these images is that they embody the powerful interaction between art and science, demonstrating how archaeologists think and express their ideas visually. On one level reconstructions are faithful to the scientific data and arguments, making every effort to be accurate. However, on another level they have a life of their own, making use of a range of interpretative devices not accessible to verbal or written expression. The idea that the accuracy in reconstructions is an indication of professional ability to see the past is analogous to the misplaced belief that archaeological facts speak for themselves so long as they are systematically recorded. This is clear at another level of appreciation where these images, as consciously authored documents, represent attempts to make sense of unfamiliar data. This point, that images, just like text, are theory-laden, can be illustrated by examining how such images were used to present findings from early prehistory.

The significance of the visual language of archaeology is nowhere as powerfully demonstrated as it is for the Palaeolithic. Images are more important for the Palaeolithic than for other periods of prehistory because they so effectively deal with the problem of communicating the vast time

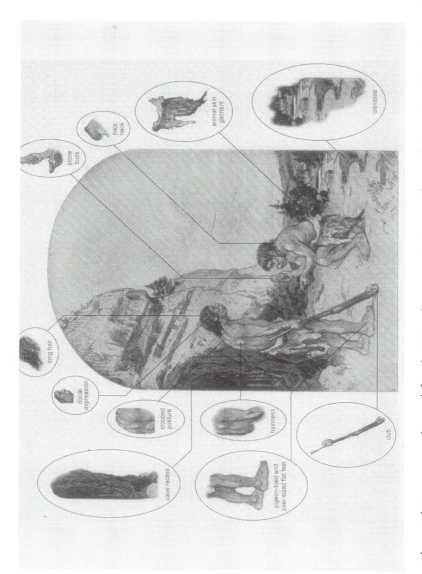

Figure 9.1 The attributes commonly used for depicting human antiquity are featured here in Osborn's image from *Men of the Old Stone Age: their Life, Environment and Art* (1915). Painted by the American Museum of Natural History's anatomical and animal illustrator Charles R. Knight, this picture demonstrates how reconstructions are characterized by a set of visual icons.

Table 9.1 A list of the icons of antiquity and their basis in scientific evidence.

| Icon | Evidence | | |
	archaeological	anatomical	environmental
club	none		
animal skin garment	none		
stone tools	yes		
long hair		none	
hairiness		none	
docile expression		none	
thick neck		none	
stooped posture		none	
flat feet		none	
cave recess (signifying a wild place)			yes, but open sites commonly inhabited
crevasse (as a symbolic gulf between us and them)			no

scale of human antiquity. Furthermore, artistic reconstructions not only make visible life-forms for which there are no modern analogues, they also play a critical role in facilitating our understanding of how we became human.

The icons of human antiquity

A major characteristic of reconstructions is the way in which they use a common set of attributes or icons for depicting the past. At this point we should have preferred to present our argument using multimedia because the icons we will describe could then be clicked on in order to open windows onto the nature of archaeological interpretation. Once opened, these windows would reveal the composite, repetitive nature of many reconstructions. However, since we are text-bound, we will identify the generic icons in one famous Neanderthal picture. This image was painted in 1915 by Charles R. Knight, under the instructions of the eminent American palaeontologist, Henry Fairfield Osborn. It appeared as the frontispiece to Osborn's well known *Men of the Old Stone Age: Their Environment, Life and Art* (1915). Backed by such a pedigree, the picture has been reproduced and copied many times since. However, this scientifically authenticated reconstruction, like many similar ones, was essentially a collage of icons and pictorial motifs deriving from earlier visual traditions.

In Figure 9.1 we identify eleven icons commonly used in the reconstruction of early prehistory. All are used to convey primitiveness and the idea of an ancient human existence. These are listed in Table 9.1, where an assessment of their archaeological validity reveals that only the manufacture of stone tools can be supported as a widespread, common trait.

But, compare our assessment of the mismatch between evidence and image with Osborn's stated intention in commissioning Knight's reconstruction.

> In these models, and in all the restorations of men by Charles R. Knight under my direction, the controlling principle has been to make the restoration as *human* as the anatomical evidence will admit. This principle is based upon the theory for which I believe very strong grounds may be adduced, that all these races represent stages of advancing and progressive development; it has seemed to me, therefore, that in our restorations we should indicate as much alertness, intelligence, and upward tendency as possible.
>
> (1915:xii, Osborn's emphasis)

The evidence available to Osborn was essentially the same as that available to us today. What has changed is that archaeologists no longer overtly support in their writings his theory of upward tendency. But while such progressive evolution has fallen out of fashion, the eleven icons we have identified in Figure 1 can be seen time and time again in the pictures of the past. These images are still authenticated and commissioned by archaeologists. Our question is, therefore, to what extent the theoretical agenda of earliest prehistory has changed (Gamble 1993).

'Clicking on' the icons labelled in Figure 9.1 reveals all sorts of theoretical baggage. Nakedness, hairiness, expression, and posture lead us directly into the eugenic assessments of capabilities based on spurious science (Gould 1984). 'Double click' on the chin in that docile expression, and this could be a hypertext link

> The form of the chin seems to be wonderfully correlated with the general character and energy of the race. It is hard to say why, but as a matter of fact a weak chin generally denotes a weak, and a strong chin a strong, race or individual.
>
> (Laing 1895:395)

Or click on that club to open a window which notes that at this time cricket provided a metaphor for a lost England and, appropriately, a Romantic past. In his best selling *The Jubilee Book of Cricket* (1897) Prince Ranjitsinhji, aided by C.B. Fry, writes of cricket thus,

> There is generous life in it, simplicity and strength, freedom and enthusiasm, such as prevailed before things in general became quite as complex and conventional as nowadays. *One gets from cricket a dim glimpse of the youth of the world.*
>
> (Kynaston 1990:7, our emphasis)

Click again, and our Neanderthal 'going out to bat for evolution' in Knight's picture could be juxtaposed with this diametrically opposed view from J.H. Rosny Aîné's Palaeolithic saga *La guerre du feu* (1992 (1911)) where two brutal Neanderthals battle it out.

> Now there was nothing but the clubs. These were raised simultaneously; both were made of oak. Aghoo's had three knots; it had been polished with time and gleamed in the moonlight. Naoh's was more rounded, less old, and dark in colour. . . . Each recognized in the other a formidable adversary; each knew that if he weakened for the space of a moment's motion he would enter death.
>
> (Rosny Aîné 1992 (1911):136)

The icons used in pictures of prehistoric life summarize wider views and theories of our ancestry. They are assembled into a limited set of scenarios including: *cave or camp life*, where ancient humans are gathered around a hearth; *man versus beast*, where prehistoric men defend themselves against vicious cave bears and sabre-toothed tigers; *the mammoth hunt*, where ancient men are featured stalking or spearing large woolly mammoths; *tool making*, where figures are shown making stone implements; *cave painting*, where people were depicted decorating cave walls; and *burial*, where our ancestors are shown grieving over their dead.

One of the most striking characteristics of these pictures is that the ancient humans tend to be identified in terms of their ecological settings. The prevailing story is one of perpetual struggle, where our prehistoric relatives were constantly challenged by the environment and the beasts that inhabited it. Clicking on this window would initiate a multimedia excursion through the nineteenth-century fascination with chivalry. Here nakedness, clubs, and living as outlaws in wild places could be seen as the necessary accoutrements for defining the knight in shining armour bent on his quest of bettering civilization at the expense of the primitive.

THREE WINDOWS ONTO THE PAST

The suite of icons described above is the core component of three visual traditions (Romantic, archaeological, comic) used to illustrate life in the Stone Age. All traditions offer different views of the past and can be associated with different scholarly traditions and trends of representation. Despite these differences, all three make use of the same basic repertoire of icons and scenarios.

The Romantic tradition

The idea that humans' ancestors lived in truly ancient times was first communicated in geological and palaeontological reconstructions of earth history. Some scenes were based on the discovery of artifacts together with human remains, but essentially, the geological and palaeontological scenes were produced before the concept of human antiquity was universally accepted by the scientific community. These images were produced in order to convey the idea that humans were the last to make their appearance on the stage of the earth's history.

The first scene of 'deep geological time' in which ancient humans were featured appeared in Unger's (1851) book *Die Urwelt in ihren verschiedenen Bildungsperioden* [The primitive world in the different periods of its formation] (Fig. 9.2). Significantly, this scene is not based on scientific evidence or related to debates about human evolution. It is essentially an Edenic scene, with fully modern people, who are white and European. It represents the day of Creation when the noble creature, man, appeared on the earth's stage. However, despite the noble and civilized appearance of the figures, some of the icons for depicting human antiquity are clearly featured. For instance, the figures are naked, the male holds a stick or staff, he is bearded, and the vegetation is wild or exotic. Here our ancestors are portrayed as living an idyllic existence in harmony with nature. Another image of ancient humans produced in the context of geological and palaeontological research, was that created by Figuier (1863) in *La terre avant le Deluge* [The earth before the deluge] (Fig. 9.3). Figuier's illustration, like Unger's, is titled 'Appearance of man' and supports the theory of creation. The image also uses the basic suite of icons to communicate human origins. The figures are naked, apart from the leafy loincloth the man appears to be wearing. The male holds a stick or staff and the vegetation is dark and wild in appearance. However, and as Rudwick (1992:208) shows, by the time Figuier's book was published more secure data had been found convincing the scientific community of human antiquity. Subsequently, Figuier radically revised his image (Fig. 9.4). The new picture incorporates many icons of antiquity, including the cave recess, the animal skin garments, the crevasse separating humans from the wild animals, and wild and exotic vegetation. Human confrontation with wild beasts is introduced as a major new theme for presenting prehistoric life. The significant difference in this image is the animals. Gone are the frolicking horses seen in Unger's image, and the cows and sheep from Figuier's original. Here are woolly mammoths, rhinos, sabre-toothed tigers, cave bears, and hyenas. Our ancestors have gone from being idyllic pastoralists to primitive warriors. While more icons of primitiveness are used in Figuier's revised image, the vision of the past remains essentially Romantic. Well muscled heroic men scare away the savage beasts with the large weapons they have

Figure 9.2 Unger's illustration of the first humans from *The Primitive World in the Different Periods of its Formation* (1851). Entitled 'The period of the present World', and painted by the landscape artist Josef Kuwasseg, this image presents our early ancestors as living in an idyllic, Edenic setting. Despite the frolicking horses in the background, the vegetation suggests that our ancestors inhabited a wild landscape. Icons such as nakedness have been used to suggest primitiveness, but it is a gentle and noble primitiveness that is conveyed here.

crafted. The Romantic vision of our earliest ancestors was fully established in a series of thirty scenes of primitive life produced by Figuier in his book *L'homme primitif* [*Primitive man*] (1870). Here all the icons for representing human antiquity are paraded in their glory. Scenes of people gathered around fires, holdings clubs, wearing animal furs, manufacturing tools, fighting beasts, producing art, and burying their dead, are presented. The frontispiece serves as the classic example of the Romantic vision of the past (Fig. 9.5). Here a heroic male leans against his cave home, looking out across the landscape he has come to master. Alongside him are his 'wife' and 'children'. In defending the validity of the images, the English translator refers to the 'Raffaelesque idealism of their style', but asserts that 'they are in the main justified by the soundest evidence, the actual discovery of the objects of which they represent the use' (Figuier 1870:vi).

Figure 9.3 Figuier's image of early humans appearing in *The Earth Before the Deluge* (1863). Entitled 'Appearance of Man', and painted by the landscape artist Edouard Riou, this image presents ancient humans living alongside nature. The setting evokes a wild and untamed landscape, but the animals and grassy foreground give the picture a pastoral feeling. In this sense the image suggests that ancient humans have domesticated their environment. While the figures in Unger's image stand in a clearing, these figures appear to be associated with a cave or dark recess. Along with the leafy covering on the man, this gives the picture a less civilized atmosphere.

In summary, the initial scenes of ancient human life were not used to endorse archaeological theories about evolution, they were an appendage to the geological and palaeontological reconstructions of extinct animals and ancient landscapes. Since these images were aimed at communicating geological theories about the history of the earth, the depiction of humans was made within the Biblical framework. Furthermore, they presented a Romantic vision rooted in antiquarian traditions of representation, where the ideological framework of primitivism shaped perceptions of life before 'civilization'. Despite this, these images went on to incorporate archaeological evidence, thus creating a new vision of the past. Significantly however, the discovery of a new chronology for human history did not lead to the revision of icons for depicting ancient human life.

Figure 9.4   Figuier's revised image of the arrival of humans in the history of the earth, appearing in a later edition of *The Earth Before the Deluge* (1867). With the same title, 'Appearance of Man' and by the same illustrator (Riou), this picture presented the idea that humans were truly ancient. A set of specific icons have been used to give the picture its new primeval aspect. The cave is now occupied by people, the men hold stone axes instead of sticks, they wear animal fur garments, and they are separated from the wild animals by a crevasse. The vegetation has totally lost its pastoral element, and animal bones are strewn around the cave entrance.

The archaeological tradition

Artistic reconstructions of ancient human life started to appear in texts on human evolution and early prehistory as the idea of human antiquity became more universally accepted. These images were presented as a result of the discovery of artifacts in stratigraphic association with the skeletal remains of extinct animals and/or humans. Prehistorians used these images to show that humans lived in times so far distant that the animals they coexisted with, and the environments in which they lived, were totally different from the present or more recent historical periods. While they did create a new vision of the past, archaeological images essentially used the same icons and interpretative frameworks that had been used previously.

Figure 9.5 The frontispiece from Figuier's *Primitive Man* (1870). Painted by the artist C. Laplante, this image encapsulates the Romantic vision of early prehistory. While the icons used suggest a primitive life, these figures could as easily be standing in a modern sitting room, with the male leaning over the mantelpiece as his wife feeds their baby, and the infants amuse themselves.

Figure 9.6 Boitard's image from *Paris Before Men* (1861). Entitled 'Anthropic period; last Palaeontological age – appearance of Man', [and illustrated by Boitard himself], this image presents a much harsher and less Romantic view of early prehistoric life. The starkness of the setting in which the figures are situated conveys a place so far away and so far distant that it is hard to imagine.

An early image produced in the context of the debates on the 'antiquity of man' was presented by M. Boitard (1861) in *Paris avant les hommes* [Paris before men] (Fig. 9.6). Conveyed here were the claims of the French flint collector, Boucher de Perthes, that humans were responsible for making the artifacts found in deposits also containing bones of extinct animals. This image provides a completely different vision from the Romantic visions of the past. Here ancient humans are presented as unheroic, almost pitiful, creatures, living in a stark and uncivilized world. However, while the vision is different, the same attributes or icons are used. Here we see the cave recess, nakedness, an animal skin, a club, and a crevasse all assembled together as they are in Figuier's heroic vision. But the new vision has a harsh edge. This bleak vision of the past is even more forcefully presented in the frontispiece of Boitard's book, where the first portrait of 'Fossil Man' appears (Fig. 9.7). Here we see the ancestor thought to be responsible for making ancient flint implements depicted as a savage simian-looking creature. The icons or

Figure 9.7   Appearing as the frontispiece in Boitard's *Paris Before Men* (1861), this image presents our early ancestors as ape-like savages. Entitled 'Fossil Man' and illustrated by Boitard, this picture recasts ancient humans in a completely different light from that of the earlier, more Romantic images. Anatomical details rather than the environmental setting take precedence among the icons used for depicting human origins.

primitiveness are all used – cave recess, weapon/tool in hand, animal skin garment, nakedness, hairiness. While the image conveys Boitard's hostility to the claims being made about human antiquity, it can be seen as an archaeologically rather than geologically inspired image.

One of the earliest reconstructions of a specific ancestor or hominid species was the image of the Neanderthals published in *Harper's Weekly* (Anon 1873) (Fig. 9.8). Here all the iconic elements have been forcefully assembled to create a statement on the nature of Stone Age life. Trinkaus and Shipman (1993:399) have argued that the practice of 'fleshing out' a fossil human and bringing it 'to life' for purposes of display was invented for the Neanderthals. However, while the archaeological tradition got under way with reconstructions of the Neanderthal fossils

Figure 9.8 This vision of ancient humans was featured in *Harper's Weekly* magazine in 1873. Based on the discovery of Neanderthal remains in France, this picture suggests that our ancestors struggled to survive rather than lived in harmony with nature. The figures are no longer situated in peaceful wooded landscapes. The focus is now on the life they lead in their cave home. The portrayal of the male figure clutching his weapon suggests that these ancestors are no longer in control; that they are constantly on guard and that they must find protection against the harsh environment.

Figure 9.9 Hutchinson's image of early life in prehistoric England appearing in Hutchinson's *Prehistoric Man and Beast* (1896). Entitled 'The eviction scene', and painted by the *Illustrated London News* illustrator Cecil Aldin, this image not only draws on classic icons of antiquity, but uses a naturalistic style of representation to reinforce the idea that our ancestors lived under constant threat from animals and the environment.

Figure 9.10 Knipe featured this illustration as his frontispiece in his classic text *From Nebula to Man* (1905). With the name of the book as its title, and painted by Lancelot Speed, this image blends elements of the Romantic tradition with those of the archaeological tradition. Here our most primal ancestors are shown hovering behind the fully evolved 'modern' humans.

Figure 9.11 Designed to introduce the new ancestor Pithecanthropus, this illustration from Knipe's *From Nebula to Man* (1905) reinforces the idea of our ape ancestry using age-old symbols of primitiveness. Painted by Lancelot Speed, this picture presents the 'missing link' as a strong character prepared for confrontation.

Figure 9.12 Entitled 'Early Palaeolithic men', this picture from Knipe's *From Nebula to Man* (1905) shows ancient humans in their cave home. Illustrated by Ernest Bucknall, and based on the Neanderthal discoveries, this image casts our ancestors as hunch-backed, thick-set figures. Again, the focus is on the activities inside the cave as opposed to those which took place outside in the 'wild'.

from Germany and France, and the Piltdown remains from England, it was not only developed for introducing new ancestors, but was introduced in order to explain what artifacts represented in terms of human behaviour. An early example of such an image appears in Hutchinson's (1896) *Prehistoric Man and Beast* (Fig. 9.9). Here the depiction of a male figure warding off beasts at the entrance to his cave is designed to show that people used Wookey Hole cave in the past. What sets the new archaeological images apart from the Romantic ones is that they characterize ancient humans as having to struggle in order to survive. Ideas about the romance of living alongside nature were replaced with the image of the prehistoric world as a harsh and inhospitable place.

The archaeological tradition became firmly established when images depicting carefully excavated sites were produced. Closely connected to this development was the 'claiming' of images by authors and prehistorians (e.g. Knipe 1905, Hutchinson 1896, Osborn 1915). Scientists now worked closely with artists to confirm, through the procedures of

Figure 9.13 This picture of a mammoth from Knipe's *From Nebula to Man* (1905) presents a very unromantic view of early prehistoric life. Painted by Joseph Smith, this almost comic reconstruction suggests our ancestors were not always the successful hunters we have envisaged them to be.

scientific accuracy, the elements they saw as important in human evolution. The fact that practitioners authorized and emphasized the validity of these pictures suggests how reconstructions became a major component of prehistorians' professional discourse. The authority of the images is also evidenced by the way in which they have been integrated with the text. Reconstructions meld together with the text, becoming part of the whole narrative. A series of images was now used to present the story of how we evolved, as opposed to an isolated image being used to reinforce a particular point in the text. An important example of this is presented in Henry R. Knipe's *From Nebula to Man*. Published in 1905, this book presents the story of human evolution in a series of six images, with each image (with the exception of the first) referred to in verse. These images blend different visual traditions of representation. For instance, the image featuring our ancestors emerging from the darkness of their primeval past (Fig. 9.10), is depicted in the Romantic style. By contrast, the images of 'Pithecanthropus' (Fig. 9.11) and 'Early Palaeolithic Men' (Fig. 9.12) are rendered in the more sombre archaeological style. Furthermore, the image entitled 'Mammoth' (Fig. 9.13), has elements of a comic vision of the past (see below). Knipe's images are character-ized by the coming together of the three traditions in a seamless blend of art and science, progress, and passion.

The comic tradition

When the prehistoric world was communicated via the geological/palaeontological and archaeological scenes of deep time, the popular media quickly seized the idea of a distant past as a new source for comic themes. The fact that the remote human past became a subject for popular treatment was reflected in the construction of an enormously powerful visual stereotype – the caveman. The caveman and his Stone Age family were a perfect target for comic representation or ridicule because they could not answer back. Closely associated with the comic vision of human antiquity were the satirical cartoons created in response to Darwin's theory of evolution, especially the idea that we evolved from apes. For example, a famous cartoon of Darwin depicted as an ape appeared in *The Hornet* in 1871, and cartoons from *Harper's Bazaar* in 1876 and *Punch* magazine in 1871 also made fun of Darwin's theory. The comic tradition of visual representation not only poked fun at the concept of human evolution, it also poked fun at the science of prehis-tory. In essence, the authors of comic representation challenged the archaeologists' bid for 'ownership' of the past; they made it their past too.

The comic tradition can be seen as starting with E.T. Reed's 'Mr. Punch's "Prehistoric Peeps"' of 1894. Here twenty-six full page cartoons range from a 'Prehistoric Lord Mayor's Show' to the 'Unsociable Mammoth' and a 'Bank Holiday of the Period' (Fig. 9.14). We witness a romp through prehistory with dinosaurs and fabulous beasts appearing side-by-side with shock-headed, bandy-legged males (but all anatomi-cally modern humans), in fur wraps and driving Heath-Robinson contraptions, usually made in stone. The elements in Reed's cartoons have been copied ever since. Significantly, the icons used in the Romantic and archaeological traditions of representation are almost the same; what is different however, is the context in which they appear.

The Stone Age has been a profitable source for cartoonists, comics, and caricaturists because it provides a means of making fun of ourselves. Cartoons of our ancestors as hairy apes and bumbling fools have been common in newspapers and magazines for over a century, and continue to be a hugely popular subject on greeting cards and in comic strips. In his review of archaeological humour, Bray (1978:223) refers to the role of *Punch* magazine, where archaeological subjects were featured from 1841. He refers to the creation of 'Archaeologyland', which is a world of fantasy peopled by stereotypes such as the cavemen, dinosaurs, Vikings, and Romans. Cavemen are by far the most popular inhabitants of

Figure 9.14 *Punch* magazine's 'Prehistoric Peeps' cartoon series was enormously popular in communicating the finds made in prehistoric research. Featured here are some of the classic icons used to present human antiquity.

Archaeologyland because the image comes from older, more established visual vocabularies. There is something so familiar about the caveman stereotype that it seems to have been in existence long before prehistoric archaeology appeared on the scene.

LOCATING THE ORIGINS OF ARCHAEOLOGY'S ICONIC VOCABULARY

Numerous traditions of representation existed from which geologists/palaeontologists, archaeologists, and the popular media could draw in order to help them produce images of ancient life. What distinguished the archaeological images was that they were presented as being based on scientific data, rather than on myths, folklore, and pictorial evidence. Significant, however, was the fact that the archaeological tradition drew heavily on the traditions of representation that used such evidence. The archaeological images were in many senses no more scholarly or scientific than the images produced without the aid of empirical data.

In seeking to locate the original sources from which an iconic vocabulary for depicting prehistory was derived, we need to consider traditions of representation from Classical times. We need to look not only at the visual traditions associated with the development of disciplines such as primatology and anthropology, but also of developments in the visual arts. As a more full investigation of these influences is presented elsewhere (Moser and Gamble forthcoming), we restrict our discussion here to a brief outline of some of the major areas of influence on the development of nineteenth-century visions of the past.

Ancestors and cultural origins

When a number of European nations became concerned with their cultural origins in the sixteenth century, they started to produce images of their distant forebears. The interest in establishing what life might have been like for these ancestors was a major characteristic of the antiquarian tradition of study from the sixteenth to nineteenth centuries. With limited historical and archaeological evidence, antiquarians turned to a vast array of sources to reconstruct pictures of their ancestors. They used material from Classical texts, medieval folklore and imagery, pictures of the people encountered in the New World, and other more mythical material. Visual material was used as primary evidence for reconstructing the past, as opposed to depending solely on historical or archaeological evidence.

The role of Greek and Roman myths and art in providing inspiration for visualizing ancestral beginnings cannot be emphasized enough. We have effectively continued to recycle a set of icons developed in Classical times. Some of these icons were constructed by Classical authors and artists to convey cultural difference and the primitiveness of other races (see Sparkes, this volume). In aiming to convey their cultural superiority, the Greeks and Romans devised visual ways of signifying their advancement. For example, barbarians and central Europeans were depicted with beards, long hair, and wearing trousers, while the Romans were portrayed as being shaven and wearing togas. Visual canons for depicting gods, such as Hercules, and mythical beings, such as giants, have also been influential in the rendition of ancestors. For example, images of Hercules highlighted his club and animal skin, and in illustrations of the battles between the gods and the giants, the more barbaric and primitive giants are depicted wearing animal skins slung over their shoulder (e.g. see Henle 1973:51). Furthermore, caves, which are a key icon in the visual vocabulary for depicting antiquity, figured prominently in Classical myths. Caves were the home of the Cyclopes, the race of savage one-eyed creatures. In this context caves were associated with, and suggestive of, wilderness and wildness.

Although they were not depicted visually, Classical descriptions of ancestral beginnings introduced many ideas about humans' early primitive existence. For example, Lucretius in his *De Rerum Natura* described our archaic forebears as living under trees, or in caves, and eating nuts and berries. Similarly, the textual descriptions of other cultures by Classical writers provided a rich source of inspiration for illustrating the archaic past. For example, Tacitus' description of the Germans as primitive people who lived in forests was influential for Renaissance scholars seeking to envisage their ancestors. Also significant were the Classical descriptions of the Plinian races, who were strange races of people thought to have lived in Africa and India (see Friedman 1981). In medieval times, the Classical icons of antiquity and cultural difference were recycled in order to construct the images of ancestors and mythical beings featured in folklore. Depictions of satyr-like figures holding clubs clearly drew on Greek iconography. Using ideas and images from Classical times, medieval folklore created the powerful and compelling image of the Wild man of the Woods (see Bernheimer 1970, Husband 1980). The Wild man of the Woods was a popular motif used not only in ancestor imagery, but also in ape imagery and landscape imagery of the seventeenth and eighteenth centuries.

Antiquarians further developed the visual language of antiquity when they started depicting European cultural origins. As Smiles (1994) has shown, images of early Britons included artifacts and the remains of prehistoric monuments. Pictures of giants who were thought to have built the megalithic monuments also contributed to the iconography of antiquity. These giants, were equipped with all the appropriate icons – they were shaggy, thick-set figures clad in furs, holding clubs (e.g. Piggott 1989:51). Of relevance here are Piggott's comments on the legacy of antiquarian studies.

> It was they [the antiquarians] who, as part of a pessimistic view of the first inhabitants of Britain, fallen from grace so far from Eden, created the stereo- type of the brutish, skin-clad, club-bearing hunter that was to flourish in popular imagination down to the present day, now silted down into the world of children's comics with The Flintstones and Stonehenge Kit The Ancient Brit.
>
> (Piggott 1989:11)

Apes, savages, and evolution

When new scientific theories about evolution were developed in the mid-nineteenth century, the iconic vocabulary for depicting antiquity was further developed. The major new sources of influence were images of the anthropoid apes and ethnographic illustrations of other peoples. With the theory that humans had evolved from ape-like ancestors came a new dimension in the representation of ancient humans. Now human ancestors were presented as having ape-like qualities. Furthermore, with the idea that humans had progressed from a state of savagery to one of civilization came images of ancient humans depicted in the manner of the 'natives' encountered in the New World.

Images of apes and monkeys had played a role in medieval folklore, being used to depict uncivilized and unchristian peoples (see Janson 1952). Not long after this they were used as source material for visualizing our ancestors. Historical images of apes were important in providing a notion of what our earliest ancestors may have looked like because they paid close attention to morphology. Significantly, the early scientific images of apes produced in the seventeenth century, were manufactured in the context of contemporary debates over whether apes were a type of human (see Corbey and Theunissen 1995). With the rise of evolutionary theory in the nineteenth century, the question of the relationship between apes and humans was resurrected and the early images of ape-like humans and human-like apes were consulted. This time, however, the question was one of whether humans were a type of ape, and the new illustrations sought to address this issue by drawing on icons from ape imagery. The icons drawn from ape imagery included hairiness, a more bestial appearance, nakedness, a docile expression, a semi-erect posture, and large hands and feet. The fact that the image of the 'Wild Man of the Woods' was being used in medieval antiquarian and primate iconography demonstrates how it served as a cross-over image in the construction of ancestors.

Antiquarians had used pictures of Virginian Indians to inform their reconstructions of ancient Britons. However, the archaeological tradition of representation treated them as a far more serious resource. Archaeologists used such images to provide information about the activities their ancestors engaged in, and more precisely, to understand how the artifacts found in archaeological deposits were used. As the 'customs and manners' of ethnographic people became the model upon which ancient human life was understood, illustrations of their lifestyles became an important source of evidence. In archaeological reconstructions, for instance, we see ancient ancestors portrayed like American Indians (e.g. Hutchinson 1896). Furthermore, images of native peoples portrayed alongside apes were used to demonstrate their lower position on the rungs of the evolutionary ladder (e.g. Haeckel 1876). It is here that we see the two visual traditions being fused to provide an image of ape-like savages.

Landscape

Another major source from which icons were drawn for the depiction of human antiquity were the visual traditions pertaining to the representation of landscape. In seeking to reconstruct the settings and landscapes that prehistoric peoples inhabited, geologists, palaeontologists, and archaeologists were strongly influenced by motifs from contemporary

European art, particularly those deriving from landscape imagery. When reconstructions were first featured in texts the rustic and pastoral traditions of landscape painting were still flourishing (see Bermingham 1986, Cafritz 1988). While pastoral settings were used for the earliest images of humans, the influence of sixteenth-century landscape imagery, where images of forests and woodlands were favoured (see Bechmann 1990, Harrison 1992, Schama 1995), can also be seen. Landscape imagery, like the other visual traditions which have been discussed, was also strongly influenced by Classical sources. For instance, the interest in depicting wild landscapes was associated with the Roman preoccupation with the forest, this being demonstrated by Tacitus' vivid descriptions of wooded Germania as a primitive wild place. This, as Schama (1995) notes, recalled the Arcadian portrait of arboreal man given by Lucretius. Closely associated with this was the image of the wild man or herdsman who lived in the woods. With the Renaissance there was a renewed interest in Tacitus' portrayals, and antiquarians drew heavily on the idea of the 'wild place' in their quest to create an image of their earliest ancestors.

AUTHENTICITY AND THE DEMISE OF THE ROMANTIC VISION OF THE PAST

With the emergence of the new scientific tradition of representing human antiquity we see the Romantic images of our ancestors being replaced with new, more 'authentic', visions of the past. Images of antiquity were now based on scientific data and did not have to resort to fanciful notions of how our ancestors once lived. However, while archaeology presented itself as the new authority, promising more accurate visions of the past, it continued to recycle the same suite of icons that had been established in Classical times and which were reused from medieval times. It is a significant paradox that archaeology, in claiming to end the production of Romantic visions and thus end speculation about the past, has kept aspects of the Romantic tradition alive.

Archaeological scenes of the ancient past drew heavily on both scientific traditions and unscientific ones. Essentially, there was such a long tradition of visualizing the past that archaeology could not avoid being shaped by it. Archaeological reconstructions were rendered in a highly naturalistic style, and made every effort to incorporate the actual data that had been recovered from sites, but they still used the same basic interpretative frameworks for depicting human antiquity. Despite having a new class of material evidence for investigating the past, archaeologists were little different from previous authors and artists in their quest to envisage the past. The fact that they turned to the rich heritage of interpretative motifs as their source for inspiration is testimony to the power of iconography and the persistence of images as constituents of knowledge.

Since their inception in prehistoric archaeology, visual reconstructions have changed very little. We have added little to the suite of icons used for depicting ancestors, and we have had little impact on revising false assumptions about the distant past. However, it is true that reconstructions have changed over the past century and that some positive developments have been made in the way we visually depict past life-ways. We have seen a shift in the depiction of sex roles for instance, with the stereotype of men as hunters and women as nurturers being challenged (Moser 1993b). Similarly, we have seen our earliest ancestors redefined as passive victims or scavengers rather than aggressive hunters (Moser 1996). The point however, is that these changes are largely cosmetic. They usually achieve little more than a reshuffle of the familiar iconic elements within the picture. The complex sub-text in these reconstructions is an investigation of how many, varied factors are concisely summarized in these reworked images. For instance, Knipe's strutting ape-man and crawling ape-woman of 1905 (Fig. 9.10) is almost directly copied by Granquist in his diorama from the Prehistorama exhibition in the Ardèche, opened in 1990. Eighty-five years of archaeological discovery and excavation, changing theoretical fashions, and the invention of new media through which to explore the past, has resulted, in this instance, in almost no interpretative gain. The idea that years of scientific investigation have done little to change ideas about the past has already been made by Stoczkowski (1994), who argues that despite the enormous growth of knowledge on human origins the basic explanatory themes have not changed. We would add that this is nowhere better demonstrated than in the visualization of the past. Furthermore, we would conclude by venturing the suggestion that the reason why the ideas have held sway is because the images have encouraged us to do so.

ACKNOWLEDGEMENTS

We would like to thank Alex Jones for producing Figure 9.1. We are also grateful to Brian Sparkes, Simon Keay, Tim Champion, David Hinton, and David Peacock, who provided insights regarding various aspects of the arguments presented in the text.

REFERENCES

Anon. 1873. 'Neanderthal domestic scene.' *Harper's Weekly* 17(864):617–18.

Baigrie, B. (ed.) 1996. *Picturing Knowledge: Historical and Philosophical Problems Concerning the Use in Art in Science.* Toronto: Toronto University Press.

Bechmann, R. 1990. *Trees and Man: The Forest in the Middle Ages.* New York: Paragon House.

Bermingham, A. 1986. *Landscape and Ideology: The English Rustic Tradition 1740–1860.* London: Thames and Hudson.

Bernheimer, R. 1970. *Wild Men in the Middle Ages: A Study in Art Sentiment and Demonology.* Cambridge, MA: Harvard University Press.

Boitard, M. 1861. *Paris avant les hommes.* Paris: Passard.

Bray, W. 1978. 'Archaeological humour: the private joke and the public image.' In J.D. Evans, B. Cunliffe, and C. Renfrew (eds), *Antiquity and Man: Essays in Honour of Glyn Daniel*, pp. 221–9. London: Thames and Hudson.

Cafritz, R.C. (ed.) 1988. *Places of Delight: The Pastoral Landscape.* London: Weidenfeld and Nicolson.

Corbey, R. and Theunissen, B. (eds) 1995. *Ape Man Apeman: Changing Views since 1600.* Leiden: Leiden University, Department of Prehistory.

Figuier, L. 1863. *La terre avant le Deluge: ouvrage contenant 25 vues ideals de paysages de l'ancien monde.* Paris: Hachette.

Figuier, L. 1870. *L'homme primitif.* English translation. London: Chapman and Hall.

Friedman, J.B. 1981. *The Monstrous Races in Medieval Art and Thought.* Cambridge: Cambridge University Press.

Gamble, C. 1992. 'Figures of fun; theories about cavemen.' *Archaeological Review from Cambridge* 11(2):357–72.

Gamble, C. 1993. *Timewalkers. The Prehistory of Global Colonisation.* Harmondsworth: Penguin.

Gifford-Gonzalez, D. 1994. 'You can hide, but you can't run: representations of women's work in illustrations of palaeolithic life.' *Visual Anthropology Review* 9(1):23–42.

Gould, S.J. 1984. *The Mismeasure of Man.* Harmondsworth: Penguin.

Harrison, R.P. 1992. *Forests: The Shadow of Civilization.* Chicago: University of Chicago Press.

Haeckel, E.H. 1876. *The History of Creation.* London: Murray.

Henle, J. 1973. *Greek Myths. A Vase Painter's Notebook.* Bloomington: Indiana University Press.

Husband, T. 1980. *The Wild Man: Medieval Myth and Symbolism.* With assistance from G. Gilmore-House. New York: Metropolitan Museum of Art.

Hurcombe, L. 1995. 'Our own engendered species.' *Antiquity* 69:87–100.

Hutchinson, H.N. 1896. *Prehistoric Man and Beast.* London: Smith, Elder and Company.

Janson, H.W. 1952. *Apes and Ape Lore in the Middle Ages and the Renaissance.* London: University of London, Studies of the Warburg Institute, Vol. 20.

Knipe, H.R. 1905. *From Nebula to Man.* London: J.M. Dent.

Kynaston, D. 1990. *W.G.'s Birthday Party.* London: Chatto and Windus.

Laing, S. 1895. *Human Origins.* London: Chapman and Hall.

Lynch, M. and Woolgar, S. (eds) 1990. *Representation in Scientific Practice.*

Cambridge, MA: MIT Press.

Mazzolini, R.G. (ed.) 1993. *Non-verbal Communication in Science Prior to 1900*. Florence: Olschki.

Moser, S. 1992a. 'The visual language of archaeology: a case study of the Neanderthals.' *Antiquity* 66:831–44.

Moser, S. 1992b. 'Visions of the Australian Pleistocene: prehistoric life at Lake Mungo and Kutikina.' *Australian Archaeology* 35:1–10.

Moser, S. 1993a. 'Picturing the prehistoric.' *Metascience* 4:58–67.

Moser, S. 1993b. 'Gender stereotyping in pictorial reconstructions of human origins.' In H. duCros and L. Smith (eds), *Women in Archaeology: A Feminist Critique*, pp. 75–92. Canberra: Research School of Pacific Studies, Department of Prehistory.

Moser, S. 1996. 'Visual representation in archaeology: depicting the missing-link in human origins.' In B. Baigire (ed.), *Picturing Knowledge: Historical and Philosophical Problems Concerning the Use of Art in Science*, pp. 184–214. Toronto: University of Toronto Press.

Moser, S. and Gamble, C. (forthcoming). *Visions of Human Antiquity: Archaeological Reconstructions of Prehistory*. Sutton: Stroud.

Nixon, L. 1994. 'Gender bias in archaeology.' In L.J. Archer, S. Fischer, and M. Wyke (eds), *Women in Ancient Societies*. pp. 1–23. London: Macmillan.

Osborn, H.F. 1915. *Men of the Old Stone Age*. New York: Scribner.

Piggott, S. 1989. *Ancient Britons and the Antiquarian Imagination*. London: Thames and Hudson.

Rosny-Aîné, J.H. 1982. *Quest for fire (La guerre du feu* (1911)). Harmondsworth: Penguin.

Rudwick, M.J.S. 1976. 'The emergence of a visual language for geological science 1760–1840.' *The History of Science* 14:149–95.

Rudwick, M.J.S. 1992. *Scenes from Deep Time: Early Pictorial Representations of the Prehistoric World*. Chicago: University of Chicago Press.

Schama, S. 1995. *Landscape and Memory*. London: Harper Collins.

Shanks, M. 1992. *Experiencing the Past: On the Character of Archaeology*. London: Routledge.

Shanks, M. and Tilley, C. 1989. 'Archaeology into the 1990s.' *Norwegian Archaeological Review* 22(1):1–54.

Shanks, M. and Hodder, I. 1995. 'Processual, postprocessual and interpretive archaeologies.' In I. Hodder, M. Shanks, A. Alexandri, V. Buchli, J. Carman, J. Last, and G. Lucas (eds), *Interpreting Archaeology: Finding Meaning in the Past*. pp. 3–29. London: Routledge.

Sherratt, A. 1993. 'Archaeology and post-textuality.' *Antiquity* 67(255):195.

Smiles, S. 1994. *The Image of Antiquity*. New Haven, CT: Yale University Press.

Stoczkowski, W. 1994. *Anthropologie naïve anthropologie savante: De l'origine de l'homme, de l'imagination et des idées reçues*. Paris: CRNS.

Stringer, C. and Gamble, C. 1993. *In Search of the Neanderthals*. London: Thames and Hudson.

Tilley, C. 1993. 'Introduction: interpretation and a poetics of the past.' In C. Tilley (ed.), *Interpretative Archaeology*. pp. 1–27. Providence, RI: Berg.

Trinkaus, E. and Shipman, P. 1993. *The Neandertals*. London: Jonathan Cape.

Unger, F. 1851. *Die Urwelt in ihren verschiedenen Bildungsperioden*. Vienna: Beck.

CHAPTER TEN

THE POWER OF THE PICTURE

The image of the ancient Gaul

TIMOTHY CHAMPION

INTRODUCTION

Archaeology has a long history of using non-verbal media for projecting ideas about the past, but it is only quite recently that we have become aware of the need to study these means of communication. Some are comparatively obvious, with an apparently simple relationship to the past, such as the exhibition of surviving material culture in museums or the presentation of sites and monuments to the public, but even these raise further questions about the meanings they convey and the messages that are understood by the spectator. Others are much more complex and problematic. The representation of the past at one further remove through painting, sculpture, and graphic illustration falls into this latter category. In addition to questions about the sources of inspiration and their authenticity, and about the active and creative role of the artist, these representations prompt further enquiries about their power to convey a message. With the development of new technologies of communication in the last two hundred years and the growth of new social mechanisms for the dissemination or even inculcation of ideas, these images can take on a new resilience and a new power; they can pervade society and prove very lasting as they are continually projected, repeated, and renewed, and they have the capacity to exert an influence and to leave a legacy beyond the time and place or the narrow cultural sphere in which they were first created.

This study is concerned with one set of such images, first produced in the 1860s in France. They are concerned with the Celtic population of France immediately before the Roman conquest, and portray historical events and people, including individuals known by name, such as Vercingetorix, the leader of the final, doomed resistance to Julius Caesar's conquest in the 50s BC. The prime focus of attention here is the production and dissemination of the images, though that cannot be divorced from a consideration of the political and ideological context (Viallaneix and Ehrard 1982; Simon 1989).

REPRESENTATION OF THE BARBARIAN GAULS

Before the emergence of a detailed understanding of the later prehistoric archaeology of Europe in the second half of the nineteenth century, the image of the pre-Roman population was shaped by the prevailing knowledge of the Classical writers and by attitudes to primitive peoples (Piggott 1989; Smiles 1994). To the Classical world they were known mostly as barbarian warriors, who had invaded Italy and sacked Rome, and later invaded Greece and sacked Delphi. Their representation in Classical art is overwhelmingly dominated by images of the noble savage,

Figure 10.1 Wood engraving after W.B. Scott, 'The free northern Britons surprising the Roman Wall between the Tyne and the Solway' (*Illustrated London News*, 12 August 1843).

Figure 10.2 Aquatint by R. Havell after C.H. Smith. 'A Briton of the interior' (Meyrick and Smith 1815).

frequently shown as a warrior in defeat and death at the hands of Rome (Andreae 1991).

In Romantic art, a similar emphasis prevails. In Britain, for example, considerable attention was paid to bards and druids, but otherwise the dominant image was of warriors (Smiles 1994:129–64). The cartoon produced by W.B. Scott in 1843 for the competition for pictures to decorate the new Houses of Parliament, showing Britons in conflict with the occupying Romans, is typical in spirit, in its portrayal of semi–clad warriors in a rugged environment (Fig. 10.1). Representations with a greater reliance on archaeological authenticity are rare; one example is the collection published by Meyrick and Smith (1815). Their image of

A Briton of the interior contains passably accurate portrayals of a late Bronze Age shield and socketed axe, though what appears to be a sword has been mounted as a spearhead (Fig. 10.2).

Archaeological knowledge of the first millennium BC improved rapidly from about the 1830s with the increase in the quantity of material recovered, and the quality of information recorded about it. The rich Iron Age graves of the Rhineland began to be known in the 1830s, Ramsauer's excavations in the Hallstatt cemetery began in 1848, and the site of La Tène was discovered in 1856. In France, Napoleon III sponsored archaeological excavations in the 1860s in the Marne region and at other sites, especially those identified with the events of the Roman conquest. In Scandinavia, the Danish archaeologists Engelhardt and Vedel elaborated a relative sequence for material of the Nordic Iron Age, and by working backwards from Roman horizons could provide a tentative absolute chronology. Their Swedish colleague Hans Hildebrand extended this work to a wider geographical scale, and in the 1870s suggested a scheme for the division of the European Iron Age into two phases, the first named after Hallstatt and the second after La Tène, providing for the first time a secure means of organizing the material of the later first millennium. The material culture which we now know to have been used by the Celtic peoples of western Europe in the later Iron Age had first been recognized as a homogeneous group in the 1860s, but its true chronology was not certain; some attributed it to the Romans, the Etruscans, or even the post-Roman Merovingians. It was not until the work of Hildebrand in the 1870s, confirmed by the excavations of the French archaeologist Gabriel de Mortillet in Italy, that Iron Age archaeology began to rest on a sure footing.

In the 1860s, therefore, at the time when the images which are the object of this study were being composed, archaeological knowledge was in a state of flux; many objects had been recovered and museums were beginning to make them available, but their true origin and chronology was very uncertain.

GUIZOT'S *HISTOIRE* AND ITS IMAGES

It is against this background of a gradual consolidation of archaeological knowledge, as well as of the political events of the time in France, that the images which form the focus of this study must be understood. They are some of the illustrations used in Frédéric Guizot's *Histoire de la France*, the first volume of which appeared in 1872. Guizot was a distinguished historian who had also pursued a political career, culminating in a short period as Prime Minister in 1847–8. His politics were basically conservative, and he supported the concept of a constitutional monarchy. With the collapse of the monarchy in 1848 his political career was ended, and he devoted the rest of his life until his death in 1874 to the writing of history. The collapse of the Second Empire in 1870 after the catastrophic defeat of Napoleon III in the Franco-Prussian War and the establishment of the Third Republic in 1871 provided the opportunity for, or perhaps even demanded, an attempt to rebuild the idea of the French nation.

Any history written and published in these circumstances, especially one by a historian with a career of high office behind him, must be seen as conveying a political message. Guizot certainly had such a message to impart, but this particular work was one of the first of a series of more popular histories which were aimed at a wide readership and were not only shorter than many of the standard works, but were also illustrated. The illustrations were the work of Alphonse de Neuville, an artist who was already establishing his reputation as one of France's foremost military painters. Some are full-page illustrations of critical events in the history of France, others are small vignettes at the beginnings and ends of chapters.

The illustrations which de Neuville provided draw on a fascinating

Figure 10.3   Untitled engraving after A. de Neuville (Guizot 1872:14).

variety of sources and inspirations. One vignette (Fig. 10.3), from the foot of Chapter 1 (Guizot 1872:14), harks back to the Romantic iconography of the barbarians. It shows them half-dressed in what appears to be a mixture of clothes and furs, with little pretence at detail of weapons or other equipment. The only clearly visible detail is the winged helmet. This is a motif which has a long history in the representation of the barbarians and owes more to the post-Roman period, or to the references in Diodorus Siculus to the helmets surmounted by birds and animals worn by the Celts, than it does to any known prehistoric archaeological evidence (Guerrier 1982).

Other images draw on a very different world of inspiration, being closely related to the historical art of the 1860s. Another vignette (Fig. 10.4), from the foot of Chapter 4 (Guizot 1872:71), is simply entitled 'Vercingétorix', and is in fact a representation of a huge bronze statue of the Gaulish leader recently erected at Alesia, the site of his final defeat. The statue was the work of the sculptor Aimé Millet, commissioned and paid for by Napoleon III himself; the details of the face were modelled on the Emperor's. The statue had been exhibited at the annual Salon in 1865, and then installed at Alesia (Pingeot 1982:256). It has been much reproduced, in later statues and in drawings and photographs, and has become an icon of French national mythology and of Napoleon III's self-image. Even by the time of Guizot's book, it had become accepted as the archetypal representation.

Two of the set-piece tableaus derive their inspiration from a similar source. The picture of the *Cavalier gaulois* (Fig. 10.5; Guizot 1872:opp. 54) is taken directly from a bronze equestrian statue by the famous artist, Emmanuel Frémiet, one of France's best animal sculptors, who was also well known for his statues of horsemen. This statue (Pingeot 1982:278, unnumbered plate; Eluère 1993:152), a version of which is now in the Musée des Antiquités Nationales, had been exhibited at the Salon of 1863 as a plaster cast from the clay model, in bronze at the Salon of 1864 and again at the Universal Exposition of 1867. The other tableau (Fig. 10.6; Guizot 1872:opp. 68) depicts the surrender of Vercingétorix to Caesar, a scene which had been represented in a picture exhibited by Emile Lévy at the Salon of 1861, and was to become a stock scene of historical imagery.

As we will see below, these images took on a considerable historical resonance, and the power of their symbolic meaning was rooted partly in their claims to historical realism. This realism was based to some extent on the fact that they represented historically known events and people, sometimes even named individuals such as Vercingétorix, rather than purely mythological or allegorical figures. But it was also based on an apparently authentic representation of the details of weapons, costumes, and equipment drawn from the evidence of archaeological discoveries. Frémiet is known to have taken the details of his equestrian chief from

VERCINGÉTORIX

(D'après la statue de M. Millet.)

Figure 10.4 Engraving after A. de Neuville, 'Vercingétorix' (Guizot 1872:71).

Figure 10.5 Engraving after A. de Neuville 'Cavalier gaulois' (Guizot 1872:opp. 54).

Figure 10.6 Engraving after A. de Neuville 'Vercingétorix se livre en personne à César' (Guizot 1872:opp. 68).

ancient bronzes in the Louvre, and other artists took similar care; Bartholdi, the sculptor of the Statue of Liberty, was congratulated for the archaeological accuracy of his equestrian statue of Vercingétorix exhibited in 1870 (Pingeot 1982:256–7). One standardized version of the representation of ancient Gauls thus emerged, showing them with a crested helmet, bronze breastplate, sword and dagger, with or without a spear, mounted or on foot. Variants of this sometimes show them without the breastplate.

The claims to authenticity were misplaced, however. In the light of our currently much improved knowledge of the archaeology of the first millennium BC, we know what the artists of the 1860s could not have been expected to know, that most of the items with which they furnished their Gaulish warriors belonged not to the end of the Iron Age, but to its very earliest stages or to the end of the Bronze Age. Not only was chronology then still very imprecise, but those earlier phases were better known: more material had been recovered, especially from burials furnished with weapons and other goods, than from the final stages of the Iron Age, when there were in any case few burials recoverable. Thus the swords and daggers belonged mostly to the Bronze Age; the breastplate is from the Hallstatt phase of the early Iron Age; and the distinctive crested helmet owes more to examples from the end of the Italian Bronze Age than to contemporary examples from France. The individual items, though each reasonably accurate in archaeological detail, were on average six or seven hundred years too old for Caesar's opponents in the middle of the first century BC, and in some cases were drawn from originals which were too widely distributed in space or time ever to have been worn by the same person. Thus the pedantic authenticity of archaeological details of typology, chronology, and distribution was brought into opposition with the imaginative authenticity of how a real Gaulish chief should have been equipped, and with the accurate portrayal of an eclectic choice of symbolically significant items.

Another version of the Gaulish warrior also existed alongside the historical realism of these putatively authentic figures. This harked back to the Romantic portrayal of barbarians, as in Guizot's vignette, and was characterized in particular by the continued use of the archaeologically unverified winged helmet. One of the most prominent examples of this version is Jules Bertin's statue of Ambiorix, the chief of the Eburones, exhibited at the Universal Exposition of 1867 and now erected in Tongres (Piggott 1975:Fig.106; Pingeot 1982:263; Smiles 1994:Plate 13); Bertin produced another very similar version of this statue as a representation of Vercingétorix, now lost (Pingeot 1982:281).

THE PROJECTION OF THE IMAGE

The phenomenal success of the images of Celtic warriors such as those described above, whether of individuals or of generalized stereotypes, was derived partly from their apparent claims to historical and archaeological authenticity. Another important factor was their potential capacity for being projected to the public in a variety of media appropriate to the social circumstances of the time; we have already seen how de Neuville's drawings for the illustrations to accompany Guizot's text drew on sources from sculpture and painting. This flexibility helped to spread the images through society and the variety of contexts and forms in which they reappeared helped to reinforce the power of their message.

As we have seen, one of the most important media, and perhaps the one which was central to their primary appearance, was statuary. Throughout Europe, and indeed in other countries influenced by European fashions, such as the United States, nineteenth-century sculpture was marked by the production of portrait statues to an extent not witnessed since the Roman empire. The selection of the individuals to be memorialized in this way varied from country to country and time to time with the political and ideological context: royalty, political leaders, military and naval heroes, reformers, figures from the past or the present, historical individuals or allegorical abstractions; all could be represented within a widely recognized code of symbolic meanings, whatever the precise nuance to be conveyed. Although such statues were not unknown in earlier times, their popularity reached a peak in the middle and later decades of the nineteenth century; figures collated by Cannadine (1983:164) show that in London and Washington the height of the fashion for the erection of such statues was in the period from the 1860s to the early years of the twentieth century.

The styles of the statues, whether standing or equestrian, were clearly derived from Classical prototypes and were remarkably standardized: Frémiet's Gallic horseman, like many others, can be traced back to Roman antecedents such as the famous equestrian statue of Marcus Aurelius, while Millet's Vercingétorix was simply one among many of the stone or bronze heroes who stood gazing into the distance, or perhaps surveying the future which their life's achievements had helped to shape. The pose is familiar and repeated: head up, eyes on the horizon, one leg straight, the other forward with the knee bent, and in one hand an item appropriate to the particular person and his deeds; a weapon for a warrior, or a book for a scholar or politician (Read 1982:147–71).

The images of the ancient Gauls were therefore part of an increasingly familiar and easily understood mode of representation in the middle of the nineteenth century, and one to which the public could be expected to have a ready response. Many of the statues were, of course, intended for display in public places, and indeed large numbers were installed in the streets and squares of European cities, and as decoration on the outside of major public buildings. In France there were also other opportunities for the public projection of these images; many were acquired by museums and art galleries, aided by government policy to support official art; some went to national institutions in Paris, but many others were destined for the museums and galleries springing up in many of the smaller provincial towns, especially if they were the work of local artists or depicted locally significant people. There were also other chances to reach a large public: the annual Salon attracted much attention, but even that was outdone by the huge exhibitions which formed one of the dominant forms of cultural activity in Europe following the Great Exhibition in London in 1851. The Universal Expositions held in Paris in 1867, 1878, 1889, and 1900 incorporated displays of art, including some statuary of Gaulish warriors. As we have seen, Frémiet's equestrian Gallic chief was displayed at the Salon of 1864 in bronze and again at the Universal Exposition in 1867 (Pingeot 1982:272). For those who could not see the statues in the street, the gallery, or the exhibition, an increasing flood of printed material, especially cheap postcards, helped to disseminate the image ever more widely.

Closely related to these statues produced in the sphere of high art were other representations of the ancient Gauls created in a different genre, as museum displays. Particularly important was the Musée de l'Armée, which contained a characterization of the ancient Gaulish warrior, drawing once again on the same set of images and the same repertoire of archaeological sources (Brunaux 1988:99).

One important element that enhanced the meaning of the image was a sense of place. There was a particular resonance attaching to monuments which celebrated a local hero of the town or region where they were displayed. Although there were a number of statues of Vercingétorix in other places such as Bordeaux, there was a special significance to the huge equestrian statue of this Arvernian hero by Bartholdi, exhibited in 1870 but not finally installed in Clermont-Ferrand in his homeland of the Auvergne until 1903.

Many of the statues were destined for urban locations, either public streets or museums, but in some cases monuments were erected at places of critical importance in the history or mythology of the nation. Thus monuments were erected at the places identified with Caesar's Alesia and Gergovia, two of the key sites in the history of the final Gallic resistance to Rome and in the subsequent national mythology of France. That at Alesia was, of course, Millet's statue of Vercingétorix. These places took on a new significance as they came to be more widely known outside their own locality, through the growing number of visitors travelling to see them and through pictorial representation in books or on postcards.

Although sculpture was the primary medium in which these images were created and disseminated, they were also powerfully reinforced by other methods, especially painting and graphic illustration. Historical themes were a regular part of French painting in the later nineteenth century, encouraged by government policy under both the Second Empire and the Third Republic which favoured the purchase of pictures with appropriately nationalistic themes for display in provincial museums; appeals to the past of France were particularly popular in the early 1870s, the years when France was trying to rebuild its idea of national identity in the aftermath of the traumatic defeat in the Franco-Prussian War of 1870–71. Alongside figures such as Joan of Arc and Bertrand du Guescelin, the remoter heroic past of the Gauls, Merovingians, and Normans was regularly portrayed by painters such as Evariste Luminais (see, for example, *The Gauls in Sight of Rome* (Eluère 1993:65) or *Battle between Romans and Gauls* (Eluère 1993:78)). These paintings drew on the same stock of warrior images, with the same archaeologically authentic but anachronistic details of helmets, armour, and weapons. One of the most impressive of these paintings was the *Chef gaulois à la Roche-Salvée* by Jules Didier, painted as late as 1896, which shows a Gaulish warrior standing at the symbolic site of Mont Beuvray in the pose of Millet's Vercingétorix and in the accoutrements of Frémiet and de Neuville's equestrian chief (Bertin and Guillaumet 1987:Plate IV). Thus the image and its meaning were reinforced by its projection through another medium.

Another channel for the diffusion of these images was graphic illustrations in books. From about the 1860s books were increasingly illustrated with engravings, many of them directly representing the images created in statuary or painting, and others drawing indirectly on the same repertoire of symbols and mythology. We have already seen some of Alphonse de Neuville's illustrations for Guizot's history of France, and a similar format and style of abundant illustration was adopted for other popular histories such as those of Henri Martin and Lavisse. Certain scenes, especially the surrender of Vercingétorix to Caesar, became standard themes for such books, and were repeatedly reproduced with minor variations on the original iconography established by de Neuville.

These stock scenes were also regularly included in materials prepared for use in schools. School textbooks, and in particular illustrations designed for display on schoolroom walls, commonly contained representations of the surrender of Vercingétorix (Simon 1989:99).

These graphic and pictorial images did not exist in isolation. The texts of the history books and school texts contained detailed accounts of the Gauls, and of the role of Vercingétorix as a national hero in the defence of the nation and independence. Vercingétorix himself was also the hero of a considerable outpouring of creative literature in the second half of the nineteenth century, in poetry, novels, and especially verse dramas, and at least one ballet–pantomime, for the theatre (Simon 1989:74–80). These stage performances would no doubt have provided yet another opportunity for the public acceptance of the image of the ancient Gaul, now brought alive in theatrical re-enactment.

The proliferation of these various modes of representing the image of the ancient Gaulish warrior cannot, of course, be separated from the social and political context of France in the middle and later years of the nineteenth century. Their success was dependent on developments of that period, without which their impact would have been severely restricted or even impossible. Foremost among these was the rising standard of education and literacy, which allowed the commercial success of illustrated popular histories, as well as the publication of more scholarly texts of limited appeal. The state's promotion of education was also the occasion for the mass production of text books and pictures. Another important factor was the increase in the available leisure time which people were able to devote to the enjoyment of spectacles such as the annual artistic Salon and the Universal Expositions. A total of 48,000,000 visitors are reported to have seen the displays at the Paris Exposition of 1900, where Bartholdi's equestrian statue of Vercingétorix, later to be installed in Clermont-Ferrand, was on show.

As well as such social factors, recent technological innovations also played an important part. The rapid development of faster and cheaper methods of printing, particularly for the reproduction of graphic images, was essential for the easy dissemination of these ideas, in books, newspapers, pictures, and postcards. The latter were also an outcome of the organization of an efficient postal service, and this, together with the growth of the railway system in the 1850s and 1860s played a critical role in the rapid spread of ideas and the potential for people to travel to see the great spectacles of the time, whether public statues, museums and galleries, or the huge universal exhibitions.

THE LEGACY

The image of the Gaulish warrior thus created and projected, and of Vercingétorix in particular, took shape in the very specific historical context of the 1860s and 1870s, and drew part of its power from its historical authenticity and the apparent accuracy of its archaeological detail. The meanings attached to these images, and their importance for the national myths being worked and reworked in those decades, were clearly also specific to those historical episodes. The images were indeed sufficiently flexible for their meanings to be subtly revised with the glory and collapse of the Second Empire, the defeat by the Prussians, the Paris Commune, the establishment of the Third Republic, and the changeable politics of the 1870s. The myths, however, and the images which helped to give them their ideological force, lived on into later years, when the specific nuances of the time of their origin had long since faded. The statues and monuments in the public squares and the paintings in the civic museums were a physical legacy of that time and a permanent reminder of the values they enshrined. School books and popular histories helped to imprint a lasting image. As we have seen, the production of these images continued to the end of the century, as in the case of Didier's painting of the *Chef gaulois*, and new sculpture on this theme was being exhibited at least up to 1914 (Pingeot 1982); the anachronistic images persisted despite the much surer foundation of archaeological knowledge available by then. The importance of Vercingétorix as a symbol of French independence continued to be adapted to the needs of later generations (Simon 1989:94–139). It was no coincidence that a number of the public statues of Gauls were destroyed in the Second World War, including three of Vercingétorix himself (Pingeot 1982:262). Even today we can find the Gaulish warrior with the winged helmet reincarnated in a modern hero of French independence, Asterix.

But the power of the image was not confined to its role in the wider cultural sphere of French political and intellectual life; nor was the relationship of archaeology to that wider sphere a simple one, with ideas passing in one direction only to provide the scholarly underpinning for a social or political ideology. On the contrary, the image was powerful enough, and so all-pervasive, that it came in turn to influence the narrower field of archaeology and to shape the way in which the Iron Age has been perceived.

At one level, its effect was to reinforce the vision of the pre-Roman Celts as warriors, and to reassert the importance of weapons and armour as an important focus of archaeological research. It has, of course, not been the only theme of research, and others such as the study of art and ornament have been given great importance, but a concern for these subjects and a series of research publications, especially on swords and helmets, has been a notable feature of more recent work. Arms and armour have also played a major role in a series of exhibitions of Celtic art and archaeology, and in the accompanying catalogues, which have been promoted in recent years.

More specifically, the image itself has proved persistent, not only in non-archaeological genres such as the Asterix strip cartoons, but also in the archaeological sphere. We can, for instance, follow its effect in England. Towards the end of the eighteenth century, the Celts of pre-Roman Britain enjoyed a comparatively favourable coverage in the ideology of the nation. Heroic individuals, especially leaders of the opposition to Rome such as Boudicca, were regular subjects of pictorial representation in various Romantic guises with little pretence at archaeological accuracy; Caratacus was shown in chains before the Emperor Claudius in an iconographic precursor of the scenes of the surrender of

Vercingétorix (Smiles 1994:129–64). In the nineteenth century, such sympathetic treatment disappears and images are much rarer; attitudes to the Celts had changed, perhaps influenced by prevailing concepts of race and contemporary problems with Ireland, and national ideology was obsessed with imperial ambitions to rival Rome and an Anglo-Saxon origin for English institutions. Mid-century images such as those produced in France were rare; the splendid statue of Caratacus from 1856 by Foley (Smiles 1994:Plate 81), reminiscent of the more Romantic of the standing warriors of French art, stands out for its very rarity.

When images of the pre-Roman Celts begin to reappear in the twentieth century, they are predominantly derived from the Gaulish warrior type. Alternative sources of inspiration were available by then. British archaeologists had begun to excavate settlement sites, which produced a very different set of objects from the weapons and ornaments that dominated the burials that formed the main focus of attention on the continent. The excavation of the so-called 'lake-village' at Glastonbury, with its remarkable preservation of organic material, played a central role in establishing the potential of such settlement excavations and in shaping ideas about domestic life in the period (Coles and Minnitt 1995). Early reports of the work were illustrated with some remarkable drawings by A. Forestier; some are reproduced by Coles and Minnitt (1995:e.g. Figs 1.5, 1.6, 7.3, 8.3, 8.12), and show scenes of domestic architecture, house interiors, and everyday life. However, in one illustration (Coles and Minnitt 1995:Fig. 8.4), the causeway is dominated by a group of warriors straight out of nineteenth-century France. Indeed, the central figure, standing in typical pose with spear, sword, breastplate, and Italian crested helmet, could almost have been inspired directly by Didier's painting of 1896. Thereafter, the warrior figure recurs regularly. In a popular and widely read and reprinted book, *Everyday life in the New Stone, Bronze and Early Iron Ages* (Quennell and Quennell 1922), domestic scenes derived from or inspired by Glastonbury were certainly used, but alongside versions of the warrior (e.g. Figs 1 and 56).

Perhaps the most striking re-embodiment of the Gaulish warrior has been in the life-size model of a Celt made for the Museum of the Iron Age at Andover in southern England (Fitzpatrick 1995:Fig.16.4). He stands with his spear, gazing at the horizon like many before him; although the individual items with which he is fitted out are all now authentically of the Iron Age, they are drawn eclectically from an impossibly wide chronological and geographical range, like many of his nineteenth-century predecessors in France. The authentic Celt, equipped with all the gear that a true warrior ought to have, has triumphed again.

REFERENCES

Andreae, B. 1991. 'The image of the Celts in Etruscan, Greek and Roman art.' In V. Kruta, O.H. Frey, B. Raftery, and M. Szabo (eds), *The Celts*, pp. 61–9. London: Thames and Hudson.

Bertin, D. and Guillaumet, J.-P. 1987. *Bibracte: une ville gauloise sur le mont Beuvray*. Paris: Ministère de la culture et de la communication.

Brunaux, J.L. 1988. *The Celtic Gauls: Gods, Rites and Sanctuaries*. London: Seaby.

Cannadine, D. 1983. 'The context, performance and meaning of ritual: the British monarchy and the "invention of tradition", *c.*1820–1977.' In E. Hobsbawm and T. Ranger (eds), *The Invention of Tradition*, pp. 101–65. Cambridge: Cambridge University Press.

Coles, J. and Minnitt, S. 1995. *'Industrious and Fairly Civilized': the Glastonbury Lake Village*. Taunton: Somerset Levels Project and Somerset County Council Museums Service.

Eluère, C. 1993. *The Celts: First Masters of Europe*. London: Thames and Hudson.

Fitzpatrick, A.P. 1995. '"Celtic" Iron Age Europe: the theoretical basis.' In P. Graves-Brown, S. Jones, and C. Gamble (eds), *Cultural Identity and Archaeology: the Construction of European Communities*, pp. 238–55. London: Routledge.

Guerrier, J. 1982. 'L'imagerie des Gaulois à Sens.' In P. Viallaneix and J. Ehrard (eds), *Nos ancêtres les Gaulois*, pp. 283–94. Clermont-Ferrand: Faculté des Lettres et Sciences Humaines de l'Université de Clermont-Ferrand II.

Guizot, F. 1872. *L'Histoire de France depuis les temps les plus reculés jusqu'en 1789*. Paris: Hachette.

Meyrick, S.R. and Smith, C.H. 1815. *The Costume of the Original Inhabitants of the British Islands*. London: Havell.

Piggott, S. 1975. *The Druids*. London: Thames and Hudson.

Piggott, S. 1989. *Ancient Britons and the Antiquarian Imagination: Ideas from the Renaissance to the Regency*. London: Thames and Hudson.

Pingeot, A. 1982. 'Les Gaulois sculptés (1850–1914).' In P. Viallaneix and J. Ehrard (eds), *Nos ancêtres les Gaulois*, pp. 255–82. Clermont-Ferrand: Faculté des Lettres et Sciences Humaines de l'Université de Clermont-Ferrand II.

Quennell, M. and Quennell, C.H.B. 1922. *Everyday Life in the New Stone, Bronze and Early Iron Ages*. London: Batsford.

Read, B. 1982. *Victorian Sculpture*. London: Yale University Press.

Simon, A. 1989. *Vercingétorix et l'idéologie française*. Paris: Imago.

Smiles, S. 1994. *The Image of Antiquity: Ancient Britain and the Romantic Imagination*. London: Yale University Press.

Viallaneix, P. and Ehrard, J. (eds) 1982. *Nos ancêtres les Gaulois*. Clermont-Ferrand: Faculté des Lettres et Sciences Humaines de l'Université de Clermont-Ferrand II.

CHAPTER ELEVEN

FOCUSING ON THE PAST

Visual and textual images of Aboriginal Australia in museums

LYNETTE RUSSELL

INTRODUCTION

Before the first contact with Europeans, Aboriginal people in Australia had a consistent mode of production coupled with enormous variation in most other aspects of society. Through more than a hundred years of research, however, scholars have constructed a collective ethnographical entity called the 'Australian Aborigine' (Attwood 1989; Reece 1987). This construct first relied on ideas of race and racist doctrines formulated in the nineteenth century (see Stocking 1968); more recently, prehistoric archaeology and material culture studies have supplied the necessary technological evidence.

European representations of Aborigines, in texts and images, popular and scholarly, have always conveyed a sense that Aborigines are the same across the continent and have changed little through millennia – that they are relics of an ancient time. Today, however, the struggle of indigenous people for control of their own culture, as seen in claims for lost tribal lands, the repatriation of museum objects, and the objection to the display of sacred objects and images, has caused a substantial shift in the way indigenous and non–indigenous communities represent Aboriginal culture. Aborigines often reject previous representations, especially those the white community have offered, as part of their attempts to de-hegemonize established power structures. Contemporary indigenous people may even reject the collective term 'Aborigine' in favour of a specific group name or a more collective term, such as 'Koorie', which is used in the southeast (see Fesl 1990).

In this chapter I will explore a range of museum and catalogue images of Aborigines. I am concerned with how and to what extent the textual and iconographic descriptions of indigenous people have been instrumental in their subjugation and colonization, how they have in effect become a forgotten people, timelocked in the past where they remain repressed and undeveloped (cf. Berkhofer 1979). At the same time, I shall examine the ways that Aboriginal people have used texts and images to provide alternative views of the past more consistent with their culture and current aims. In place of the old-fashioned European concept of 'Aborigines', the contemporary Koorie community has developed a new style of representation using information from prehistoric archaeology to support its views of the ancient past – this is ironic, as Koorie people have also at the same time criticized archaeology for its disturbance of Aboriginal sites and general intervention in Aboriginal life (e.g. Langford 1983, Marrie 1989). This discussion will therefore expose the historical and situational aspects of representations of Aborigines in Australia.

INVENTING THE OTHER

The English sailor William Dampier described the indigenous Australians as the 'Miserablest People in the World' (Dampier 1697:312). He coined the phrase 'antipodean ignoble savages' and regarded them as not only materially and culturally impoverished but also unenterprising and incapable of advancement. Dampier set the scene for generations of observers to see indigenous Australians as one of the earliest forms of humanity, little changed since the dawn of time. Captain James Cook's often quoted musing on the state of the original Australians' happiness and sense of 'Tranquillity . . . [in their] pure state of nature' (quoted in Beaglehole 1955:357) added an element of Rousseau-like nobility to Dampier's primitive image. Aborigines became noble savages, yet they remained unchanged and unenterprising.

Throughout the colonial history of Australia, academic and popular representations of the indigenous Australians wavered between these noble and ignoble constructions, with their assumptions of homogeneity in time and space. Early observers emphasized the antiquity and primitivism of Australian Aboriginal culture. David Collins, in the first fleet of colonists, described how Aborigines of the Sydney district exploited their land to acquire food. Their rudimentary existence, as he described it, was an important marker of their place as the most primitive of 'all mankind' (Collins 1798–1802:460). Ironically, little has changed since. Australia's best known historian, Manning Clark, in the first volume of his work *A History of Australia*, observed that the primitivism of Aborigines ensured that they were socially passive and subject to the whims of nature (Clark 1962:3). Such notions have 'rarely been absent from constructions of Aboriginality, whether popular or official' (Becket 1988:194).

Constructing and representing 'the other' as primitive has been an important concern of European colonial discourse. Said (1978,1993) argues that the concept of 'primitive' is a construct of European colonial encounters and that Western society, scholarship in particular, has contrived a homogeneous, inferior, and oppositional view of indigenous cultures. Within his specific field, orientalism, such representations have relied on notions of 'unimaginable antiquity . . . [and] boundless distance' (Said 1978:167). This focus on the imagined space and time occupied by the 'other' is central to my reading of Australian museum representations and archaeology. Timelessness and spatial sameness have been constant referents in these materials, whether the portrayals emphasized the 'native' as noble or ignoble, savage or brute. Their use is an inherently political act, condemning colonized peoples to the timeless fringes, the edges of history (Fabian 1983:85–7).

The relationship between representations of indigenous people, expressions of time, and archaeology is a complex one. Bruce Trigger (1980,1984,1985,1986) argues that colonial archaeology and culture history aimed 'to denigrate native societies and peoples by trying to demonstrate that they had been static in prehistoric times and lacked the initiative to develop on their own' (Trigger 1984:362; see also McGuire 1992). The situation in Australia is, however, more subtle than this. The first archaeological study of Australia's past was conducted in the first years of the colony (Mulvaney 1961:56) and yet it was more than one hundred years before the academic establishment treated archaeology as a legitimate exercise. They clearly thought that research into Aboriginal Australia was fruitless because the Aborigines showed so little evidence of 'progress'. As anthropologist Baldwin Spencer put it:

> So far, no fossil remains of man have been discovered in Australasia; but there is no need to seek there for fossil forms. Ancient and primitive man still survive – more primitive than any fossil form of modern man yet found in Europe.
>
> (Spencer 1921:29)

This neglect of archaeological research is ironic, as there was widespread interest at the time in both the antiquity and origins of the Aborigines. But scholars sought answers to these questions through affinity studies of indigenous languages and social systems rather than through archaeology and material culture studies (McBryde 1986:13). Their images and texts were therefore based on ethnographic observations that both minimized cultural differences and emphasized temporal and spatial homogeneity. As archaeologists were not (yet) interested in research, Aboriginal material culture was simply collected and exhibited in Australian museums.

The legacy of this approach is an enduring impression of Aborigines in museum displays and texts as a people defined through ethnographic and – later – archaeological research, responding ultimately to Western, as opposed to Aboriginal, sentiments and sensibilities.

MUSEUM TEXTS AND DISPLAYS, PAST AND PRESENT

Beginning in the early colonial period, museum displays pictured Aborigines as pristine, noble savages little changed through time. Such images were geographically restricted: colonization and dispossession ensured that no 'pure' Aborigines remained in the south and east of the country. Aborigines were also a people without a history, in spite of the frequent appeals in museum texts to the great antiquity of Aboriginal culture. The past was merely the ethnographic present endlessly revisited in static glass cases. Virtually all the material displayed came from anthropological or ethnographic contexts but, ironically from today's perspective, Aboriginal people were not consulted or acknowledged as having a legitimate claim to question such representations. Real Aborigines could only exist in the past; after contact they became hybridized and, hence, inauthentic. Consultation was therefore an irrelevancy.

A leading figure in the development of these and other ideas about the Aborigines was W. Baldwin Spencer, the Director of the National Museum of Victoria (hereafter the Museum) in Melbourne (Fig. 11.1) from 1899 until his death in 1929. With F.J. Gillen, a central Australian postmaster, Spencer conducted field work and research over thirty years, documenting the Arunta and several other central Australian tribes in popular and academic publications (Spencer 1928; Spencer and Gillen 1899,1904,1927). In 1901 Spencer wrote Australia's first ethnographic exhibition catalogue for the Museum, the *Guide to The Australian Ethnographical Collection in The National Museum of Victoria*. This was a significant event within the history of Australian Aboriginal studies; it took over half a century before another museum prepared an exhibition catalogue (Mulvaney 1961:63). The structure of Spencer's original and subsequent catalogues (Spencer 1901,1915,1922) serves as an interesting template for the way that scholars in general perceived, represented, and constructed Aboriginal people.

The *Guide* displays Spencer's strong belief in a typological framework, based on an assumption of linear social evolution, that placed the indigenous Australians on the lowest rung. The antiquity of the Aborigines was never questioned. Spencer argued that

> The Australian aborigines [sic] are regarded as belonging to one of the most primitive of existing races. They are true savages, living by fishing and hunting, never cultivating the land over which they roam, nor domesticating animals. How far the fact that . . . there are no animals useful for domestic purposes in Australia has been an element in retarding the development of the race is impossible to say.

> (Spencer 1901:7)

He also considered their 'primitive' state pristine, and not showing any signs of having deteriorated; their retarded development was due to environmental influences and low population numbers:

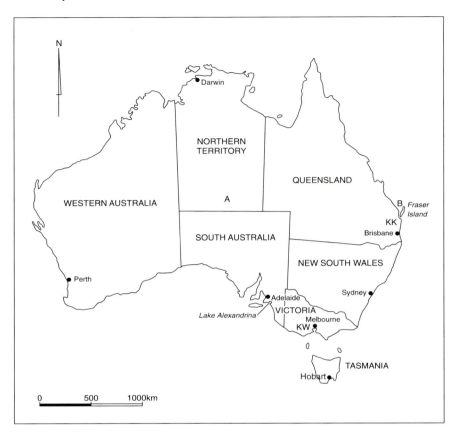

Figure 11.1 A map of Australia indicating locations mentioned in the text. Legend A = Arunta, B = Badtjala, KK = Kabi Kabi, K = Kerrup-Jmara and W = Wurundjeri.

> The Australian aborigines may be regarded as a relic of the early childhood of mankind left stranded in a part of the world where he has without the impetus derived from competition, remained in a low condition of savagery; there is not the slightest evidence either in his customs, social organization, weapons or implements to show that he has retrograded from a higher state of civilization.
>
> (Spencer 1901:12)

Spencer also assumed that Aboriginal culture was spatially homogeneous. He stated, for example, that social organization was essentially the same across the continent (Spencer 1901:9). But his position was inconsistent when it came to material culture. He wrote, for example, that the returning boomerang was absent from 'large areas of the continent' (Spencer 1901:11).

Figure 11.2   The 'Native Camp Scene' diorama from the Museum of Victoria, ethnological gallery 1915 (published in Spencer 1922). Reproduced with permission of the National Museum of Victoria.

Spencer's lifesize reconstruction of a 'Native Camp Scene' (Fig. 11.2), set up in 1915, shows how the Museum conveyed this temporal and spatial homogeneity to the public. The diorama, representing a habitation site occupied by four adults and an infant, claimed to show a typical view of 'traditional' pre-European camp life across the continent – but it was actually designed with information from the ethnographic present. The exhibit also used a hodgepodge of cultural material from various groups: the shelter, shields, canoe, boomerang, and possum cloak were from South Australian (especially Lake Alexandrina) and Victorian people and representing the rest of Australia were a spear and headband from central Australia (Spencer 1915).

The interpretive texts exacerbated the confusion, as these came from Spencer's fieldwork among the Arunta of central Australia. This material did not convey any sense of change or history – and yet appealed to the notion that the culture was extremely old. Spencer wrote that it was the camp site of a people who had 'not reached the agricultural stage of civilization' (Spencer 1922:136), people who a year earlier he had described as a 'fossil form' of modern humanity (Spencer 1921:29).

The spatial organization and content of the Museum itself virtually guaranteed that visitors would pick up the generalized ideas of the 'Native Camp Scene' and attach them to a specific cultural group. The diorama was literally surrounded by over ninety cases of artifacts, most from the region inhabited by the Arunta in Central Australia. The Arunta also supplied the ethnographic information for other representations of Aboriginal Australians within the Museum.

Together the diorama and display cases provided the model for all representations of Australia's native people. The impression was that indigenous people were noble, and worthy of display, but lacked specific homelands and settlements and seemed to live in an ageless world. The only pretence to historical depth was the notion that over time, a generalized Central Australian culture had emerged as the quintessential Aboriginal culture, representing the end point in the history of the Australian continent prior to European colonization.

Spencer's bias towards the ethnographic present and the exclusion of a sense of history clearly influenced the Museum's presentations, but such ideas were widespread. The Australian Museum in Sydney represented Aborigines in a similar way in 'The Aboriginal Culture Exhibition'. This was a long-running display, co-sponsored by the Australian National Committee for UNESCO, that was developed between 1949 and 1953 and sent on the road to the United States and Canada, returning to Australia in mid-1957 (McCarthy 1965:1).

The display was accompanied by a brochure entitled *Australian Aboriginal Culture*, written by F.D. McCarthy, Curator of Anthropology at the Australian Museum and an experienced archaeologist. The brochure pointed out that indigenous Australians were a diverse group of peoples, and indeed, a key feature of the display was a map of six hundred and eighty ethnographically observed 'tribes' – although fewer than ten of them were named. But despite this vast range of social groups, the exhibition – like Spencer's diorama – used central Australian images to represent them all. This bias is shown in the photographs surrounding the tribal map (Fig. 11.3). One shows a man, identified as a central Australian, decorated for a ritual; another portrays a woman carrying a bowl on her head and a child on her hip, identified as 'The water carrier, central Australia'; and a third shows a group of men from the northern central region.

McCarthy and the UNESCO exhibition also emphasized that Aborigines were largely the same across time and space. The promotion of this static model was surprising, as McCarthy had excavated archaeological sites such as Lapstone Creek (McCarthy 1948) that had evidence of chronological changes and distinct culture phases (McCarthy 1948:28–31). Despite archaeological indications of dynamic change in Aboriginal cultures, McCarthy chose to show the past in light of judgements and assumptions made about the (ethnographic) present.

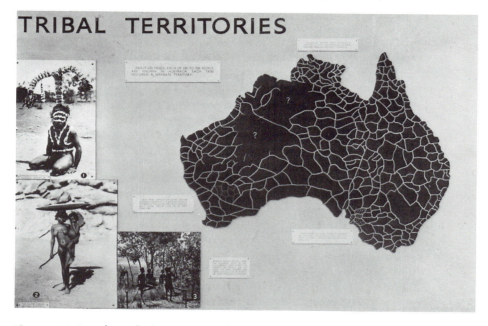

Figure 11.3 The tribal territories display, UNESCO exhibition from the 1940s and 1950s. Reproduced with permission of the Australian National Commission for UNESCO.

During the 1950s the UNESCO exhibition continued to represent Australian Aboriginal culture in a manner established by Spencer more than forty years earlier. These outmoded depictions of an Aboriginal culture frozen in time and space were consumed by an even larger audience through the UNESCO booklet *Australian Aboriginal Culture*. It circulated widely, was re-published in 1953 and revised with some changes in content by an anthropologist, Robert Edwards. The impact of this document was considerable: by 1973, more than one hundred thousand copies had been sold.

By the end of the 1970s, however, such museum fantasies began to conflict with the Aboriginal reality. When Spencer and McCarthy produced their exhibitions, no-one consulted contemporary Aboriginal people about their own pasts. Archaeologists and anthropologists regarded them as inauthentic because contact with Europeans corrupted their genetic, cultural, and material heritage. Because museum displays misrepresented Aborigines by relegating them to a generalized, sterile past, it is not surprising that such installations have become sites of contention for contemporary indigenous researchers and activists.

Since museums in Australia – and around the world – entered the debate over the ownership and control of ethnographic objects and information (e.g. Terrell 1993, Clifford 1988) museum protocol has changed significantly. Museums now routinely consider indigenous views through the hiring of indigenous permanent staff or by liaising with relevant groups. At the Victorian Museum, for example, three Aboriginal curators are responsible for the ethnographic section and display, negotiating with specific Koorie communities over the storage, handling, and display of their material culture.

Archaeologists are now being criticized for their lack of consultation with indigenous communities, from within the profession (e.g. Layton 1989) and by indigenous commentators. This problem has been a factor in the escalating demands by Aboriginal groups for the return of archaeological material. Although the archaeological community's reaction has perhaps been slower than that of the museum community, changes in procedure are taking place.

In response to the need for a more accurate picture of Aboriginal culture, the Commonwealth Government of Australia issued a third edition of the UNESCO booklet, still under McCarthy's original title of *Australian Aboriginal Culture*, in 1989. An indigenous scholar, Marji Hill, wrote this revised edition (reprinted in 1991 and 1993) (Hill 1989:v). Through personal contacts and community involvement Hill sought and incorporated the views of contemporary Aboriginal people, and she made significant editorial and structural alterations in line with contemporary Aboriginal and Western thinking.

She avoids value-laden terminology, for example, replacing gender-specific designations and stereotypes such as 'man the hunter' with a more balanced view – pointing out that women occasionally catch 'small animals and reptiles' (Hill 1989:38). She likewise amends visual representations to include images such as men caring for children (Hill 1989:37). And she replaces the traditional term in Australian history for the coming of Europeans, colonization, with a term appropriate to the Aboriginal perspective: 'invasion'. The most significant changes, however, concern the representation of past and present Aboriginal culture. Hill's treatment is markedly different from the versions presented in the first and second editions of the booklet and in Spencer's and McCarthy's museum displays and accompanying catalogues, in that she emphasizes change, progress, and development.

Hill writes that the dynamic nature of the relationships between the indigenous occupants and their land was a constant factor in the images of Aboriginal life in the pre-European contact period. She first points out that in the forty to fifty thousand years of Australian history, Aboriginal culture survived and adapted to changes in climate and sea level (Hill 1989:3). Then she uses archaeological evidence to suggest that significant changes in economic, social, and trading relations had taken place in Aboriginal society approximately five hundred years before the arrival of the Europeans – seeming to imply that the Aborigines were moving toward incipient farming and sedentism. Although the text does not acknowledge the archaeological work of Harry Lourandos, the arguments draw upon his research (e.g. Lourandos 1977,1980,1983,1987, 1988). Lourandos suggests that radical changes, which he terms intensification, took place in Aboriginal society prior to contact with Europeans: increases in population, sedentism, inter-regional alliance networks, and large scale ceremonial gatherings. This hypothesis deliberately challenges the traditional stereotypical view of a static pre-contact period, replacing it with a model of long term and short term trends – each having local, regional, and general applications (Lourandos 1993:80).

Despite the gestures towards political correctness, and the desire to show Aboriginal Australia as a dynamic and fluid entity, however, the latest edition of *Australian Aboriginal Culture* promotes a view of traditional Aboriginal culture that differs little in orientation from the views promoted in the Spencer and McCarthy catalogues. The problem is that the indigenous community has uncritically adopted Lourandos' reasonable model of dynamic changes in the pre-contact period because it is suggestive of progress – in an explicit attempt to demonstrate that Aboriginal society was more 'advanced' than previously thought. In effect, Hill and other Aboriginal writers are using these findings to slot indigenous culture into a structure predicated on European constructed markers of social development.

Hill's approach in the 1989 *Australian Aboriginal Culture* pamphlet does not engage with the contemporary debate over whether or not such measures are appropriate for comparing and judging cultures. It merely reinvents traditional Aboriginal society and, by characterizing sedentism as a progressive step, locks it into nineteenth-century social evolutionist precepts of progress and linear, hierarchical development. The result is that the indigenous community is actually promoting an idealistic, outmoded set of notions now commonly associated in Western scholarship with racism.

It is clear that for the most part Western representations of indigenous Australians have emphasized the temporal and spatial states described in the traditional homogeneity paradigm. Input from contemporary Koories, as in the pamphlet *Australian Aboriginal Culture*, has altered the image, but rather than attempting to de-hegemonize the previous representations, indigenous scholars have appropriated Western scholarship and reiterated its fundamental historicist tenets.

The influence of traditional museum structures and ideas of the Aboriginal past on the contemporary indigenous community is evident in museum displays that Koories have themselves created.

AN ABORIGINAL-DESIGNED MUSEUM EXHIBITION

In December 1988 an exhibition entitled *Koorie* opened at the Museum of Victoria. It was designed by the Koorie Heritage Trust, an independent autonomous body of contemporary Aboriginal people that operates within the Museum's building. *Koorie* was 'devoted to over 40,000 years of Aboriginal cultural heritage in south-eastern Australia' (Koorie Heritage Trust 1991:n.p.), using dioramas, information boards, and display cases to present an Aboriginal view of the past and so challenge the received Western notions of Aboriginal life.

Koorie is a remarkable example of how difficult and challenging indigenous self-representation can be. The display blended information from anthropology, archaeology, oral history, and documentary history in order to demonstrate the continuity between past and contemporary Aboriginal culture in Victoria. In the traditional section several large poster boards covered topics such as religion, social life, health, and healing. Nineteenth-century images included photographs and texts on life at government mission stations. A stark map represented violence between colonists and Aborigines, showing sixty-eight massacre sites. And there was a display of the artworks of William Barak, a Wurundjeri elder, using Western paints and canvas. The section dealing with contemporary Aboriginal society showed Koorie business ventures, arts and crafts, nutrition, and health problems.

In using such information, however, *Koorie* perpetuated the stereotypes that it was intended to overcome. An image painted in the 1870s portraying the resolution of a dispute, for example, conveys the classic image of the noble savage, with an Edenic background, lush foliage, and a muscular warrior (Fig. 11.4). Unfortunately, nineteenth-century iconography such as this compels the viewer to infer that contact images are valid models for depicting Aboriginal life in prehistory. Paradoxically, in an attempt to historicize – and idealize – Aboriginal occupation, such images purvey the timelessness of Rousseau's noble savage, resurrected and transported into Australia's deep past.

In addition, the attempt by Aboriginal people in the *Koorie* exhibition to challenge the stereotypical view of their people as nomadic, desert dwellers resulted in a replication of Western stereotypes – as in Hill's (1989) third edition of the *Australian Aboriginal Culture* booklet. In place of images of mobile hunter–gatherers, these representations showed Aboriginal groups as semi-sedentary, leading a complex hunting–gathering lifestyle centred on the cultivation of the land through fire-stick farming. A model of one of these 'villages', reconstructed as a diorama display, focuses on male activities, including a number of men fishing at eel traps (Fig. 11.5). Women are simply pictures in the painted background, caring for children. A leisurely life is implied; although it is clearly day, numerous adults sit and talk together and an adult sleeps

Figure 11.4   A painting from the 1870s used in the Koorie exhibition at the Museum of Victoria as an example of traditional dispute resolution. Reproduced with permission of the Mitchell library, State Library of South Wales.

inside one of the huts in the foreground. The impression given is that the basalt plains of the Victorian western districts, home to the Kerrup–Jmara people, were 'villages of several hundred people for long periods of time' (Koorie Heritage Trust 1991:8).

Archaeologists in the region do not dispute the possibility that there were in fact villages housing substantial numbers of people possibly for short periods of time (Clarke 1994), but they do challenge the Aboriginal notion that they occupied such villages permanently prior to European contact. Frankel (1991:92–3) suggests that these houses were a post-contact phenomenon resulting from the Kerrup–Jmara being forced onto the basalt plains area. Another recent interpretation (Clarke 1994) suggests that these houses were at best transiently occupied in the pre-contact period. Significantly, the *Koorie* exhibition ignored these alternative interpretations.

By presenting the 'village' representation, however, the *Koorie* exhibition implied that traditional Aboriginal society conformed to the European constructed concepts of complexity and sedentism. This was

Figure 11.5 The Kerrup-Jmara village diorama, Koorie exhibition. Reproduced with the permission of Mr J. Berg of the Koorie Heritage Trust.

the greatest irony: in order to debunk the myths associated with popular stereotypical Aboriginal images, the Aborigines who developed *Koorie* played into the framework established and controlled through Western institutions. In attempting to document the diversity and complexity of pre-contact Aboriginal culture, the *Koorie* exhibition merely reconfirmed European notions of social progress and social evolution, touting sedentism and village life as markers of social progress. The result was a reduction of the complexity of the pre-contact Aboriginal society to a form immediately identifiable by a late twentieth-century audience.

The Hill pamphlet and the *Koorie* exhibition both illustrate that contemporary Aboriginal people working within the institutional structures of government departments and museums are handicapped in their attempts to challenge hegemonic practices. By and large their attempts to interact with and usurp the power structure result in little change in representational style. Authorized representations of Aboriginal Australia as found in museums and government publications are images (visual and textual) in which the native artisan is both subject of study and subject person. Substituting Koorie curators therefore fails to overturn the oppression of colonial instrumentalities: the presence of these Aborigines simply reinforces the place of the museum as part of the colonial power structure – a place where Aboriginal people are institutionalized as research objects and workers (cf. Molyneaux 1994:8). The problem is structure, not personnel.

What, then, is the effect of these Western notions of history and development on the way that Aborigines represent themselves when they are outside the ideological influence of museums and other governmental institutions?

CORPORATE SYMBOLISM: ABORIGINES REPRESENT THEMSELVES

The examples of the third edition of *Australian Aboriginal Culture* (Hill 1989) and *Koorie*, the museum exhibition, indicate that the social and political agendas at work in the representation of the Aboriginal past are highly complex. On the one hand, Aborigines reject the depictions of the past contained in traditional archaeology and anthropology, as expressed in Western museum texts and installations, and on the other, they include archaeological information in their cultural representations – however uncritically – because they rightly and reasonably accept that it contributes to an understanding of the time before European settlement (see Aldred 1993 for parallels in representations of and by the Waccamaw–Siouan peoples of North America). This strategic use of Western and Aboriginal symbolism is clearly evident in the symbols that contemporary Aboriginal corporations choose to signify their social groups (or corporate identities) (Fig. 11.6).

The corporate logo of the Kabi Kabi Aboriginal Corporation, for example, depicts two popular signifiers of Aboriginal Australia: the black silhouette of a hunter, standing on the arch of a boomerang. The image of a dusty hunter perched on one leg (usually) wistfully gazing out across the panorama has been endlessly reproduced in popular journal, magazine, and film representations (and see Fig. 11.3) and the boomerang is one of the global symbols of Australia. This logo therefore represents the deliberate use of an image that the non-Aboriginal community recognize as distinctively Aboriginal.

The logo on the letterhead of the Tasmanian Aboriginal Land Council, an abalone shell and mutton birds, asserts the integrity of past and present culture – a response to the once popular notion that Tasmanian Aborigines were extinct. The design seems traditional, or at least emphasizes traditional activities, as both shellfish and birds were resources exploited prior to European contact. It seems odd that such prehistoric resources would be depicted, however, for archaeological evidence shows that numerous terrestrial mammals probably formed a much more important aspect of the traditional economy than either the abalone or mutton birds (e.g. Jones 1971). During the post-contact period, however, these items were staple food-stuffs and are still collected today by islanders (Bass Strait) and Tasmanian Aborigines alike (D. West personal

Tasmanian Aboriginal Land Council
Aboriginal Corporation

Thoorgine Educational & Culture Centre

Figure 11.6 Letterheads from the Kabi Kabi Aboriginal Corporation, the Tasmanian Aboriginal Land Council, and the Thoorgine Educational and Cultural Centre.

communication 1992). They represent, therefore, a tangible link between past and present indigenous Tasmanians.

The letterhead of the Thoorgine Educational and Culture Centre, established in 1986 by the Badtjala people on Fraser Island, emphasizes a similar link between past and present. The logo is a black and white circular motif enclosing a black silhouette map of Fraser Island (with fish on the left) encircled by shells. These shells, which the Badtjala call *wongs*, represent the numerous shell middens found along the east coast of the island. The letterhead explicitly promotes what, in other contexts, would be a highly controversial image of the past: a vision of past life-ways using the evidence of archaeological sites.

The intentional use by Aborigines of archaeological information for their corporate symbolism indicates that archaeology continues to play an important role in their ideas of the past – but here, a role that the Aborigines themselves determine, as they respond to the shifting demands of their political and economic situation.

CONCLUSION

The analysis of representations of Aboriginal Australia in museum displays and texts allows us to develop insights into the role of representations and the communication of ideas about the past as expressed within specific political and social agendas. Such images are invariably conservative (see Lutz and Collins 1993) and tend toward confirmation of complacent and frequently self-congratulatory hegemonies.

I have identified two general phases of Australian Aboriginal museum representations. Western scholars developed the first of these as the colony and nation developed. Australian settlers did not see the indigenous people as providing valuable labour sources or mercantile expertise (as in India); instead, Aborigines were an impediment to progress. Within this sociopolitical milieu, the indigenous Australians came to be represented as 'the other': timeless, stateless, childlike, and primitive. Museums sealed their traditional culture in glass cases without the benefit of archaeological or historical information. The second phase consists of representations produced by (or in conjunction with) contemporary Koorie people. These representations make direct appeals to the authority of archaeological research only when Aborigines see that it provides a more positive and dynamic interpretation of their past.

Both types of representation have assumed continuity with the pre-European contact population and contemporary Aboriginal people. They have done this, however, in very different ways. The images of Aboriginal Australia constructed by Western authors moved from the perpetuation of racial stereotypes to a reliance on empirical data from archaeological sites, while maintaining the restrained attitudes of Western science; Koorie-constructed representations are more explicitly political, accenting the relationships between past and present indigenous peoples regardless of the scientific reliability of archaeological or ethnographic evidence.

Archaeological information, sites, and insights into past Aboriginal lifeways are now commonly included in representations produced by contemporary Aborigines. This information endures, in spite of the controversies surrounding archaeological practice in general, because it promotes urban Koories as legitimate inheritors of an archaeologically determined legacy – the use of which has become an essential aspect in eliminating the hegemony of Western representations and therefore securing authenticity for a self-determined Aboriginal past.

ACKNOWLEDGMENTS

I would like to thank Patrick Wolfe and Ian McNiven for critical comments; also Clive Gamble for encouraging the contribution and Brian Molyneaux for the opportunity.

REFERENCES

Aldred, L. 1993. 'No more cigar store Indians: ethnographic and historical representation by and of the Waccamaw–Siouan peoples and their socio-economic, legal and political consequences.' *Dialectical Anthropology* 18:207–44.

Attwood, B. 1989. *The Making of The Aborigines*. London: Allen and Unwin.

Beaglehole, J. (ed.) 1955. *The Voyage of the Endeavour 1768–1771*. Cambridge: Cambridge University Press.

Beckett, J. 1988. 'The past in the present; the present in the past: constructing a national Aboriginality.' In J. Beckett (ed.), *Past and Present*. Canberra: Australian Institute of Aboriginal Studies.

Berkhofer, R.F. 1979. *The White Man's Indian*. New York: Vintage Books.

Clark, M. 1962. *A History of Australia, Volume 1, From Earliest Times To The Age Of Macquarie*. Melbourne: Melbourne University Press.

Clarke, A. 1994. '"Romancing the Stones": the cultural construction of an archaeological landscape in the Western District of Victoria.' *Archaeology in Oceania* 29:1–15.

Clifford, J. 1988 *The Predicament of Culture: Twentieth-Century Ethnography, Literature, and Art*. Cambridge: Harvard University Press.

Collins, D. Colonel. 1798–1802. *An Account of The English Colony of New South Wales*. Facsimile edition (1975), edited by Brian Fletcher. London: A. W. Reed.

Dampier, W. 1697. *A New Voyage Round the World*. London: Adam and Charles Black.

Fabian, J. 1983. *Time and The Other: How Anthropology Makes Its Object*. Baltimore, MD: Johns Hopkins University Press.

Fesl, E. 1990. 'How the English language is used to put Koories down and deny us our rights.' *Social Alternatives* 9(2):35–7.

Frankel, D. 1991. *Remains to be Seen: Archaeological Insights into Australian Prehistory*. Melbourne: Longman Cheshire.

Hill, M. 1989. *Australian Aboriginal Culture*. Canberra: Australian Government Printing Services. (Reprinted 1991, 1993).

Jones, R. 1971. 'Rocky Cape and the problem of the Tasmanians.' Unpublished PhD thesis, University of Sydney, Australia.

Koorie Heritage Trust 1991. *Koorie Exhibition Catalogue*. Melbourne: National Museum of Victoria and the Koorie Heritage Trust.

Langford, R. 1983. 'Our Heritage – Your Playground.' *Australian Archaeology* 16:1–6.

Layton, R. 1989. 'Introduction.' In R. Layton (ed.), *Conflict in The Archaeology of Living Traditions*, pp. 1–21. London: Unwin Hyman.

Lourandos, H. 1977. 'Aboriginal spatial organization and population: Southwestern Victoria re-considered.' *Archaeology and Physical Anthropology in Oceania* 12:202–25.

Lourandos, H. 1980. 'Change or stability? Hydraulics, hunter–gatherers and population temperate Australia.' *World Archaeology* 11:245–66.

Lourandos, H. 1983. 'Intensification: a late Pleistocene–Holocene archaeological sequence from southwestern Victoria.' *Archaeology in Oceania* 18:81–94.

Lourandos, H. 1987. 'Pleistocene Australia: peopling a continent.' In O. Soffer (ed.), *The Pleistocene Old World: Regional Perspectives*, pp. 147–65. New York: Plenum.

Lourandos, H. 1988. 'Palaeopolitics: resource intensification in Aboriginal Australia and Papua New Guinea.' In T. Ingold, D. Riches, and J. Woodburn (eds), *Hunters and Gatherers: History, Evolution and Social Change*, pp. 148–60. Oxford: Berg.

Lourandos, H. 1993. 'Hunter–gatherer cultural dynamics: long and short term trends in Australian prehistory.' *Journal of Archaeological Research* 1:67–88.

Lutz, C. and Collins, J. 1993. *Reading National Geographic*. Chicago: University of Chicago Press.

McBryde, I. 1986. 'Australia's once and future archaeology.' *Archaeology in Oceania* 21:13–18.

McCarthy, F.D. 1948. 'The Lapstone Creek excavation: two culture phases revealed in eastern New South Wales.' *Records of the Australian Museum* 22:1–34.

McCarthy, F.D. 1965. *Australian Aboriginal Culture*. Canberra: Australian Commission for UNESCO.

McGuire, R.H. 1992. 'Archaeology and the first Americans.' *American Anthropologist* 94:816–36.

Marrie, A. 1989. 'Museums and Aborigines: a case study in internal colonialism.' *Australian and Canadian Studies* 7:63–80.

Molyneaux, Brian L. 1994. 'Introduction: the represented past.' In P. Stone and B.L. Molyneaux (eds), *The Presented Past: Heritage, Museums and Education*, pp. 1–13. London and New York: Routledge.

Mulvaney, D.J. 1961. 'The Stone Age of Australia.' *The Prehistoric Society* 4:56–107.

Reece, B. 1987. 'Inventing Aborigines.' *Aboriginal History* 11:14–23.

Said, E. 1978. *Orientalism*. New York: Pantheon.

Said, E. 1993. *Culture and Imperialism*. London: Chatto and Windus.

Spencer, W.B. 1901. *Guide to The Australian Ethnographical Collection in The National Museum of Victoria*. Melbourne: Government Printer of Victoria.

Spencer, W.B. 1915. *Guide to The Australian Ethnographical Collection in The National Museum of Victoria*. Melbourne: Government Printer of Victoria.

Spencer, W.B. 1921. *Presidential Address At The 15th Australian and New Zealand Association for the Advancement of Science, Hobart/Melbourne*. Melbourne: Albert Mullet, Government Printer.

Spencer, W.B. 1922. *Guide to The Australian Ethnographical Collection in The National Museum of Victoria*. Melbourne: Government Printer of Victoria.

Spencer, W.B. 1928. *Wanderings in Wild Australia*. London: Macmillan.

Spencer, W.B. and Gillen, F. 1899. *The Native Tribes of Central Australia*. London: Macmillan.

Spencer, W.B. and Gillen, F. 1904. *The Northern Tribes of Central Australia*. London: Macmillan.

Spencer, W.B. and Gillen, F. 1927. *The Arunta*. London: Macmillan.

Stocking, G.W. 1968. *Race, Culture and Evolution*. Chicago: University of Chicago Press. [Reprinted 1982].

Terrell, J. 1993. 'We want our treasures back.' *Museums Journal* (March):34–6.

Trigger, B. 1980. 'Archaeology and the image of the American Indian.' *American Antiquity* 45:662–76.

Trigger, B. 1984. 'Alternative archaeologies: nationalist, colonialist, and imperialist.' *Man* 19:355–70.

Trigger, B. 1985. 'The past as power: anthropology and the North American Indian.' In I. McBryde (ed.), *Who Owns the Past?*, pp. 135–62. Oxford: Oxford University Press.

Trigger, B. 1986. 'Prospects for a world archaeology.' *World Archaeology* 18:1–20.

CHAPTER TWELVE

THE PAINTER AND PREHISTORIC PEOPLE

A 'hypothesis on canvas'[1]

WIKTOR STOCZKOWSKI[2]

> They found the portraits true to life, without knowing the subjects.
> G. Flaubert *Bouvard et Pécuchet*

Just as there are painters, such as Van Gogh, whose exemplary lives as artists are publicly better known than their work, so there are pictures whose popular success has eclipsed the personality of their authors, leaving them irrevocably in the shadows of obscurity. Such was the fate of Czech painter Zdenek Burian, who so loved the picturesque qualities of prehistory that he dedicated his life to painting scenes from a world long past. When the artist passed away in Prague in 1981, after a career spanning over sixty years, on the very day a new exhibition of his work was due to open in the Czech capital, he left behind him an impressive body of work, as well known as he himself was unknown.[3] Today his pictures are used to illustrate countless books throughout the world, and there can be few people who at one time or another, perhaps when flicking through a popular book as a child, have not come across one of Burian's stooped Australopithecus or powerful Neanderthal figures.

The remarkable art of this Czech painter has its devoted admirers and its sworn enemies. He has been accused of 'naturalism' and 'academicism'; equally he has been defended as being a noble example of 'imaginative realism' in the tradition of Courbet. But tastes and labels matter little. There is no doubt that Burian belonged to that group of artists for whom the creative and the scientific existed symbiotically together; his paintings, like Zola's ideal 'novel with a scientific dimension', drew their strength from science and tried to extend it. In Burian's pictures, a historian of prehistory would have no difficulty in recognizing many familiar objects: Venus figurines and clay animal statuettes from Dolni Vestonice, Montespan bears, Lascaux cave paintings, Predmostí ivory carvings, Magdalenian spears in a hunting scene. Well known objects in scientific publications and museum displays are here brought to life in the hands of prehistoric people, their fireplaces come alive where a small mark of ash is all that would usually appear on an archaeological plan, their huts rise up where holes for the posts used to be, and bare palynologic diagrams change suddenly into picturesque landscapes filled with vivid forms, brought back to life from centuries gone by. Exhibition catalogues term Burian's pictures 'reconstructions', and rightly so given the faithful and scholarly research which preceded their artistic creation, often dubbed a 'scientific hypothesis on canvas' as a result (Mazak 1983). In accordance with this judgement, the Czech artist's work may offer us a late example of naturalistic art, as Zola liked to call it, an art rooted in the field of scientific discovery, feeding consciously off an established body of knowledge, with additional true-to-life material that our imagination fills in occasionally only when the facts we witness prove insufficient (cf. Zola 1971:95).

In an art that sees itself as having a 'scientific dimension', the part imagination can play inspires a sense either of embarrassment or of pride: embarrassment, because this type of art lacks facts and, having to rely on the whims of imagination, it must betray the desire to be truthful to reality; pride because imagination – the moment it is based on a definite piece of knowledge – is no longer pure fantasy. The artist, wrote Zola

> starts from the reality of his surroundings and the truth of human evidence; if thereafter he develops in a certain direction, this is not due to the kind of imagination story-tellers possess but due to deduction, a scientific trait.
> (Zola 1971:227)

In the former case, imagination would be considered with suspicion because of its unpredictable and over-free nature, and therefore contrary to the principles of realism; it would become laudable in the latter, when it is methodical. It could be said, then, that there are two types of imagination: one which is wild and deceptive and despised by down-to-earth art, and the other, disciplined, deductive, and devoted faithfully to understanding.

In reality, there is yet a third type: conditioned imagination. The history of European thought provides many illustrations of its workings. To give just one example, we need only to think of the numerous flights-of-fancy and voyages to imaginary destinations which have flowed from the pens of countless authors since antiquity. In them, descriptions can be found of strange peoples and amazing monsters, said to be the work of pure fantasy but which in fact take up, time and time again, the same images, revealing a seemingly mysterious connection that shackles the flow of the human imagination. Even in the sixteenth century when voyages to the 'antipodes' had already stopped being fiction, the first explorers of America reported that they had fought Amazon women at

Figure 12.1   *Neanderthals under Kotocem hill, Moravia*

. . . a race born of the hard earth: it was built up on larger and more solid bones within, fastened with strong sinews traversing the flesh; not easily to be harmed by heat or cold. . . . And during many lustres of the sun rolling through the sky they prolonged their lives after the roving manner of beasts.

Lucretius *De Rerum Natura*. (1 BC) Liber V, 925–30

the mouth of the Rio Negro, similar to ones mentioned in Homer, and spoke of people with eyes in their shoulders and mouths between their breasts, identical to those Pliny the Elder had imagined existed.

It is often claimed that our representation of prehistory is free from such conditioning for one very simple reason: we have forgotten our roots, obscured by the mists of time, and would never have known of the ages of prehistory until science succeeded in finding fossil traces of them. Following this logic, there could not have been an imaginary prehistory before the scholarly version of prehistory. Consequently, as our vision of prehistoric life could only derive from science, our imagination, not wanting to be swallowed up by pure fantasy, had no choice but to use 'imaginative deduction' as a way of filling in the gaps in scientific understanding.

This conviction is part of a vast universe of received wisdom, as 'credible' as it is fragile. In reality, just as the first imaginary voyages came before the first geographical discoveries, so an imagined prehistory preceded the emergence of scholarly prehistory: before being discovered,

prehistoric people were invented. By forgetting the old 'figmentary prehistory', we deprive ourselves of the possibility and the pleasure of better understanding the conditioning to which our imagination is subject, and which is so often unable to go beyond a few endlessly used clichés when we think about the earliest ages of human history.

The Greek civilization left us the first indications of a naturalistic speculation which sought to explain the birth of humanity and of culture without reference to the omnipresent, supernatural forces of traditional anthropogenic myths. The most complete versions of naturalist theory reached us from the first century BC (for example in Lucretius, Diodorus Siculus, Cicero, and Vitruvius). A new expansion – in fact a veritable renaissance – of these concepts occurred in the second half of the eighteenth and at the beginning of the nineteenth century (cf. Stoczkowski 1994). What images of our ancestors and of their existence does this imaginary prehistory give us?

The *philosophes* of the Enlightenment delighted in presenting us with a picture of a primitive race of robust people who were already able to walk upright but whose appearance still bore traces of their previous animal state, such as extreme hairiness. These first people lived in the midst of a hostile environment exposed to bad weather, easy prey to wild beasts whose incessant attacks forced them to organize into groups and to make the first weapons: sticks, stones, and clubs. Despite this progress, hunger remained their primary concern, driving them into a nomadic existence, always desperately in search of food. Still subject to the most primal instincts, they never hesitated in times of shortage to eat human flesh to satisfy their hunger. Caves were their earliest shelters, often acquired after great struggles with the bears who first lived in them. Little by little, thanks to their superior intelligence, they drove back the wild beasts, perfected their tools and were able to move from the casual hunting of small animals to that of bigger game, guaranteeing them a safer and more stable existence. The turning point in the conquest of nature was the control of fire. In the beginning, fire started by lightning inspired an animal fear in our ancestors, but the human part of their nature prevailed and led people to tame it, at first only knowing how to feed the flames but soon learning to make it as well. They made the leap forward which forever separated them from nature, where fire was merely a destructive force, a cataclysm turning forests to ash and spreading panic amongst the most fearless of animals. Henceforth, neither the cold nor the wild beasts would threaten the 'Masters of Nature'

Figure 12.2 *The great Neanderthal portrait*

The majesty of his august face, the signals of intelligence, the mark of superior spirit, the sign of genius, all of this could be said to be hidden beneath the mantle of a ferocious beast.

B.G.E. Lacépède *Homme* (1821)

Figure 12.3 *Homo erectus*

For then more often would some one of them be caught and furnish living food to the wild beasts, devoured by their teeth, and would fill woods and mountains and forests with his groaning, as he looked on his living flesh being buried in a living tomb.

Lucretius *De Rerum Natura.* Liber V 990–4

anymore. Their immediate needs satisfied, they then set about creating a real culture, consisting of religion, art and everything that goes beyond the basic struggle for survival.

It is easy to see many elements of this vision in the pictures of Zdenek Burian (see illustrations). Moreover, it seems such a natural vision that the public is inclined to accept it quite naturally and consider it part of the earliest scientific truths. In reality, science can tell us very little about the hairiness of *Homo erectus*, though he is wonderfully hairy in Burian's work: a veritable monkey-man with an excessively ape-like head on top of a perfectly human body. We have no factual information to be able to maintain that *Homo erectus* walked about naked, without any covering. We have found neither large cudgels nor clubs, which Burian happily gives to *Homo erectus* and the Neanderthals. We lack the archaeological remains which would allow us to infer that a particular threat from large wildcats was of concern to prehistoric people, and the example of primates today suggests indeed that this danger was not

Figure 12.4   *Cannibals in the Krapina caves*

It is hardly surprising that, with such vulnerability, the first people often found themselves exposed to all the horrors of hunger and famine . . . and it is these terrible extremes to which they were reduced that caused them to adopt the frightful practices of many ancient peoples, devouring others.

A.Y. Goguet *De l'origine des loix* (1758)

necessarily of immediate importance (Stoczkowski 1992). We also know nothing about the circumstances in which people were able to obtain fire.

This statement of our ignorance (which could have been much longer) does not mean that Burian's vision, and others of its type which are sometimes given academic backing, are necessarily wrong. *Homo erectus* could have been hairy, Neanderthals could have used clubs, the predators could have had a taste for human flesh; lightning and conflagrations could have given the opportunity to discover fire . . . it *could* all have been thus. But it could also have been completely different. And we will never know.

What we do know is that there are countless ways, all of them plausible and at the same time equally unconfirmed by fossil evidence, to imagine the lives of prehistoric people (we need only remind ourselves of the idyllic 'noble savage' image, the reverse of the bestial savage and as old as its *alter ego*, which has declined in popularity despite several famous attempts to resurrect it in the eighteenth and nineteenth centuries,

Figure 12.5 *The first encounter with fire*

... it was the lightning that first of all brought fire to earth for mortals, and from it all the heat of the flames is spread abroad. For we see many things flare up, kindled with flames from heaven, when a stroke from the sky has brought the gift of heat.

Lucretius *De Rerum Natura*. Liber V 1091–5

and in recent times by Sahlins).[4] We also know that among these conceptions there is only one our imagination continues to favour. And it is not by chance that the conception easiest to accept is precisely the one that the naturalist tradition of European thought has carefully cultivated for over two thousand years; still alive today, it reigns in the textbooks of every country, propagated effectively not only by schools but also by the combined efforts of film, cartoons, comic strips, 'prehistoric' novels and popular scientific works (Stoczkowski 1990).

This imaginary prehistory, endurably and deeply entrenched in the universe of common sense, continues to have a life of its own today only through sheer apathy. A true 'living fossil' of the imagination, it is, however, the remnant of the intellectual efforts to take the first steps in giving a naturalistic explanation to humanity's origins, something that has happened regularly over the centuries. The naturalist vision of our origins, laid down by the founding thinkers in Antiquity and continued by Enlightenment *philosophes*, declared open war on traditional myths.

Figure 12.6   *Homo erectus pekinensis: controlling the fire*

Terrified by the raging flame, those who were about that place were put to flight. Afterwards when the thing was quieted down, approaching nearer they perceived that the advantage was great for their bodies from the heat of the fire. They added fuel, and thus keeping it up, they brought others.

Vitruvius *On Architecture*. 2:1: 'The origin of building' 1BC

But, curiously, it did not know how to rid itself of the framework that was the vehicle for these mythical conceptions.

The Bible story (Genesis I–II) as well as certain ancient myths (for example the *Georgics of Virgil*) located our ancestors in the midst of a natural paradise – Eden or a Golden Age – where food was plentiful and the lack of predators led human beings into docile passivity and a peaceful life. A 'catastrophic' event (original sin, intervention by Jupiter) occurred to disturb this original harmony and transformed the paradise setting into a hostile environment whose image was a Golden Age in reverse: constant lack replaced abundance of food; wild animals, absent until then, filled the forests and mountains to hunt down humans mercilessly; eternal Spring was transformed into severe cold and bad weather. Consequently, people had to leave their state of blissful passivity and engage in hard labour; in order to defend and feed themselves, they were forced, as stressed by Virgil, to clothe themselves, make tools and organize socially.

Figure 12.7 *Neanderthals preparing for the hunt*

They sharpened branches, they fashioned stakes, they made clubs.
B.G.E. de Lacépède *Homme* (1821)

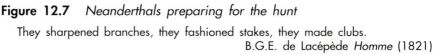

This mythic framework was taken up and 'naturalized' by philosophical speculation, representing our ancestors to begin with as living without culture in a state of animal insensibility, in an environment that possessed every heavenly quality; then came a catastrophe which rendered nature hostile. Here we are offered an image of paradise in negative, and it keeps its traditional role as a force pushing people to create a Culture. So the idea of shortage and constant search for food, or the constant threat from wild beasts that we find in the imaginary prehistory and which can be perceived in Burian's pictures, only takes over the old mythical concepts; these developed when the vision of primitive nature was created, by inverting the standard qualities of the heavenly setting. The *philosophes*' main innovation consisted of changing the cause responsible for the original disaster which turned Mother Nature into a wicked step-mother: an over-expansion in population (or a dramatic change in the climate) replaced Jupiter's decisions and the punishment for original sin. This clever touch was enough to transform a myth into a 'naturalistic' conception of prehistory.

We would have no difficulty in giving other examples of similar evolutions of myths, which end in the visions whose traces can be found in

Figure 12.8 *Hunting the cave bear*

They thus had to unite to defeat the savage beasts, so as to have safety and nourishment.

J.-J. Virey *Historie naturelle du genre humain* (1801)

Burian. The idea that people lit the first homefires thanks to a blaze caused by lightning is not without a link to the beliefs we inherited from the ancient Greeks. They believed that the first people lived without fire, which was the exclusive gift of Zeus, and that Prometheus stole fire from the gods and brought it from the heavens to earth. In the 'naturalized version of the *philosophes*' Zeus and Prometheus disappear but fire comes to humanity the same way, from the sky via the intermediary of lightning, ascribed in mythology to Zeus.

Popular culture and its influence did not remain without an impact on naive prehistory either. For example, in the descriptions by the *philosophes* as well as in Burian's pictures, particularly the *Homo erectus*, the first people strangely resemble the figure of the 'Wild Man of the Woods' from medieval imagery. Like the Wild Man, Burian's *Homo erectus* is very hairy, carries a club and his physiognomy presents a mix of human and animal characteristics, without descending totally into the purely simian (cf. Bernheimer 1970).

The Wild Man was already present in Arthurian tales, in the songs of minstrels, in medieval and renaissance sculpture and in the ritual processions of carnivals, though his counterparts were also found in ancient Mediterranean and Nordic folklore. Texts and representations put the accent on his bestial character and indicate his ignorance of fire and sometimes of speech, and depict him looking for shelter in caves and fighting ferocious beasts with a club. At a time of great geographical discoveries, the Wild Man lent his qualities to the natives of the 'Antipodes', quickly shown covered with hair and fighting large wild-cats. From this even comes the name which was given to them – savages – from the French name 'salvage' or 'sauvage' given to the Wild Man. The transfer of properties from the Wild Man onto the image of our ancestors is probably even older. In the fourteenth century when Charles V entered Bruges, the solemn cortege that welcomed him wore hairy masks and carried clubs, to represent the first inhabitants of Flanders (Bernheimer 1970).

Popular imagination painted a portrait of the prehistoric savage taking the 'salvage' from folklore as its model; thus the club, an inseparable symbol of the latter, became the faithful companion of prehistoric people, although archaeologists have never found the slightest trace of one. The symbolic sense of the big club, charged with obvious phallic connotations in popular culture, today passes unnoticed in prehistoric images: the modesty of artists such as Burian notwithstanding (he hid the private parts of the Neanderthal under small pieces of animal skin), this virile power reappears in a symbolic form when prehistoric man is discreetly covered.

In the medieval era, the Wild Man of the Woods who fought with wild animals could also confront knights: encounters with young, valiant princes who incarnated the Christian and warrior virtues became a pretext for better defining qualities of civilized people by showing their opposite, represented by the Wild Man. This role and this form of image, civilized humanity in reverse, were projected onto prehistoric people. Just as the deep virgin forest inhabited by the Wild Man was the negative pole for medieval or ancient civilization, so the first ages of humanity were often considered as the negative pole for contemporary civilization. It was necessary thus to populate it with creatures who were the opposite of today's Europeans. We wear clothes, so they must have lived naked; we cook our food, theirs must have been eaten raw; we are monogamous and strictly respect the taboo on incest, so they must have lived in total promiscuity, with hints of incest; and since eating one's own kind is the essence of horrid abomination for us, they must have naturally been cannibals.

If prehistoric people were invented before they were discovered, we must recognize that this invention owes little to the creative effort of a free and arbitrary imagination. The naive prehistory which Burian and other 'prehistoric' painters and illustrators articulate combines a mythical 'naturalized' framework with elements of folklore. This mix is the last step in an intellectual process, begun as a 'make-shift' measure, which plays with some basic concepts of traditional thought. Being originally the product of a method, naive prehistory has entered into the common fund of vernacular understanding down the centuries, and re-emerges each time our mind tries to imagine the lives of fossil humans. The earliest archaeological remains brought to light in the nineteenth century turned out to be too fragmentary to bring about large-scale change to the traditional vision of prehistory; thus they were more often than not merely props with which one embellished the old conceptions by giving them the semblance of science. If the scenes painted of prehistory translate into a theory on canvas, it is above all the one that common sense has forged and which, furthermore, has also fed into scientific thinking (cf. Stoczkowski 1994).

Burian, like all illustrators, drew freely from the wealth of naive prehistory. So did the novelist J.H. Rosny Aïné who had recourse to similar clichés in his famous book *Guerre du feu*, whose prehistoric intrigue was recently brought to the screen by J.J. Annaud without a single received idea being lost. It is striking to notice the pride and the insistence with which Rosny Aïné and Annaud, like Burian, stressed their realist ambitions when all three of them, in their own ways, were so far removed from realism in which we tend towards when accepting the current meaning of the term, which presupposes a compatibility between artistic representation and the reality it portrays. Their 'realism' is, without them knowing it, of a totally different kind, and it is the only one, possibly, that art knows: a staged realism, one that calls on the props of reality's naive vision and is fed by conditioned imagination. It is less important to reflect reality than to erect a conventional backdrop, credible both in its exoticism and its familiarity, to give the whole representation the illusion of authenticity. So that we can judge a 'true-to-life' portrait of prehistoric humanity – without knowing the subjects, as Flaubert ironically commented; our imagination demands hairy creatures, animal-skin garments, clubs, bloody attacks by predators, struggles against enormous animals, caves; an atmosphere rather than an archaeologically correct representation. Art that is termed realistic is that which is able to produce what Roland Barthes called the effect of reality, that is of creating the sense of conforming to what we believe to be real. The role of conditioned imagination in this process is thus inescapable, for artists draw on this wealth of conventional imagery, whilst the viewer uses it to judge the product's believability. Yet, this game between creator and public often remains overshadowed, and art 'with a scientific dimension' continues to boast its rigour and erudition. It remains to be seen to what extent science itself participates in the same game, with greater subtlety no doubt, yet following the same rules with the same risk of producing visions that are just as seductive and illusory and whose prestige stems only from a deceptive effect of reality.

NOTES

1   This article was first published in the picture catalogue for the Burian exhibition at the Musée de Préhistoire in Solutré, France, cf. Lagardère 1990.
2   Translated from French by Simon Terry.
3   Further details on Burian can be found in Lagardère 1990.
4   Sahlins 1968 and 1972.

REFERENCES

Bernheimer, R. 1970. *Wild Men in the Middle Ages.* New York: Octagon Books.

Flaubert, G. 1952. *Bouvard et Pécuchet.* In A. Thibaudet and R. Dumesnil (eds), *Oeuvres de Flaubert.* Paris: Gallimard.

Goguet, A.-Y. 1758. *De l'origine des loix, des arts, et des sciences, et de leur progrès chez les anciens peuples.* Paris: Desaint & Saillot.

de Lacépède, B.G.E, 1821. *Homme.* In F. Cuvier (ed.), *Dictionnaire des Sciences Naturelles.* Paris: Levrault, Le Normant.

Lagardère, G. (ed.) 1990. *Peintres d'un monde disparu: la préhistoire vue par les artistes de la fin du XIXe siècle à nos jours.* Solutré: Musée de Préhistoire de Solutré.

Lucretius 1947. *De Rerum Natura.* Translated by Cyril Bailey. Oxford: Clarendon Press.

Mazak, Z. 1983. *Pravak v dile Zdenka Buriana.* In *Vyvoj zivota na Zemi. Stala expozice obrazu Zdenka Buriana.* Prague.

Rosny Aïné, J.H. 1985. *Romans préhistoriques.* Paris: Robert Laffont.

Sahlins, M. 1968. 'Notes on the original affluent society.' In Richard B. Lee and Irven DeVore (eds), *Man the hunter.* New York: Aldine de Gruyter.

Sahlins, M. 1972. 'The original affluent society.' In *Stone Age Economics.* London: Tavistock Press.

Stoczkowski, W. 1990. 'La préhistoire dans les manuels scolaires, ou notre mythe des origines', *L'Homme* 116:111–35.

Stoczkowski, W. 1992. 'Quand la science répète les mythes.' *La Recherche* 244: 746–50.

Stoczkowski, W. 1994. *Anthropologie naïve, anthropologie savante: de l'origine de l'homme, de l'imagination et des idées reçues.* Paris: Editions CNRS.

Virey. J.-J. 1801. *Histoire naturelle du genre humain.* Paris: F. Dufrat.

Virgil 1994. *Georgics.* Edited and with commentary by R.A.B. Mynors. Oxford: Clarendon Press.

Vitruvius 1931. *On Architecture.* Translated by Frank Granger. 2 vol. London: Heinemann.

Zola. E 1971. *Le roman expérimental.* Paris: Garnier-Flammarion.

INDEX

173; *see also* Custer's Last Stand, Plains Indian art

Material Culture and Text: illustrations, discussion of the role of in 62

meaning: art and language, discussion of the relationship between 1–4; perceptual theory, its account of pictorial meaning 49; photographs, derivation of meaning from their context 80, 83; photographs, discussion of the role of collage and montage in the construction of the meaning of 83–4; shape of meaning, definition of 112; Wittgenstein, discussion of his belief of the impossibility of images existing outside of language 1–2

Men of the Old Stone Age: discussion of the use of icons of human antiquity in **9.1**, 188–90

montage: definition of 84; photographs, discussion of the role of montage in the construction of the meaning of 83–4

multimedia 92, 99

museums: exclusion of Aborigines from decisions concerning their representation in museums 236, 236; growing consultation of Aborigines in museum and archaeological representations 237–8; their representation of Aborigines as unchanged noble savages 233; *see also* National Museum of Victoria

myth: Africans, discussion of the mythological representation of in Ancient Greece **7.9**, **7.10**, **7.11**, **7.12**, 146, 148–9, 151, 153–4; Ancient Greece, discussion of the representation of foreigners in the art and mythology of 133–54; Ancient Greek myth, its preoccupation with contemporary issues 132–3; Egyptians, mythological representation of in Ancient Greece **7.10**, **7.11**, **7.13**, 149, 151, 153–4; Ethiopians, mythological representation of in Ancient Greece **7.9**, 146, 148–9; Thracians, discussion of their mythological associations in Ancient Greece 142

National Museum of Victoria: *Koorie*, discussion of the exhibition of and its representation of Aborigines **11.4**,

11.5, 240–3; *Koorie*, its reproduction of colonial stereotypes 240–2; its representation of Aboriginal culture as pristine and unprogressive **11.2**, 235, 236; representation of Aborigines as 'noble savages' 236; *see also* Spencer

naturalism: in the art of Ancient Greece 130; Burian, discussion of the naturalist vision of his representations of human antiquity 254–5, 258; definition of 2, 78; distinction of from realism 78–9; human origins, discussion of the origins of the naturalist vision of 253–4, 256–8; propagandic role of 2

nature: Renaissance, its hermetic vision of nature and landscape 11

Neanderthals: icons, discussion of the use of in the visual representation of **9.1**, **9.8**, 188–90, 198; *see also* Palaeolithic

Neuville, A. de: discussion of his representations of Gauls in Guizot's *Histoire de la France* **10.3**, **10.4**, **10.5**, **10.6**, 217–18, 222

New Archaeology: origins of xv; *see also* Binford

New Kingdom Period: ideology, representation of in the art of 109–10; power, representation of in the art of 109–10; situational analysis of ideology and social position represented in New Kingdom tomb paintings 115–21; stylistic analysis, discussion and critique of its approach to uncovering the social references of the art of 110; tomb owners, representations of in the tomb paintings of 116–120; *see also* Akhenaten

objectivity: photographs, their role in establishing objectivity 82–3; theorization of 81–2; use of the concept of in archaeological rhetoric 82

oratory: significance of in Ancient Greece 132

Osborn, H.F.: discussion of the use of icons of human antiquity in *Men of the Old Stone Age* **9.1**, 188–90

other: discussion of Said's theorization of the European construction of 231–2

paintings: perceptual theory, discussion of its theorization of pictorial meaning 49–56, 58–9